WAID FLYNN MOK FITZPATRICK MORELLI

ARCHIE

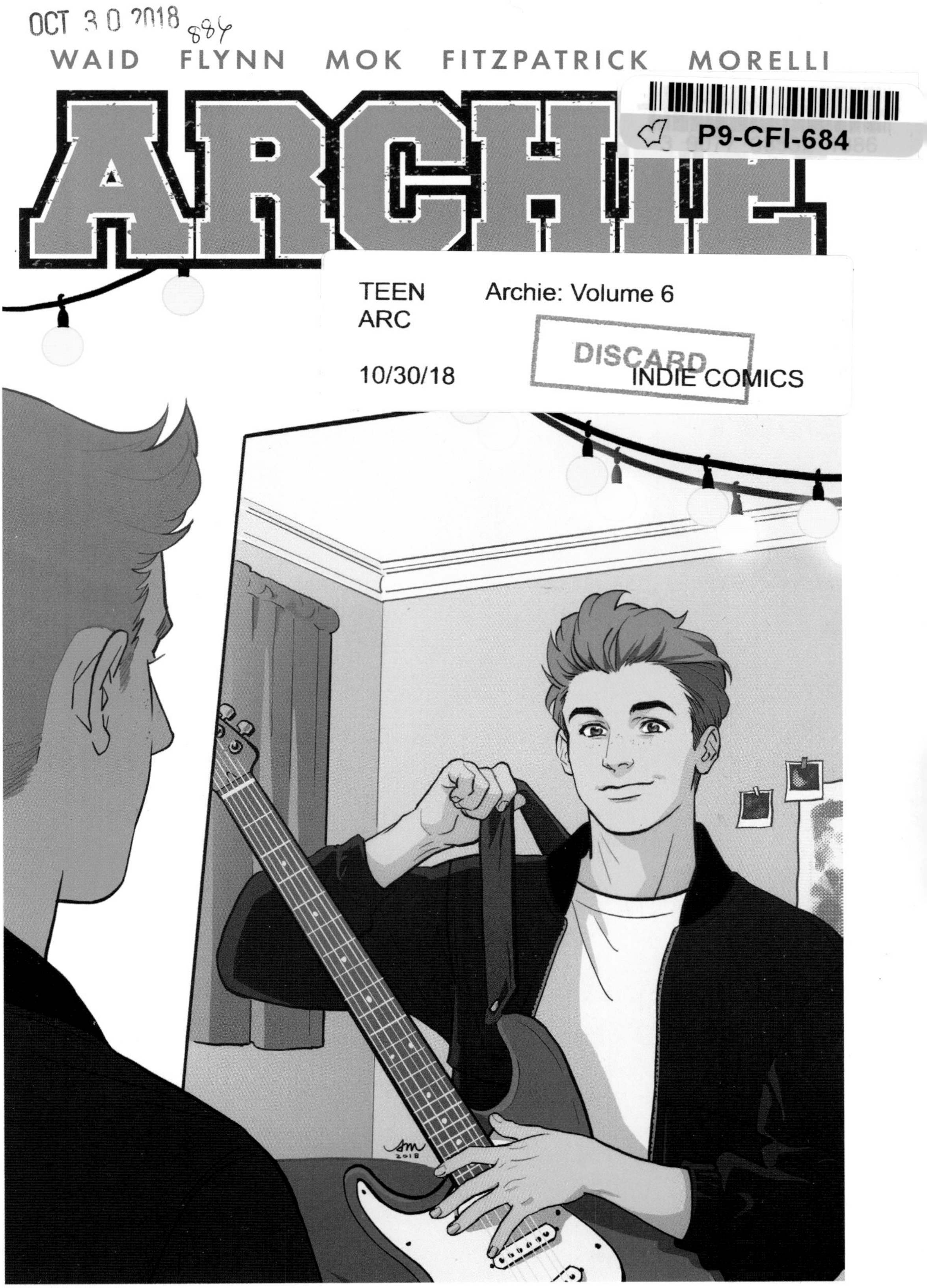

VOLUME SIX

STORY BY
**MARK WAID &
IAN FLYNN**

ART BY
AUDREY MOK

COLORS BY
KELLY FITZPATRICK

LETTERING BY
JACK MORELLI

EDITORIAL TEAM
MIKE PELLERITO
VINCENT LOVALLO
JAMIE LEE ROTANTE
STEPHEN OSWALD

GRAPHIC DESIGN BY
KARI McLACHLAN

EDITOR-IN-CHIEF
VICTOR GORELICK

PUBLISHER
JON GOLDWATER

PREVIOUSLY IN...

ARCHIE®

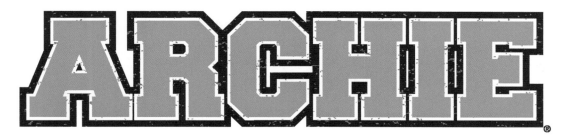

After a tragic drag racing accident landed Betty Cooper in a coma, her family and friends were all expecting the worst. But ever the trooper, Betty came out of it and made a nearly-full recovery, she was even able to walk on her own for the first time in months. Betty did her best to live her life as if nothing had changed, often refusing any help or charity from her friends. The only thing she really wanted was to see Archie Andrews again—unfortunately her father, Hal Cooper, barred Archie from the Cooper household. Thanks to some help from Jughead Jones, the two were finally able to talk and reconnect—the only problem was that Archie's girlfriend Veronica Lodge overheard their conversation and took it badly out of context. Meanwhile, Dilton Doiley's did everything he could to win Betty's affections once and for all.

Regaining her independence has been a long road, but it's allowed Betty the time to think on what's important to her—and that's being accountable for her own happiness. She rejected both Dilton Doiley and the newly-broken up Archie Andrews. With the spring dance quickly approaching, Archie will have to scramble to find a date now that Veronica Lodge is out of the picture. Plus, Reggie Mantle is out of jail and back in Riverdale, and he has some secret info he's eager to share...

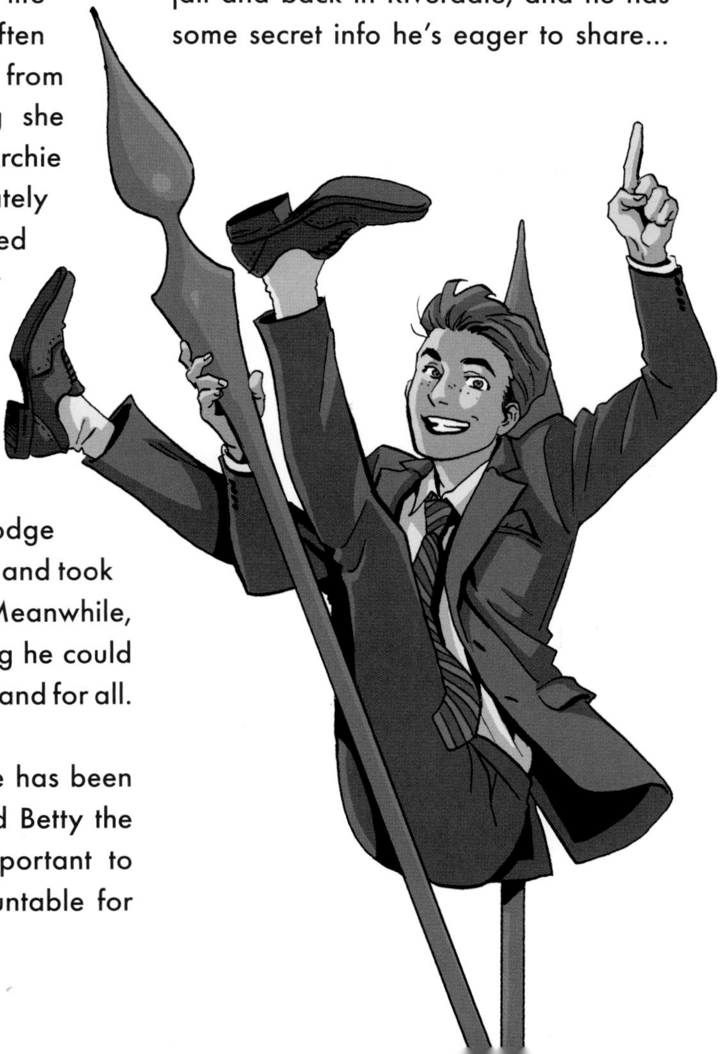

ISSUE TWENTY-EIGHT

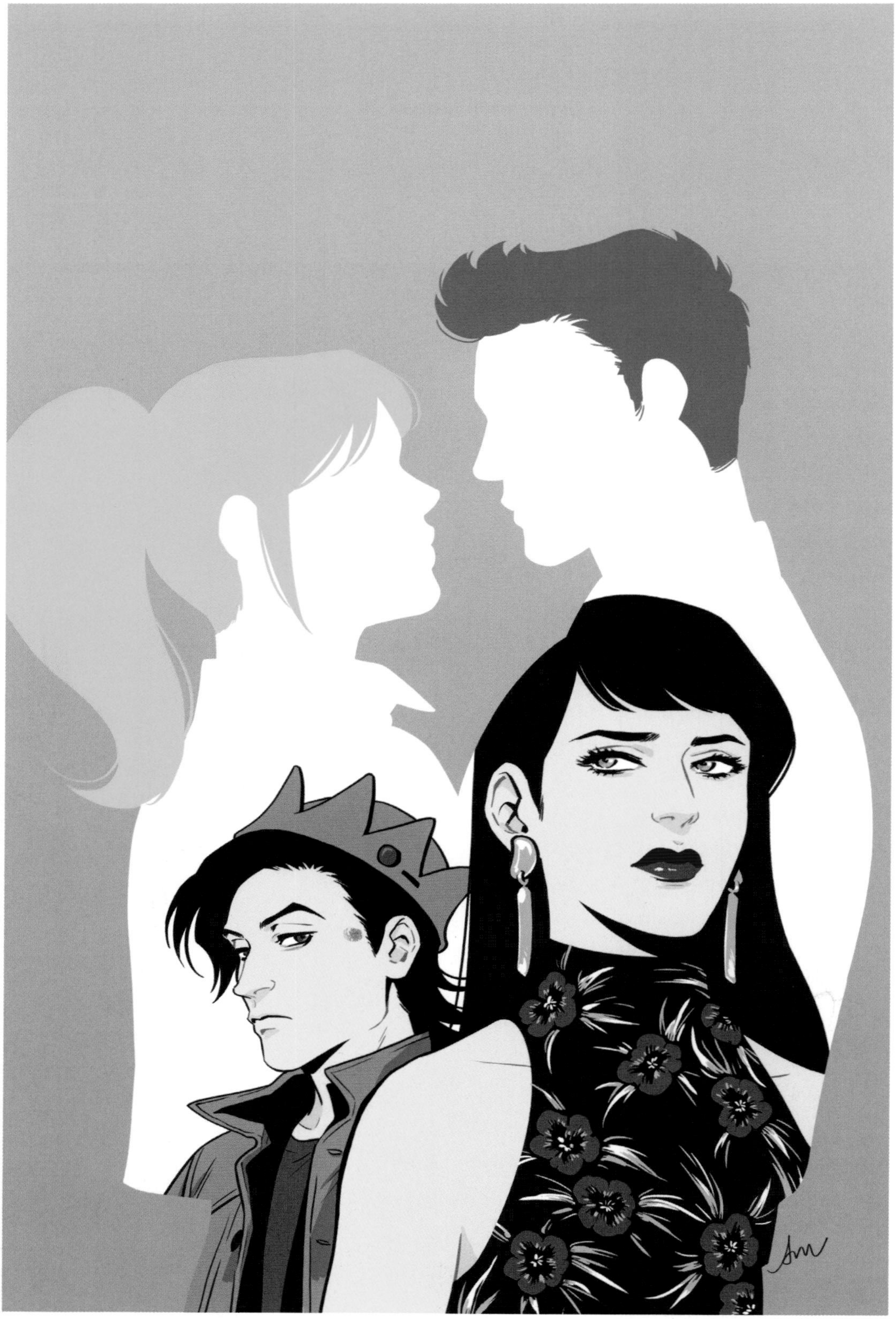

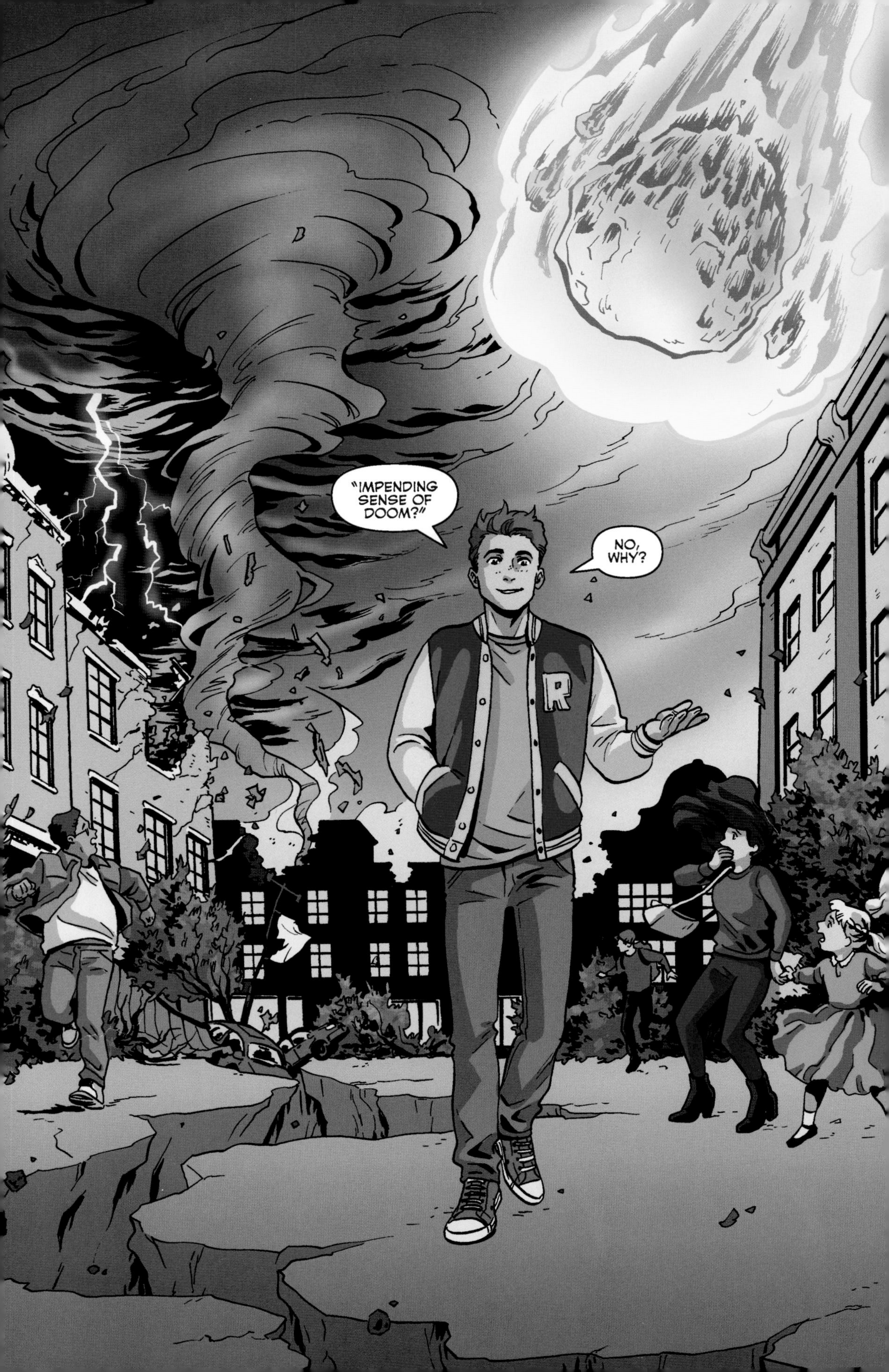
"IMPENDING SENSE OF DOOM?"
NO, WHY?

CHAPTER ONE: RIVERDALE'S: The BACHELOR

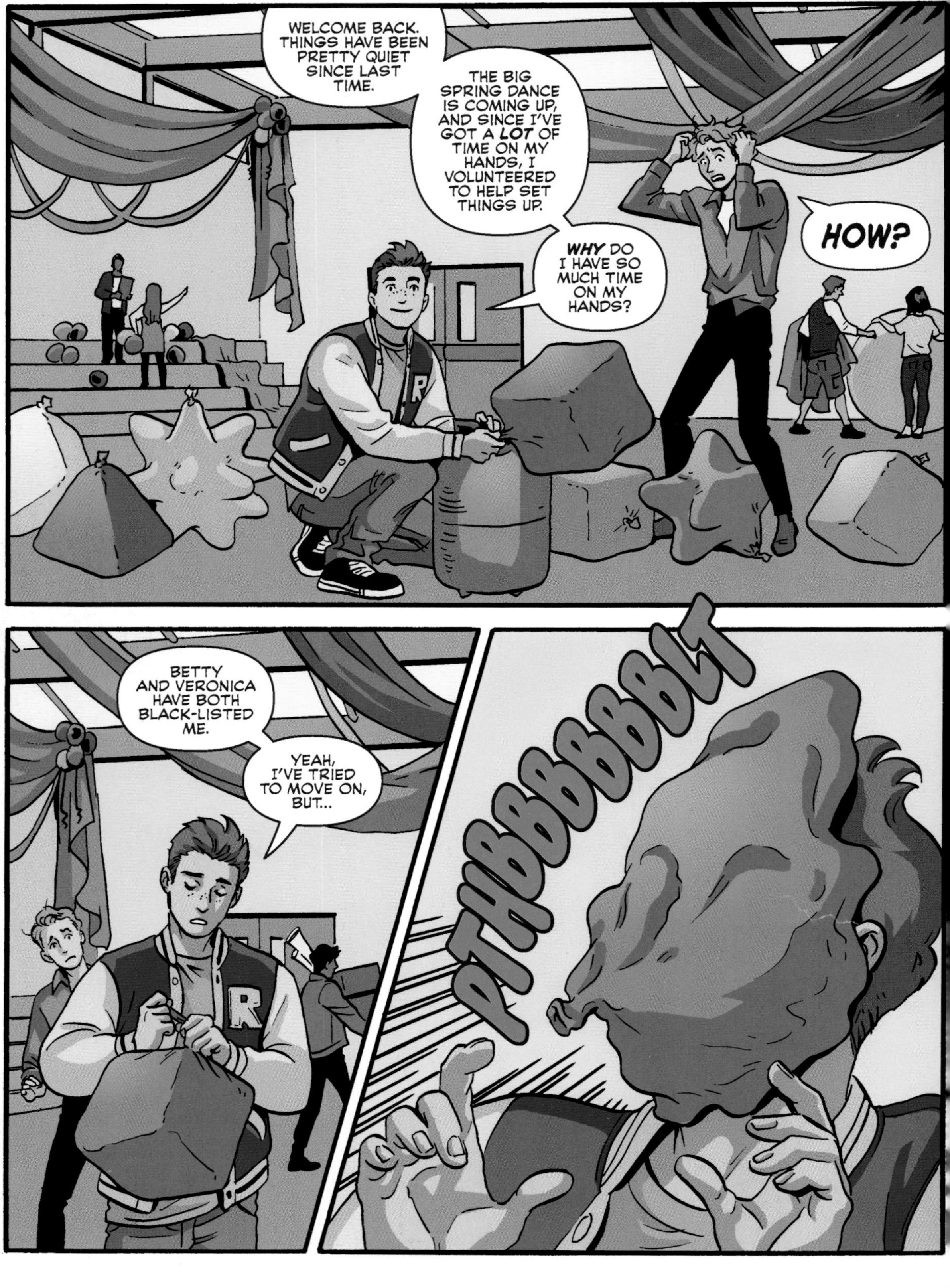
WELCOME BACK. THINGS HAVE BEEN PRETTY QUIET SINCE LAST TIME.
THE BIG SPRING DANCE IS COMING UP, AND SINCE I'VE GOT A **LOT** OF TIME ON MY HANDS, I VOLUNTEERED TO HELP SET THINGS UP.
WHY DO I HAVE SO MUCH TIME ON MY HANDS?
HOW?
BETTY AND VERONICA HAVE BOTH BLACK-LISTED ME.
YEAH, I'VE TRIED TO MOVE ON, BUT...
PTHBBBBBBLT

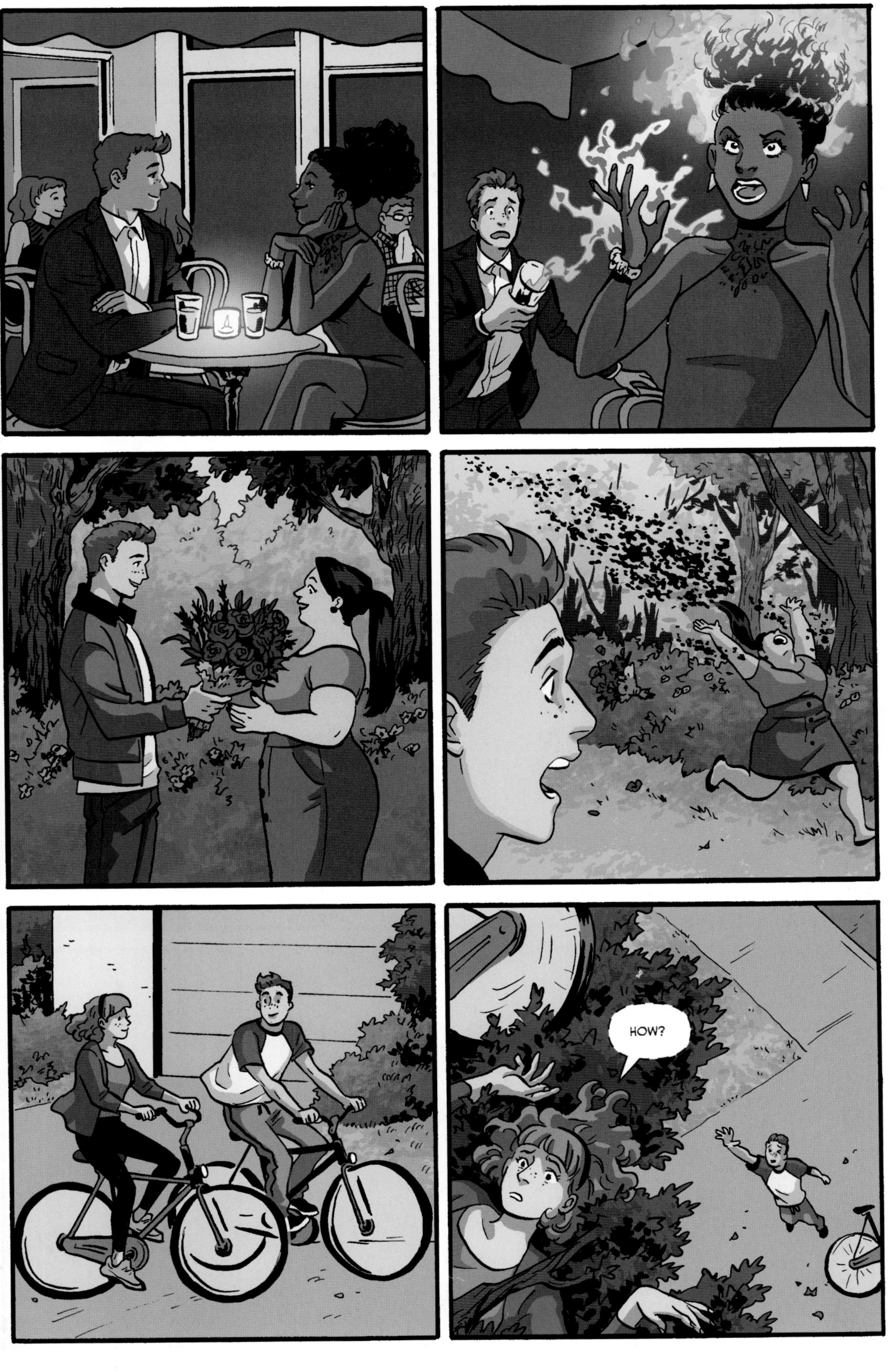
HOW?

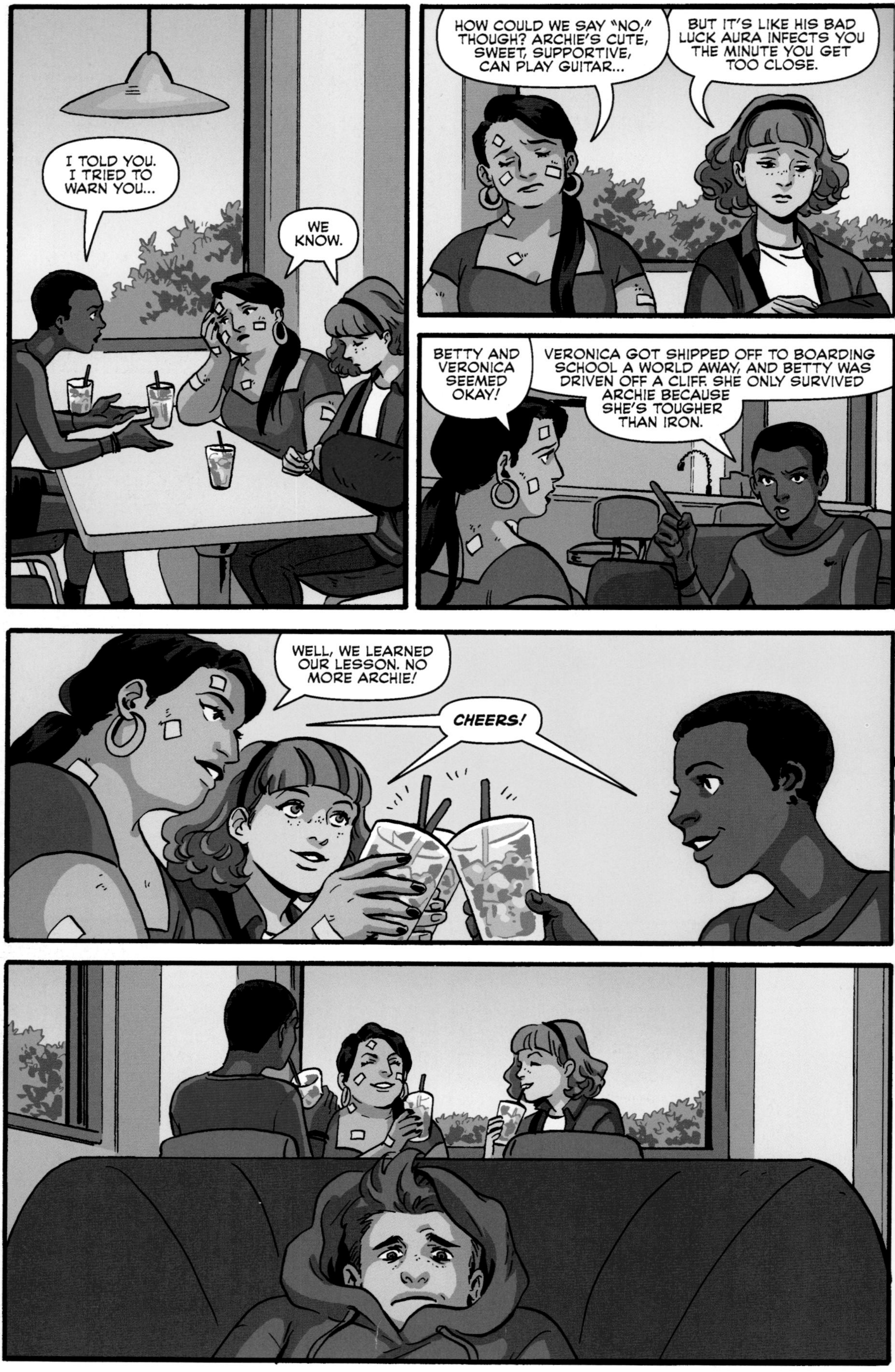
I TOLD YOU. I TRIED TO WARN YOU...
WE KNOW.
HOW COULD WE SAY "NO," THOUGH? ARCHIE'S CUTE, SWEET, SUPPORTIVE, CAN PLAY GUITAR...
BUT IT'S LIKE HIS BAD LUCK AURA INFECTS YOU THE MINUTE YOU GET TOO CLOSE.
BETTY AND VERONICA SEEMED OKAY!
VERONICA GOT SHIPPED OFF TO BOARDING SCHOOL A WORLD AWAY, AND BETTY WAS DRIVEN OFF A CLIFF. SHE ONLY SURVIVED ARCHIE BECAUSE SHE'S TOUGHER THAN IRON.
WELL, WE LEARNED OUR LESSON. NO MORE ARCHIE!
CHEERS!

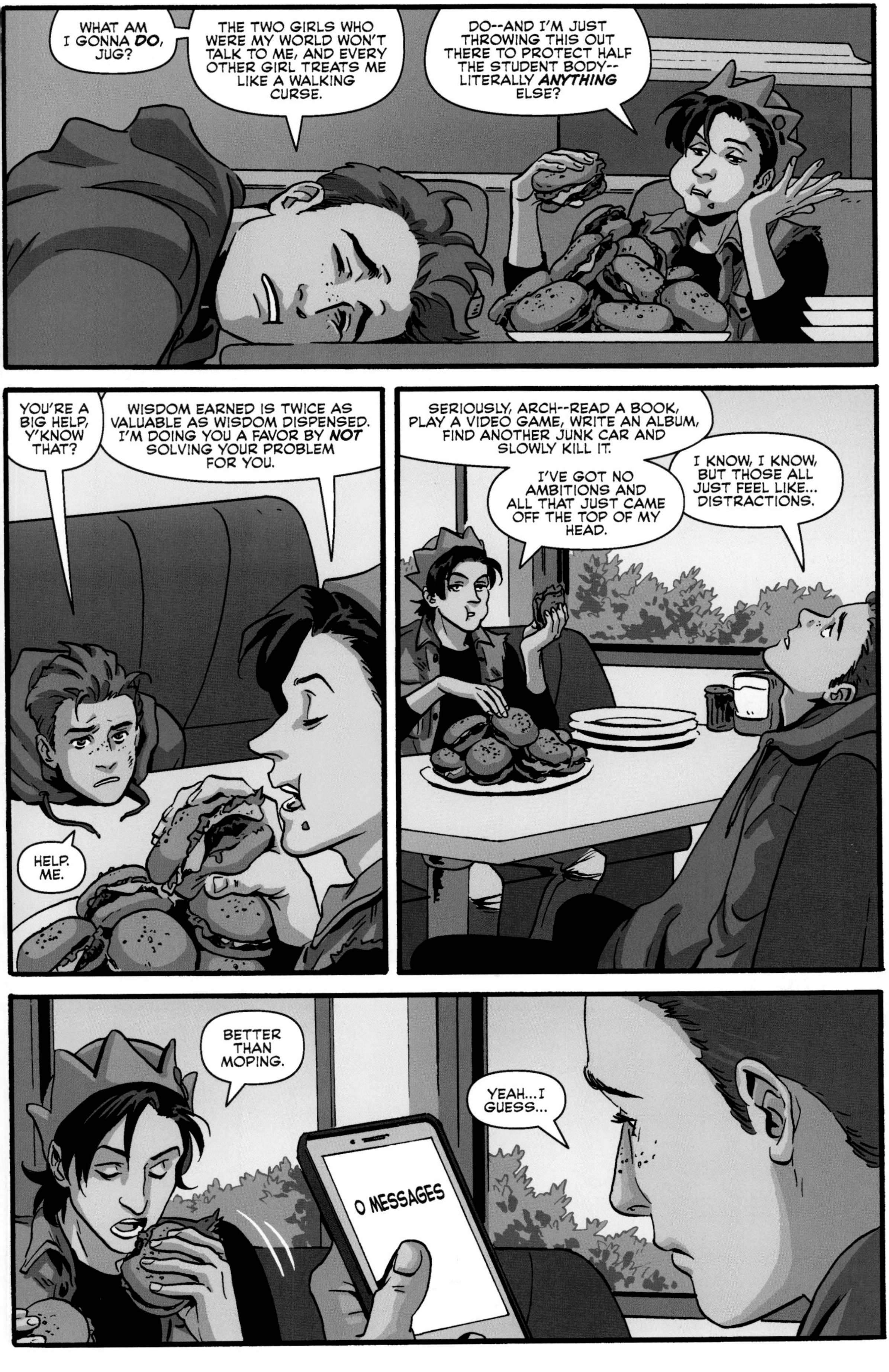
WHAT AM I GONNA *DO*, JUG?
THE TWO GIRLS WHO WERE MY WORLD WON'T TALK TO ME, AND EVERY OTHER GIRL TREATS ME LIKE A WALKING CURSE.
DO--AND I'M JUST THROWING THIS OUT THERE TO PROTECT HALF THE STUDENT BODY--LITERALLY *ANYTHING* ELSE?
YOU'RE A BIG HELP, Y'KNOW THAT?
WISDOM EARNED IS TWICE AS VALUABLE AS WISDOM DISPENSED. I'M DOING YOU A FAVOR BY *NOT* SOLVING YOUR PROBLEM FOR YOU.
HELP. ME.
SERIOUSLY, ARCH--READ A BOOK, PLAY A VIDEO GAME, WRITE AN ALBUM, FIND ANOTHER JUNK CAR AND SLOWLY KILL IT.
I'VE GOT NO AMBITIONS AND ALL THAT JUST CAME OFF THE TOP OF MY HEAD.
I KNOW, I KNOW, BUT THOSE ALL JUST FEEL LIKE... DISTRACTIONS.
BETTER THAN MOPING.
YEAH...I GUESS...
0 MESSAGES

CHAPTER TWO: DEER VERONICA

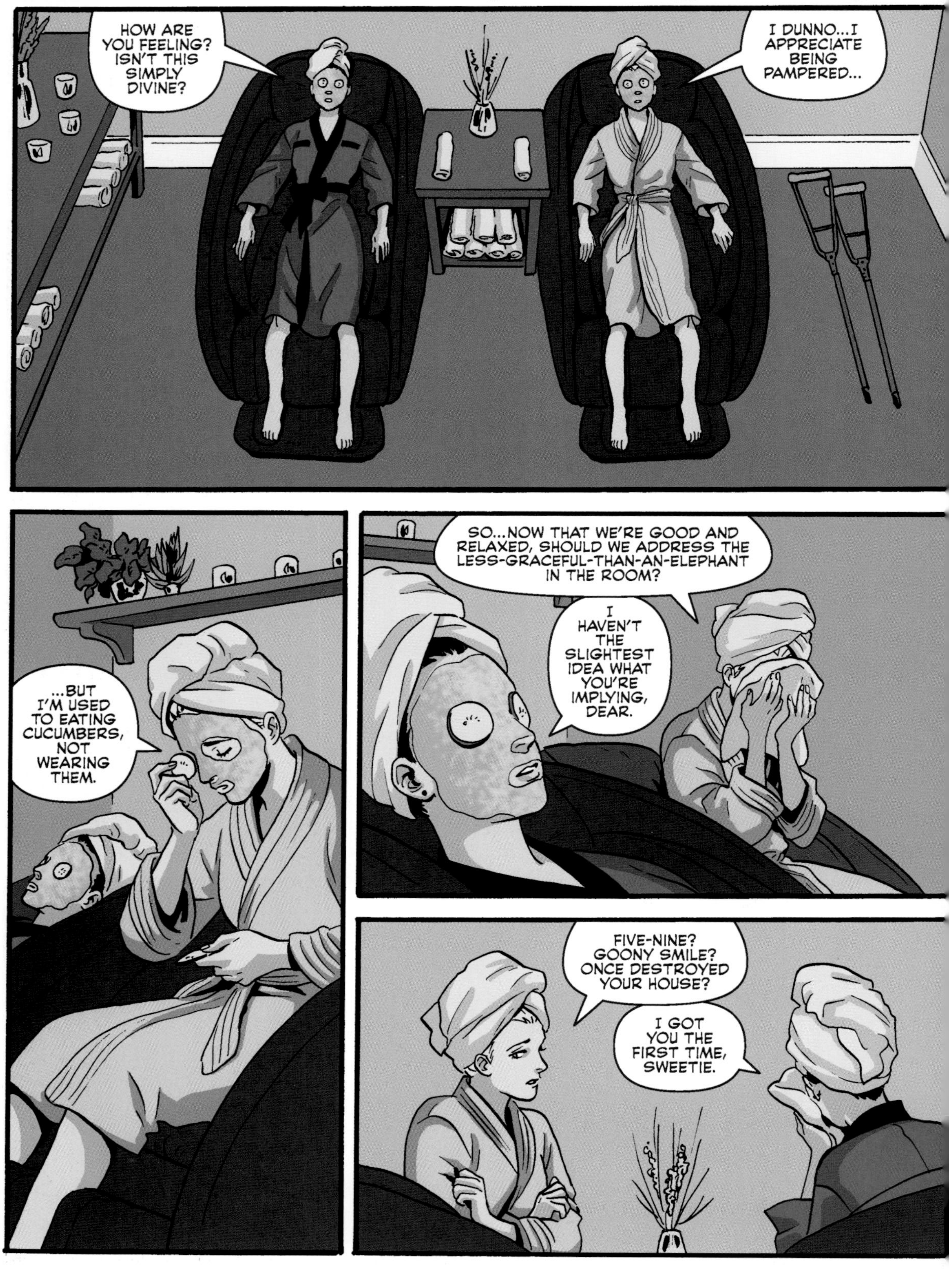
HOW ARE YOU FEELING? ISN'T THIS SIMPLY DIVINE?
I DUNNO...I APPRECIATE BEING PAMPERED...
...BUT I'M USED TO EATING CUCUMBERS, NOT WEARING THEM.
SO...NOW THAT WE'RE GOOD AND RELAXED, SHOULD WE ADDRESS THE LESS-GRACEFUL-THAN-AN-ELEPHANT IN THE ROOM?
I HAVEN'T THE SLIGHTEST IDEA WHAT YOU'RE IMPLYING, DEAR.
FIVE-NINE? GOONY SMILE? ONCE DESTROYED YOUR HOUSE?
I GOT YOU THE FIRST TIME, SWEETIE.

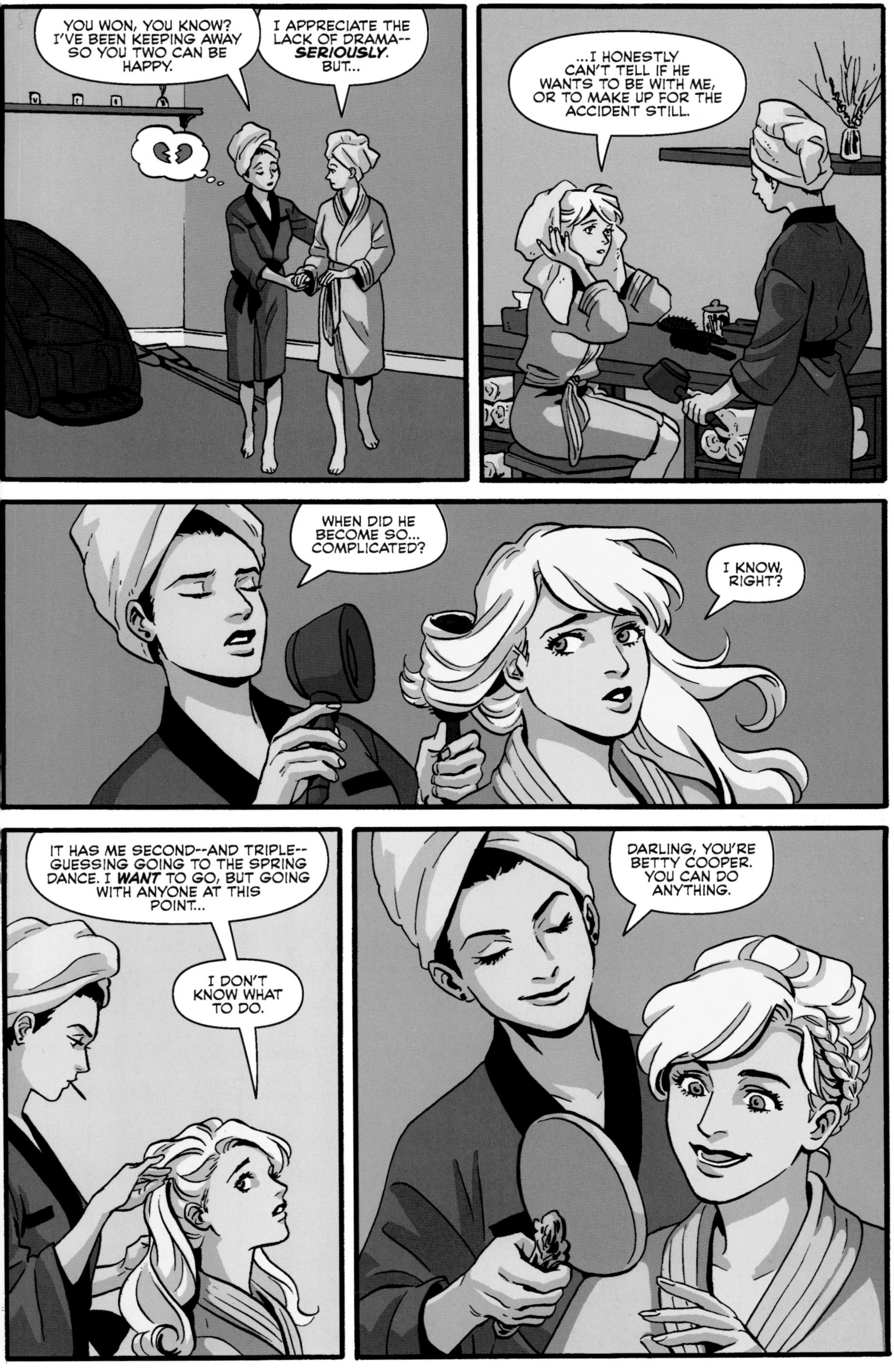
YOU WON, YOU KNOW? I'VE BEEN KEEPING AWAY SO YOU TWO CAN BE HAPPY.
I APPRECIATE THE LACK OF DRAMA-- SERIOUSLY. BUT...
...I HONESTLY CAN'T TELL IF HE WANTS TO BE WITH ME, OR TO MAKE UP FOR THE ACCIDENT STILL.
WHEN DID HE BECOME SO... COMPLICATED?
I KNOW, RIGHT?
IT HAS ME SECOND--AND TRIPLE--GUESSING GOING TO THE SPRING DANCE. I WANT TO GO, BUT GOING WITH ANYONE AT THIS POINT...
I DON'T KNOW WHAT TO DO.
DARLING, YOU'RE BETTY COOPER. YOU CAN DO ANYTHING.

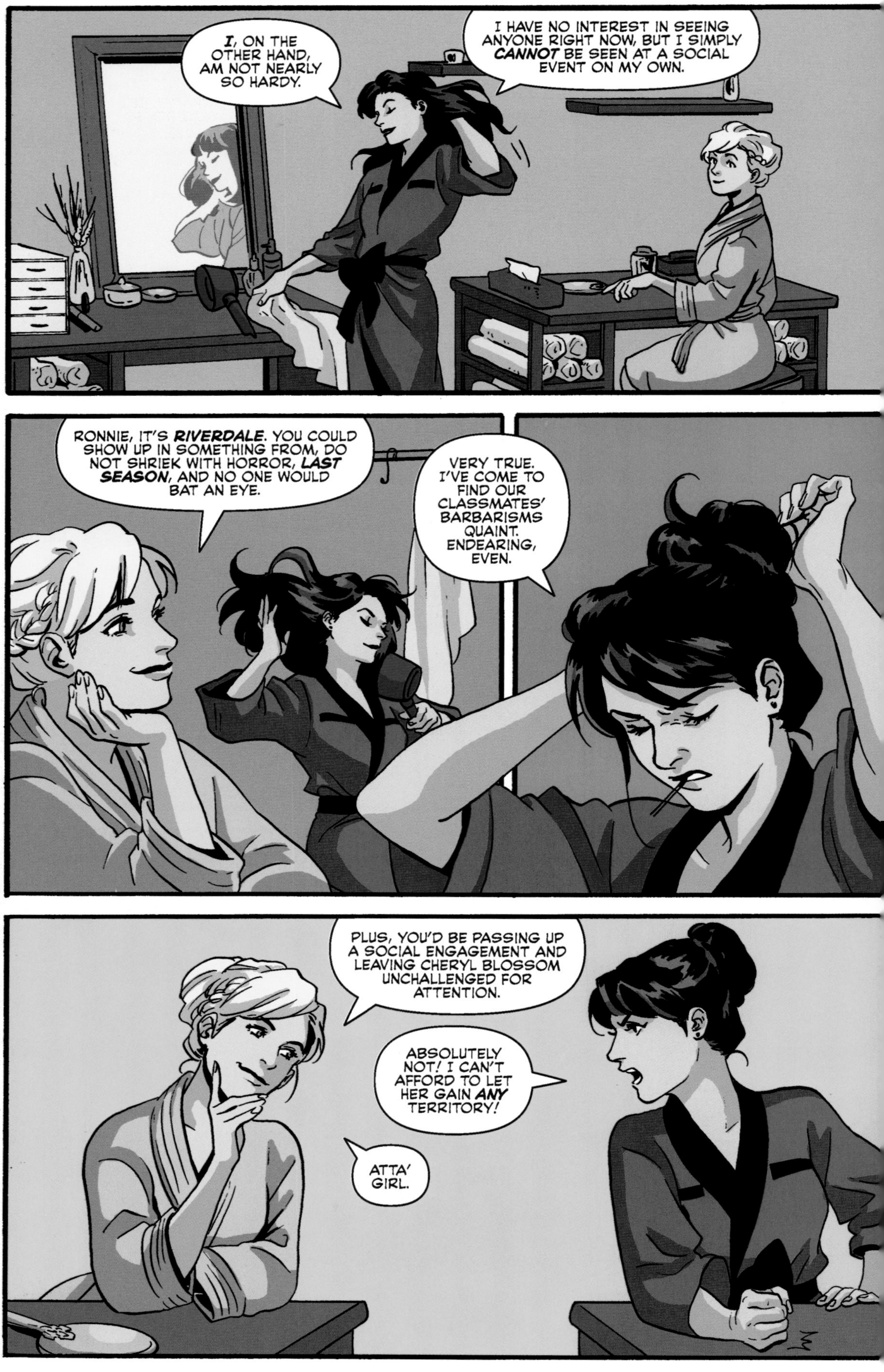
I, ON THE OTHER HAND, AM NOT NEARLY SO HARDY.
I HAVE NO INTEREST IN SEEING ANYONE RIGHT NOW, BUT I SIMPLY ***CANNOT*** BE SEEN AT A SOCIAL EVENT ON MY OWN.
RONNIE, IT'S ***RIVERDALE***. YOU COULD SHOW UP IN SOMETHING FROM, DO NOT SHRIEK WITH HORROR, ***LAST SEASON***, AND NO ONE WOULD BAT AN EYE.
VERY TRUE. I'VE COME TO FIND OUR CLASSMATES' BARBARISMS QUAINT. ENDEARING, EVEN.
PLUS, YOU'D BE PASSING UP A SOCIAL ENGAGEMENT AND LEAVING CHERYL BLOSSOM UNCHALLENGED FOR ATTENTION.
ABSOLUTELY NOT! I CAN'T AFFORD TO LET HER GAIN *ANY* TERRITORY!
ATTA' GIRL.

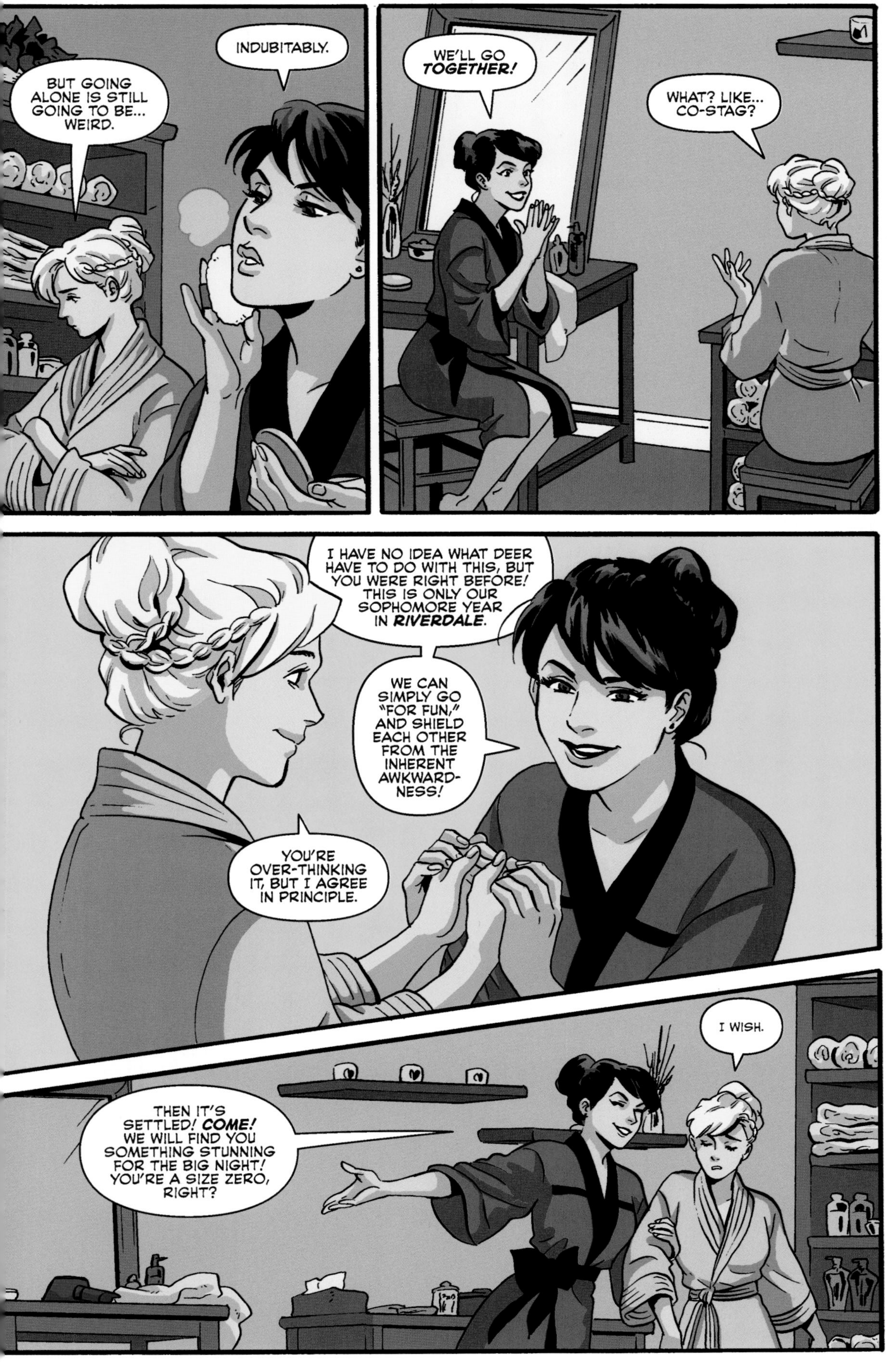
INDUBITABLY.
BUT GOING ALONE IS STILL GOING TO BE... WEIRD.
WE'LL GO *TOGETHER!*
WHAT? LIKE... CO-STAG?
I HAVE NO IDEA WHAT DEER HAVE TO DO WITH THIS, BUT YOU WERE RIGHT BEFORE! THIS IS ONLY OUR SOPHOMORE YEAR IN *RIVERDALE*.
WE CAN SIMPLY GO "FOR FUN," AND SHIELD EACH OTHER FROM THE INHERENT AWKWARD-NESS!
YOU'RE OVER-THINKING IT, BUT I AGREE IN PRINCIPLE.
THEN IT'S SETTLED! *COME!* WE WILL FIND YOU SOMETHING STUNNING FOR THE BIG NIGHT! YOU'RE A SIZE ZERO, RIGHT?
I WISH.

CHAPTER THREE: PLIGHT OF THE WEATHERBEE

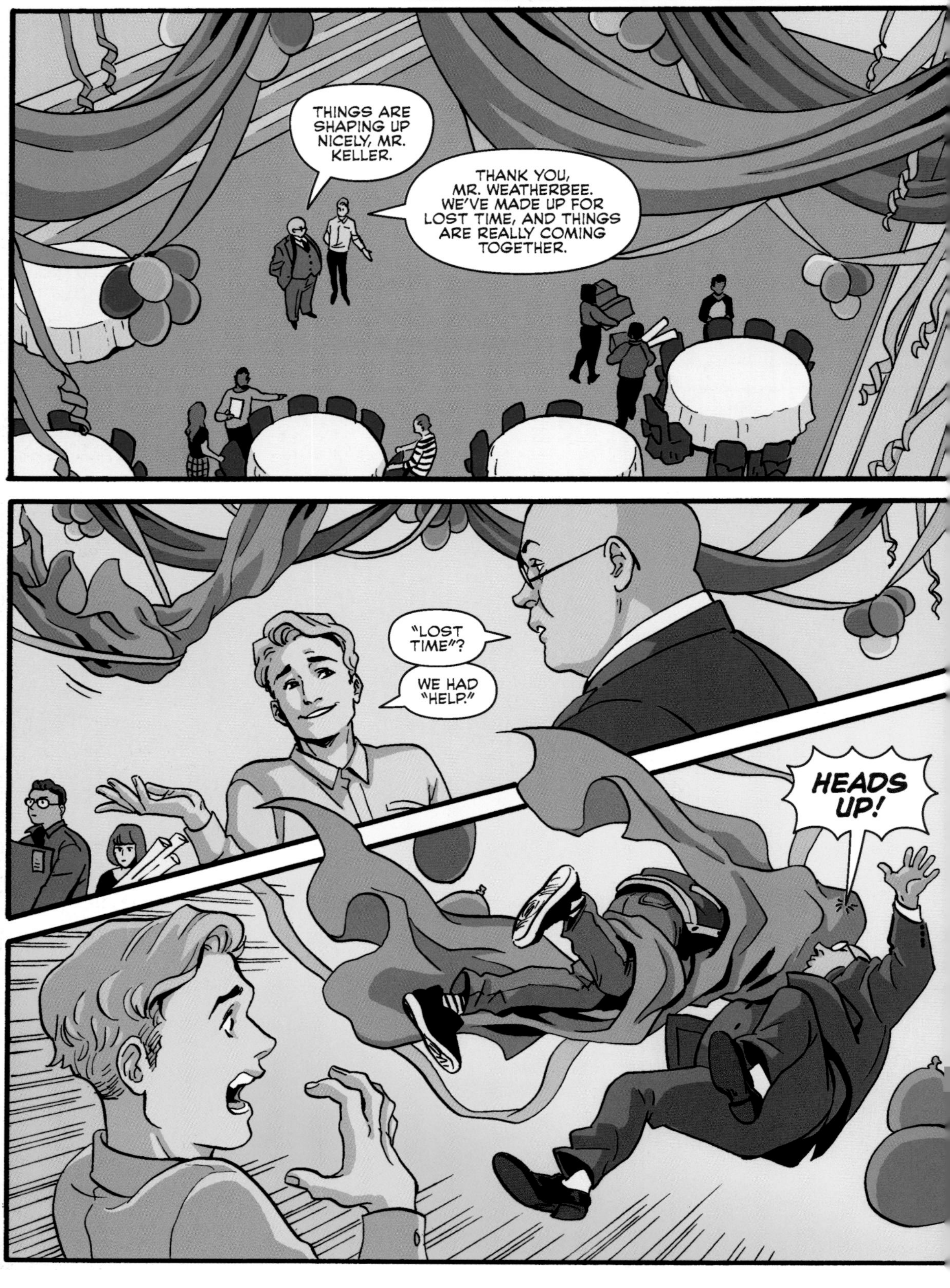
THINGS ARE SHAPING UP NICELY, MR. KELLER.
THANK YOU, MR. WEATHERBEE. WE'VE MADE UP FOR LOST TIME, AND THINGS ARE REALLY COMING TOGETHER.
"LOST TIME"?
WE HAD "HELP."
HEADS UP!

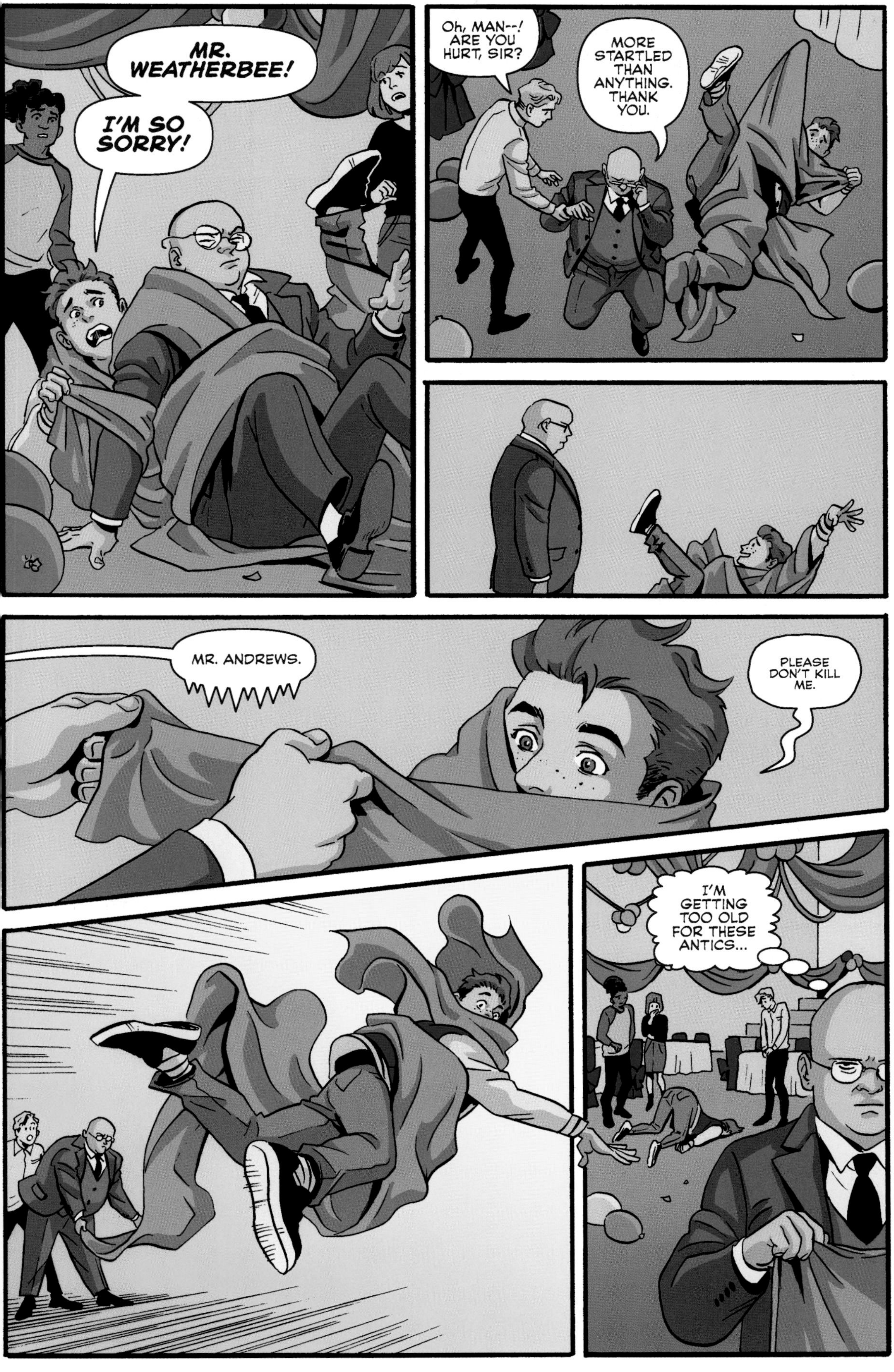
MR. WEATHERBEE!
I'M SO SORRY!
Oh, MAN--! ARE YOU HURT, SIR?
MORE STARTLED THAN ANYTHING. THANK YOU.
MR. ANDREWS.
PLEASE DON'T KILL ME.
I'M GETTING TOO OLD FOR THESE ANTICS...

CHAPTER FOUR: ONE BIG ~~HAPPY~~ FAMILY

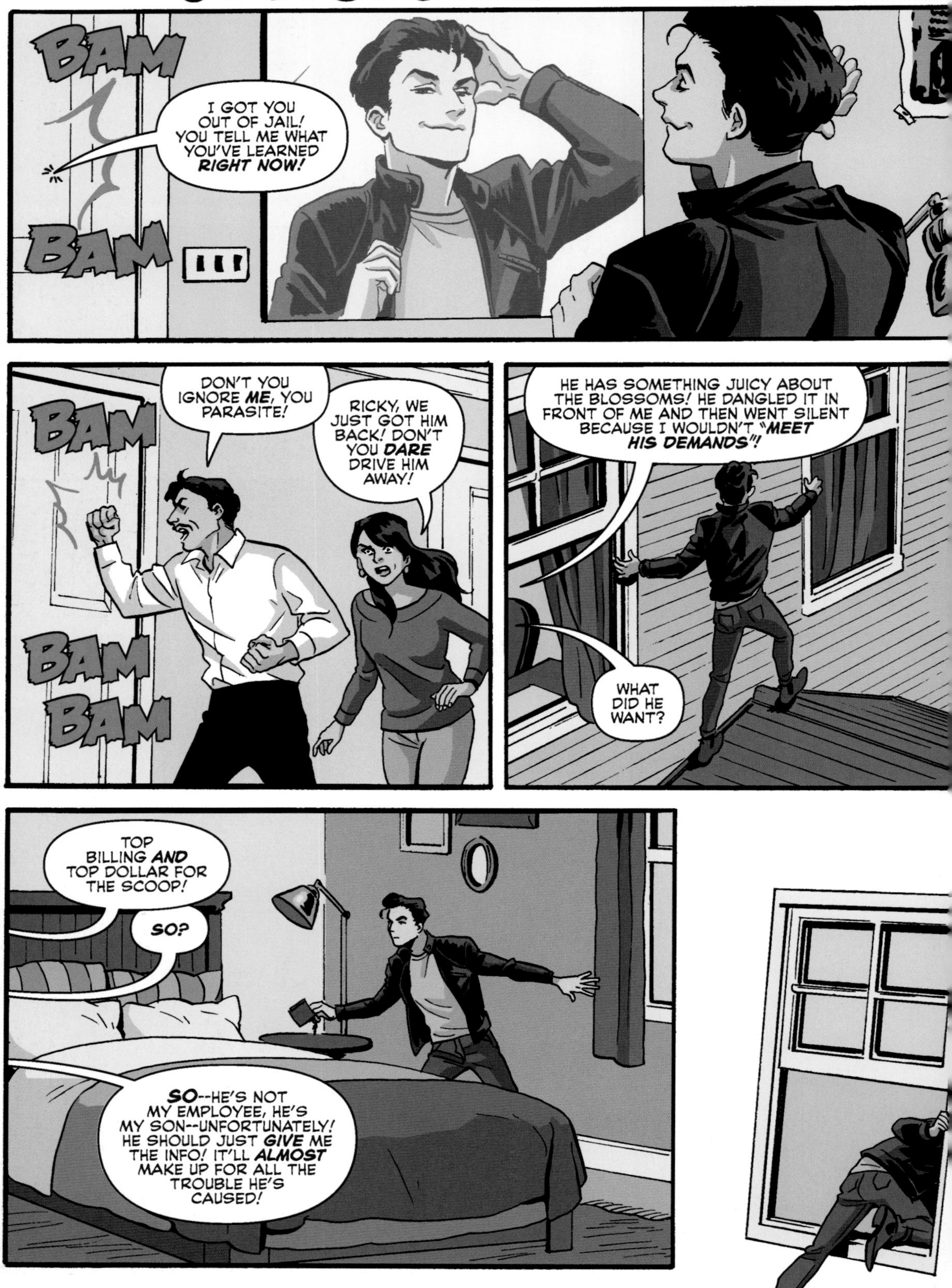

BAM
I GOT YOU OUT OF JAIL! YOU TELL ME WHAT YOU'VE LEARNED RIGHT NOW!
BAM
BAM
DON'T YOU IGNORE ME, YOU PARASITE!
RICKY, WE JUST GOT HIM BACK! DON'T YOU DARE DRIVE HIM AWAY!
BAM BAM
HE HAS SOMETHING JUICY ABOUT THE BLOSSOMS! HE DANGLED IT IN FRONT OF ME AND THEN WENT SILENT BECAUSE I WOULDN'T "MEET HIS DEMANDS"!
WHAT DID HE WANT?
TOP BILLING AND TOP DOLLAR FOR THE SCOOP!
SO?
SO--HE'S NOT MY EMPLOYEE, HE'S MY SON--UNFORTUNATELY! HE SHOULD JUST GIVE ME THE INFO! IT'LL ALMOST MAKE UP FOR ALL THE TROUBLE HE'S CAUSED!

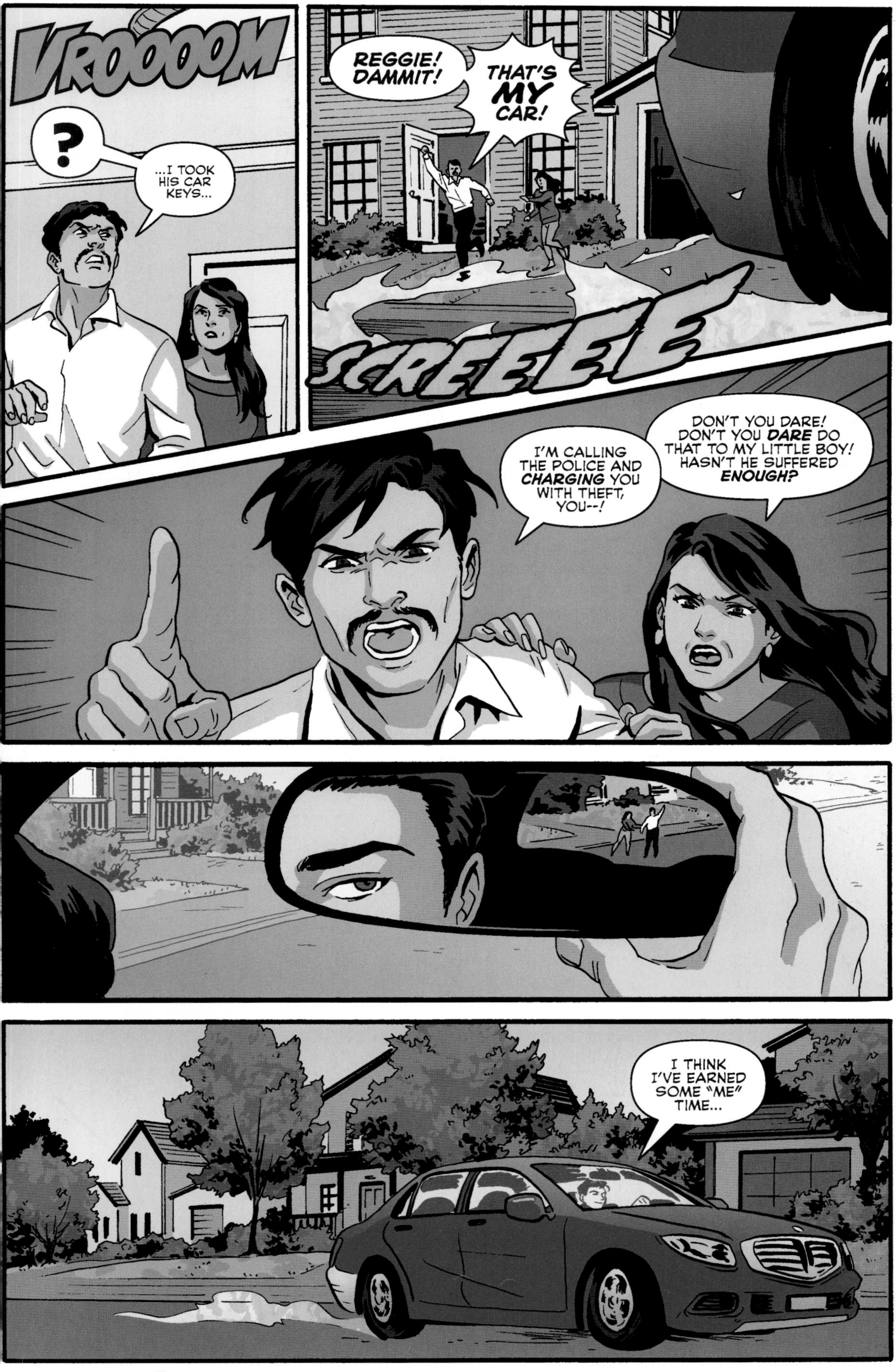
VROOOOM
?
...I TOOK HIS CAR KEYS...
REGGIE! DAMMIT!
THAT'S MY CAR!
SCREEEE
I'M CALLING THE POLICE AND CHARGING YOU WITH THEFT, YOU--!
DON'T YOU DARE! DON'T YOU DARE DO THAT TO MY LITTLE BOY! HASN'T HE SUFFERED ENOUGH?
I THINK I'VE EARNED SOME "ME" TIME...

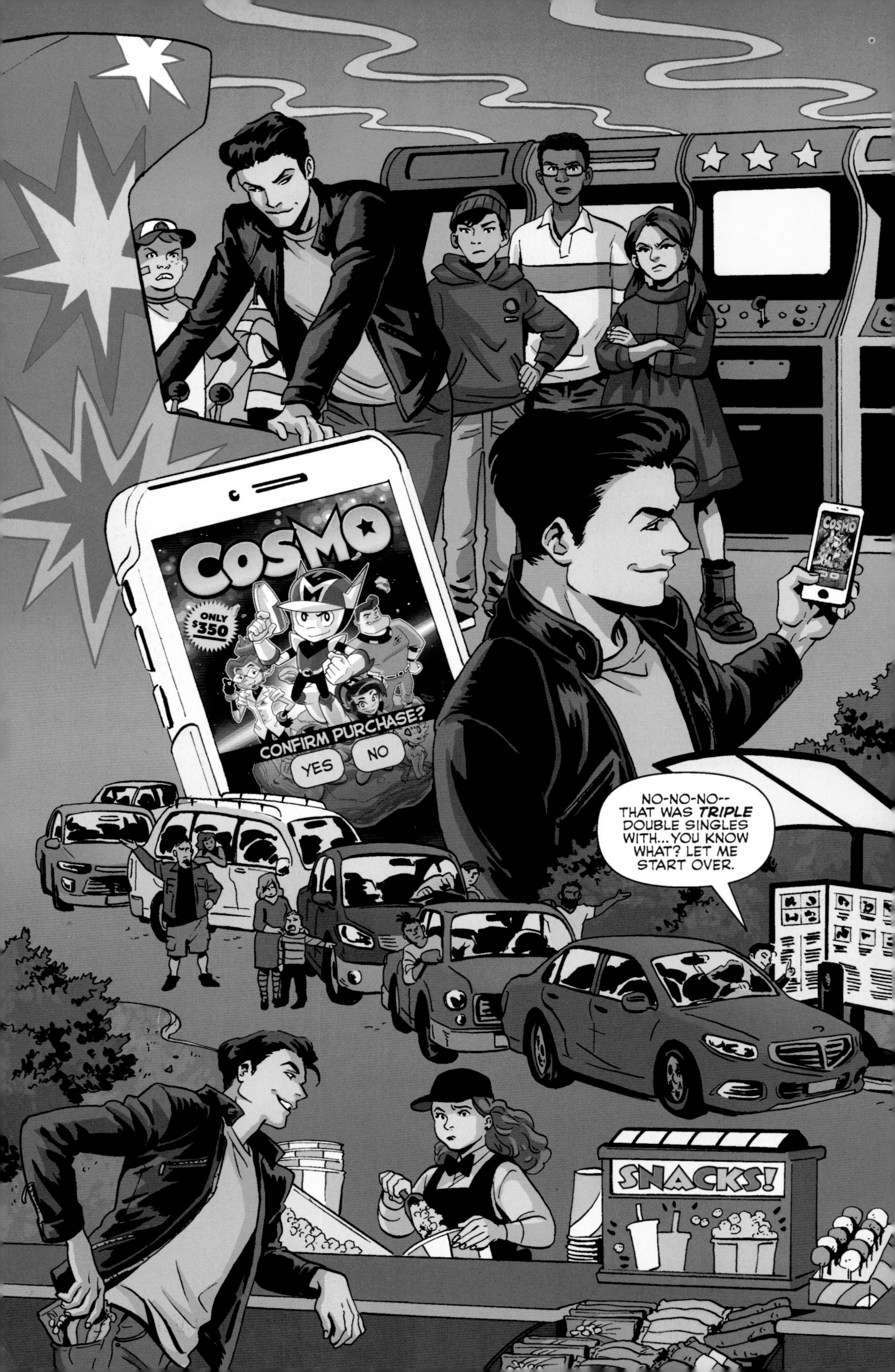
COSMO
ONLY $350
CONFIRM PURCHASE?
YES
NO
NO-NO-NO-- THAT WAS *TRIPLE* DOUBLE SINGLES WITH... YOU KNOW WHAT? LET ME START OVER.
SNACKS!

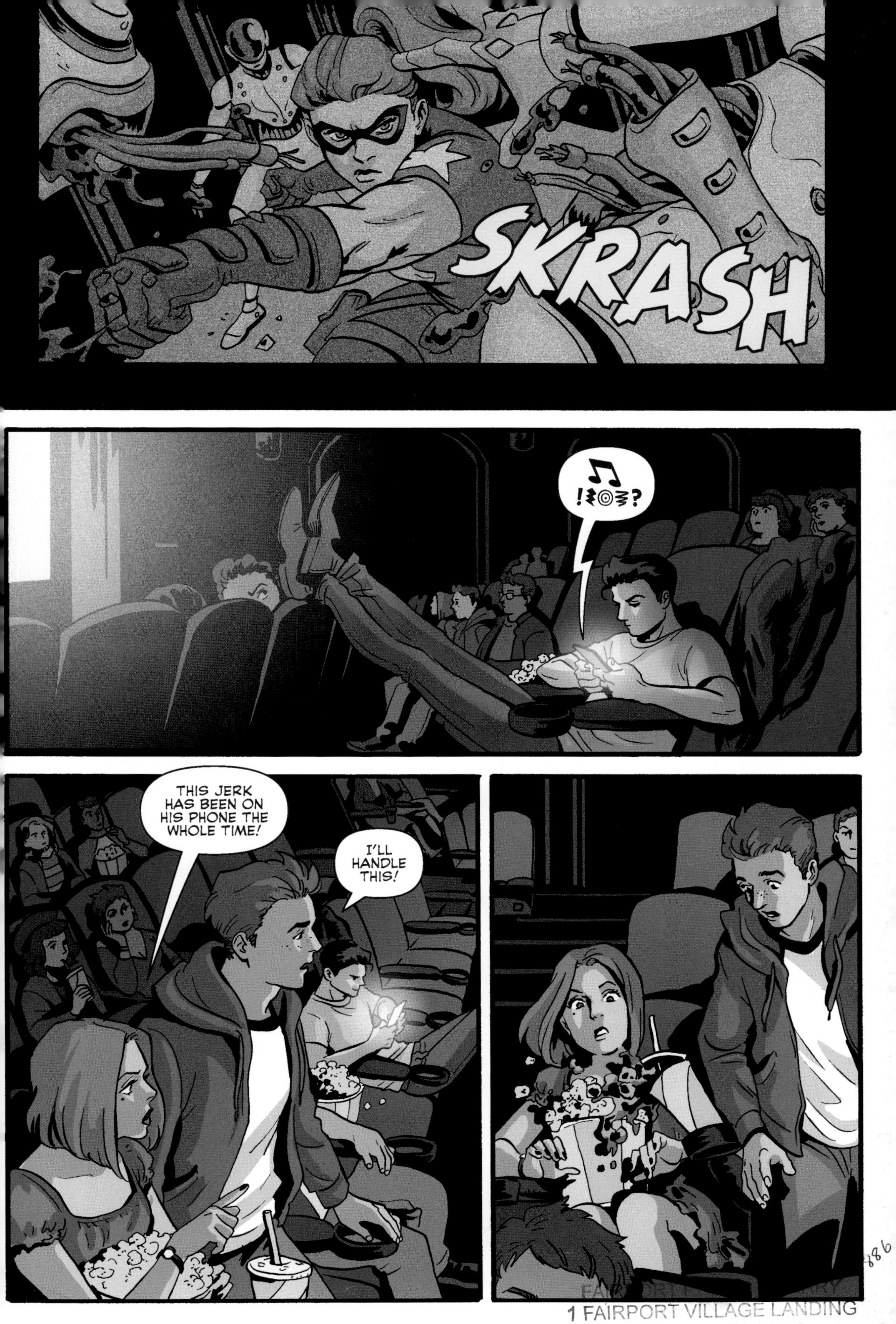
SKRASH
THIS JERK HAS BEEN ON HIS PHONE THE WHOLE TIME!
I'LL HANDLE THIS!

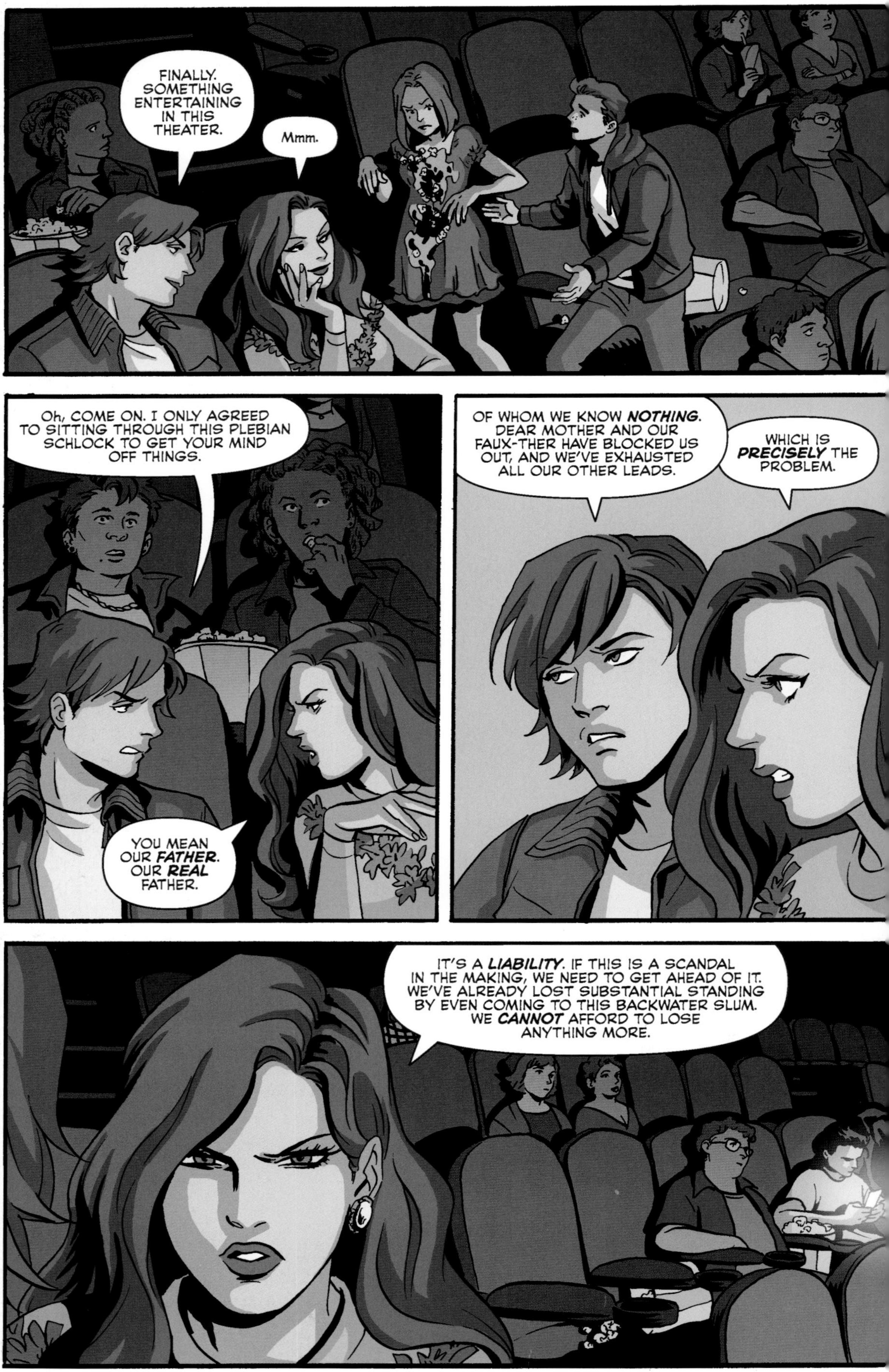
FINALLY. SOMETHING ENTERTAINING IN THIS THEATER.
Mmm.
Oh, COME ON. I ONLY AGREED TO SITTING THROUGH THIS PLEBIAN SCHLOCK TO GET YOUR MIND OFF THINGS.
YOU MEAN OUR FATHER. OUR REAL FATHER.
OF WHOM WE KNOW NOTHING. DEAR MOTHER AND OUR FAUX-THER HAVE BLOCKED US OUT, AND WE'VE EXHAUSTED ALL OUR OTHER LEADS.
WHICH IS PRECISELY THE PROBLEM.
IT'S A LIABILITY. IF THIS IS A SCANDAL IN THE MAKING, WE NEED TO GET AHEAD OF IT. WE'VE ALREADY LOST SUBSTANTIAL STANDING BY EVEN COMING TO THIS BACKWATER SLUM. WE CANNOT AFFORD TO LOSE ANYTHING MORE.

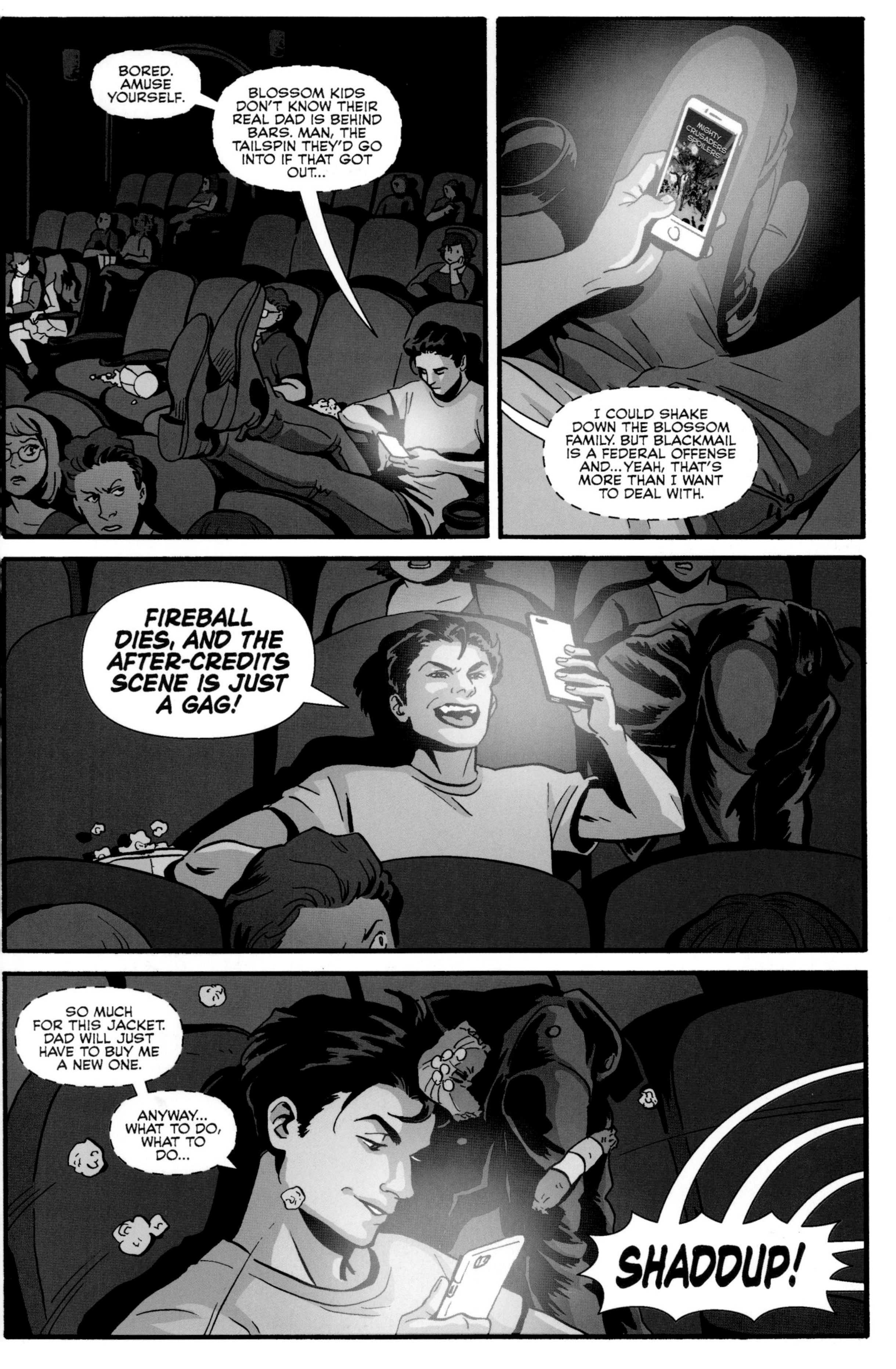
BORED. AMUSE YOURSELF.
BLOSSOM KIDS DON'T KNOW THEIR REAL DAD IS BEHIND BARS. MAN, THE TAILSPIN THEY'D GO INTO IF THAT GOT OUT...
MIGHTY CRUSADERS SPOILERS
I COULD SHAKE DOWN THE BLOSSOM FAMILY. BUT BLACKMAIL IS A FEDERAL OFFENSE AND...YEAH, THAT'S MORE THAN I WANT TO DEAL WITH.
FIREBALL DIES, AND THE AFTER-CREDITS SCENE IS JUST A GAG!
SO MUCH FOR THIS JACKET. DAD WILL JUST HAVE TO BUY ME A NEW ONE.
ANYWAY... WHAT TO DO, WHAT TO DO...
SHADDUP!

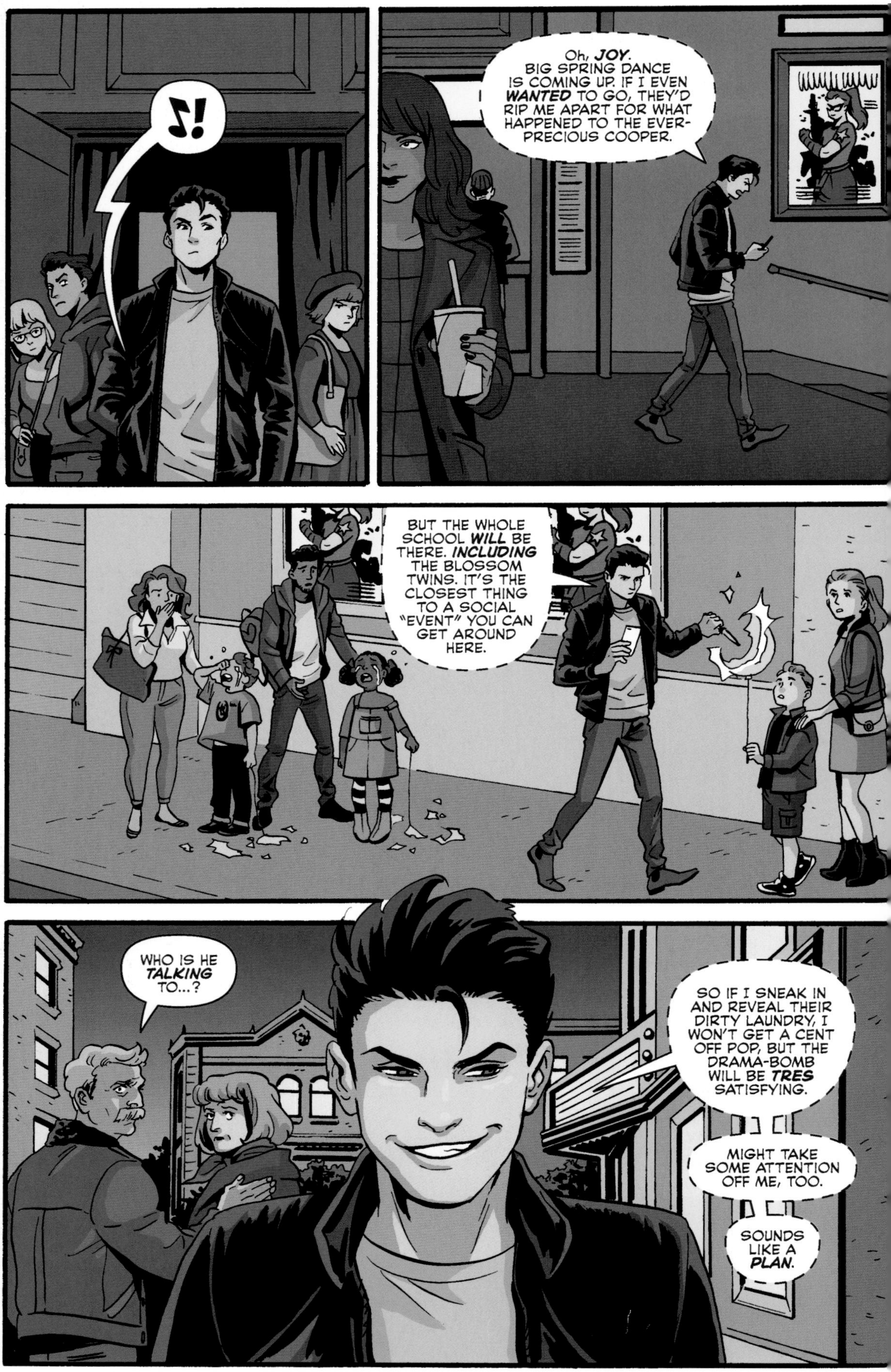
♪!
Oh, JOY. BIG SPRING DANCE IS COMING UP. IF I EVEN WANTED TO GO, THEY'D RIP ME APART FOR WHAT HAPPENED TO THE EVER-PRECIOUS COOPER.
BUT THE WHOLE SCHOOL WILL BE THERE. INCLUDING THE BLOSSOM TWINS. IT'S THE CLOSEST THING TO A SOCIAL "EVENT" YOU CAN GET AROUND HERE.
WHO IS HE TALKING TO...?
SO IF I SNEAK IN AND REVEAL THEIR DIRTY LAUNDRY, I WON'T GET A CENT OFF POP, BUT THE DRAMA-BOMB WILL BE TRES SATISFYING.
MIGHT TAKE SOME ATTENTION OFF ME, TOO.
SOUNDS LIKE A PLAN.

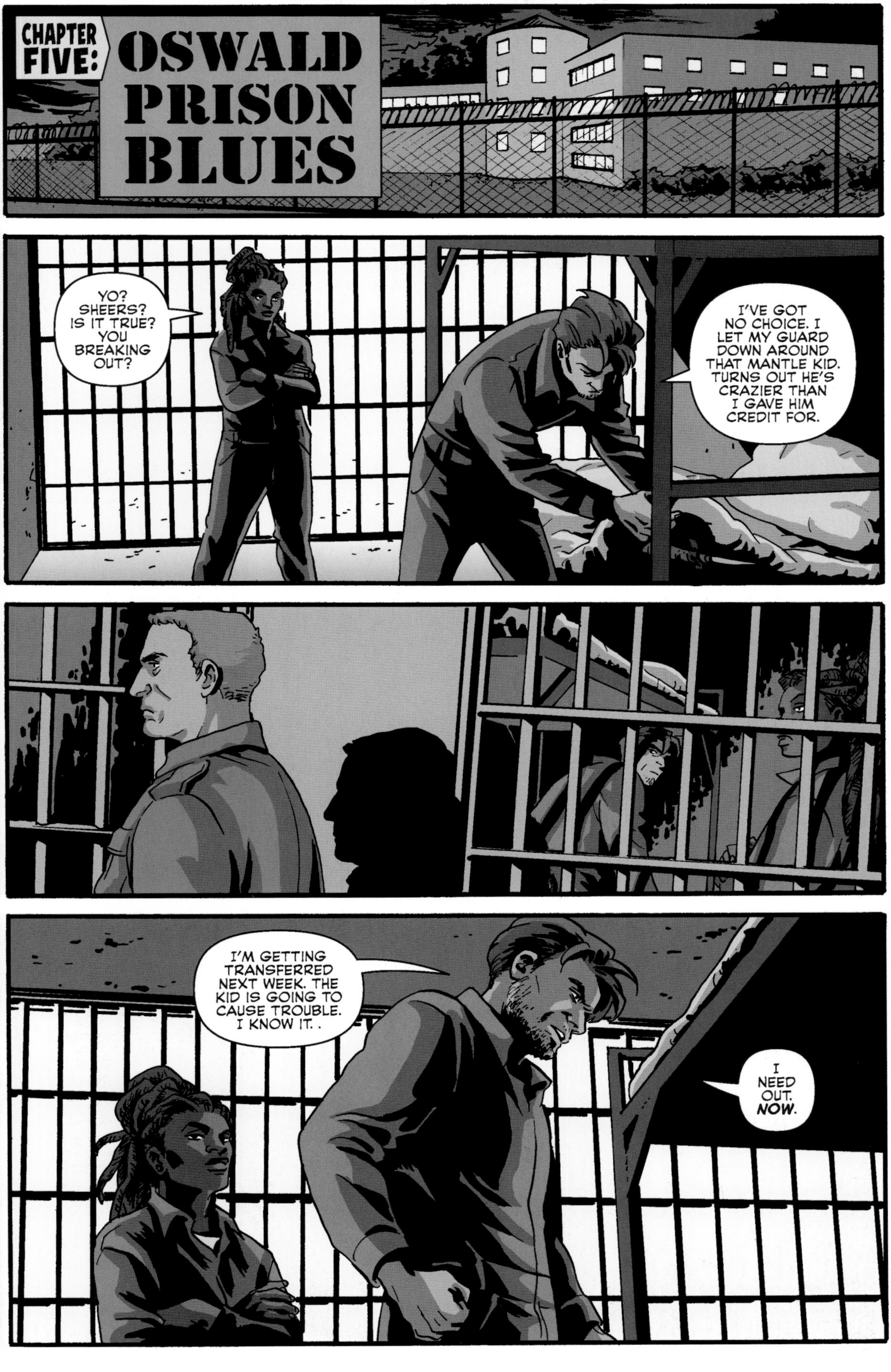
CHAPTER FIVE: OSWALD PRISON BLUES
YO? SHEERS? IS IT TRUE? YOU BREAKING OUT?
I'VE GOT NO CHOICE. I LET MY GUARD DOWN AROUND THAT MANTLE KID. TURNS OUT HE'S CRAZIER THAN I GAVE HIM CREDIT FOR.
I'M GETTING TRANSFERRED NEXT WEEK. THE KID IS GOING TO CAUSE TROUBLE. I KNOW IT. .
I NEED OUT. NOW.

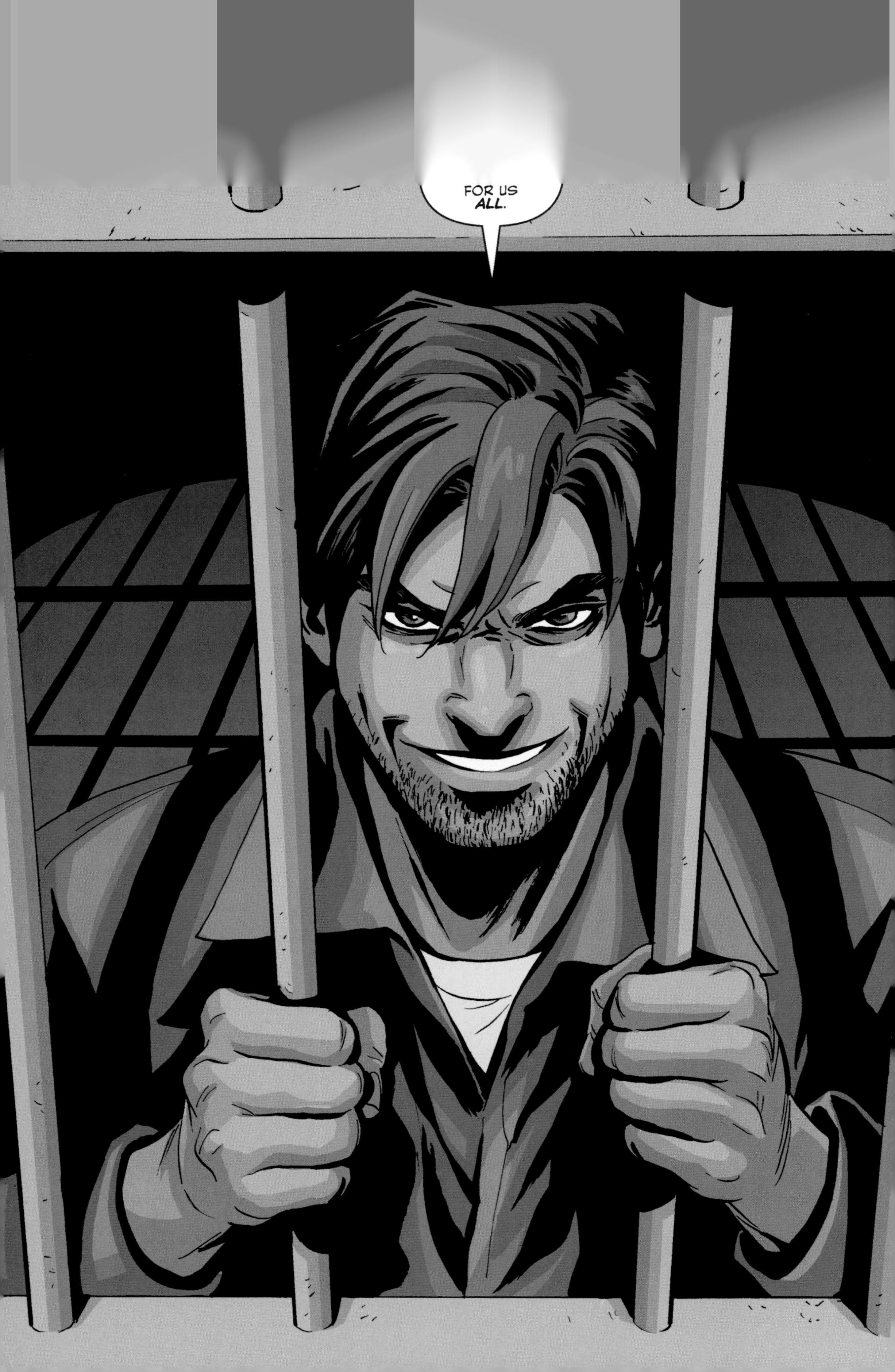
FOR US ALL.

TO BE CONTINUED...

ISSUE TWENTY-NINE

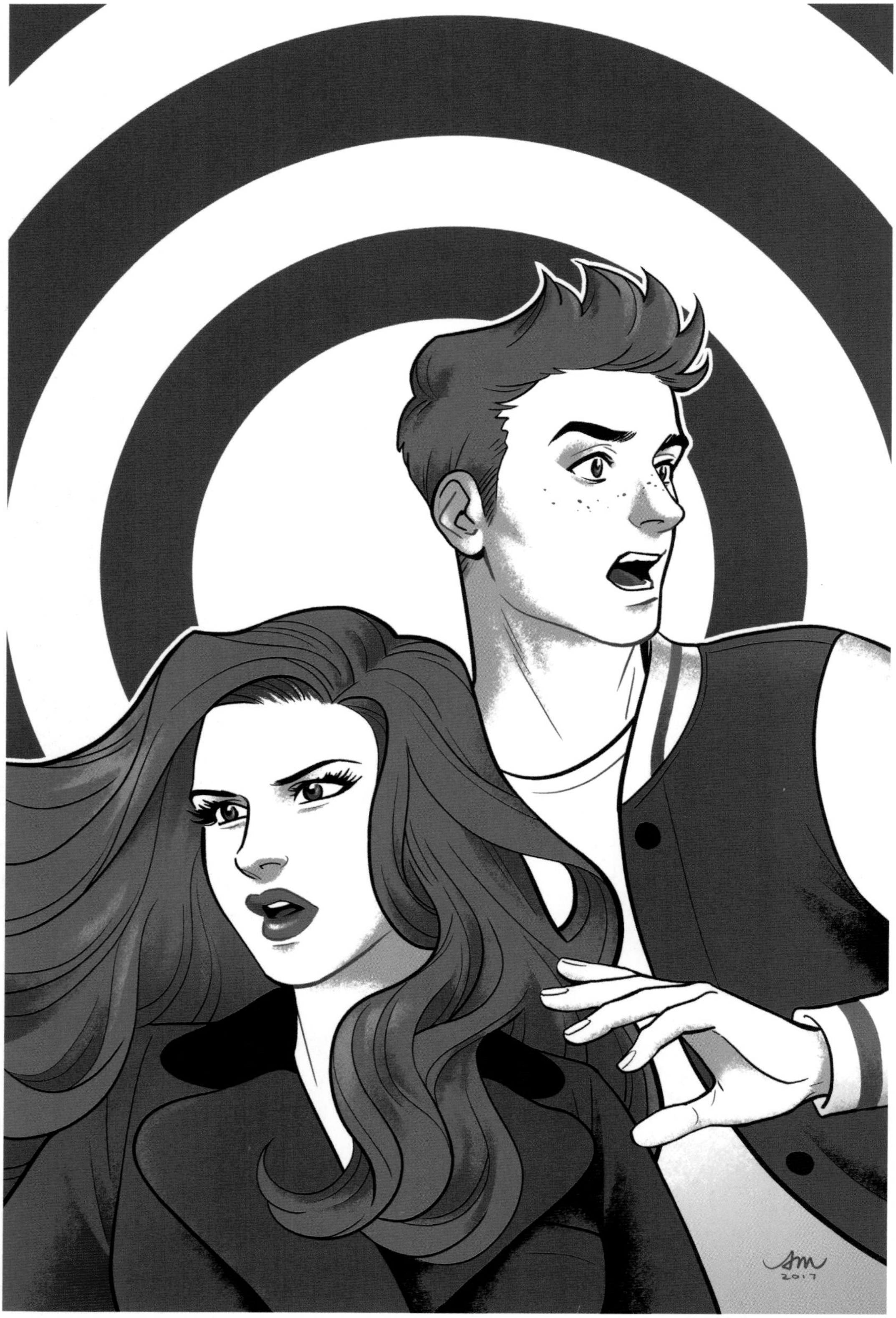

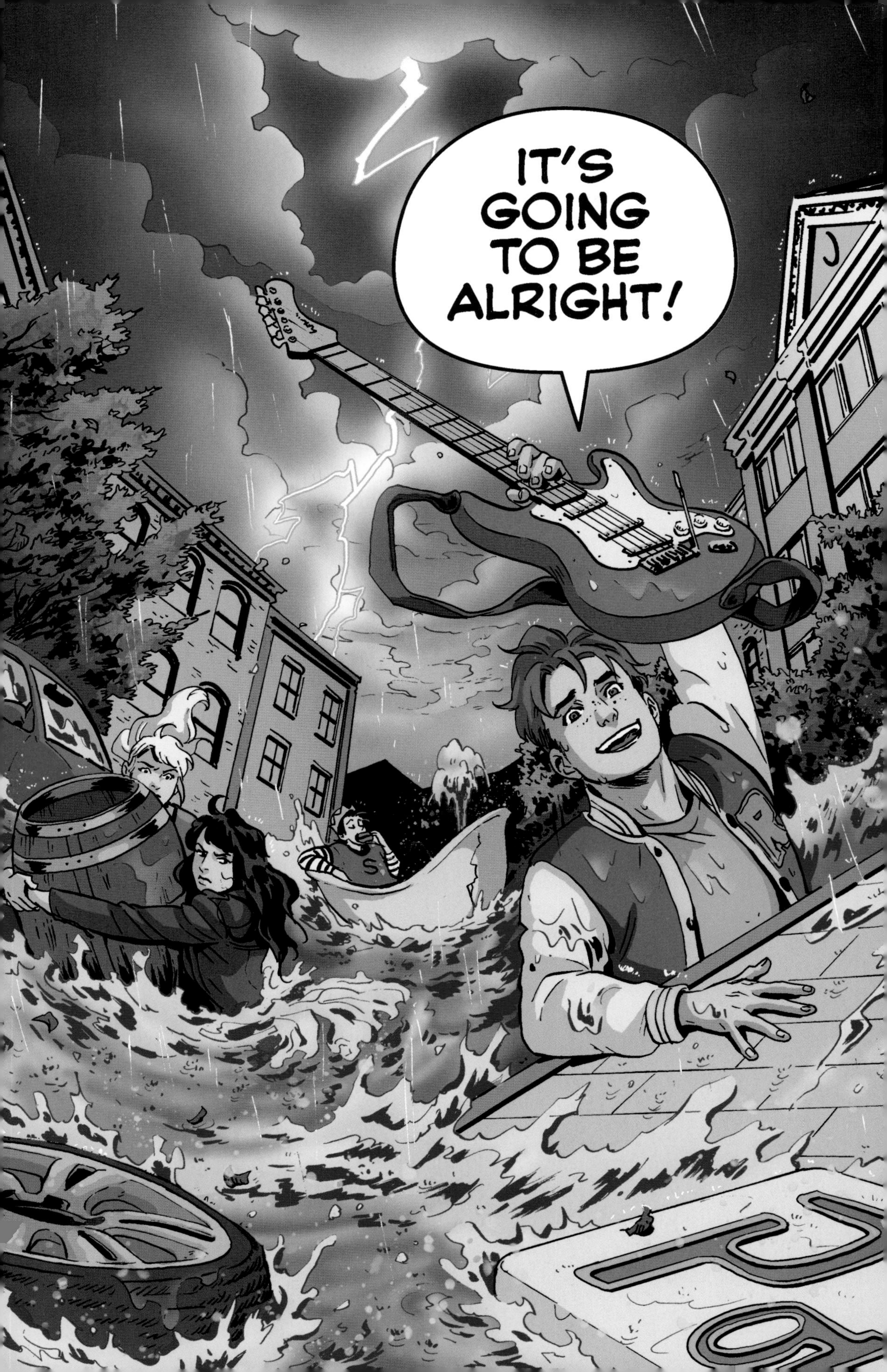
IT'S GOING TO BE ALRIGHT!

CHAPTER ONE: AND THE BEAT GOES ON

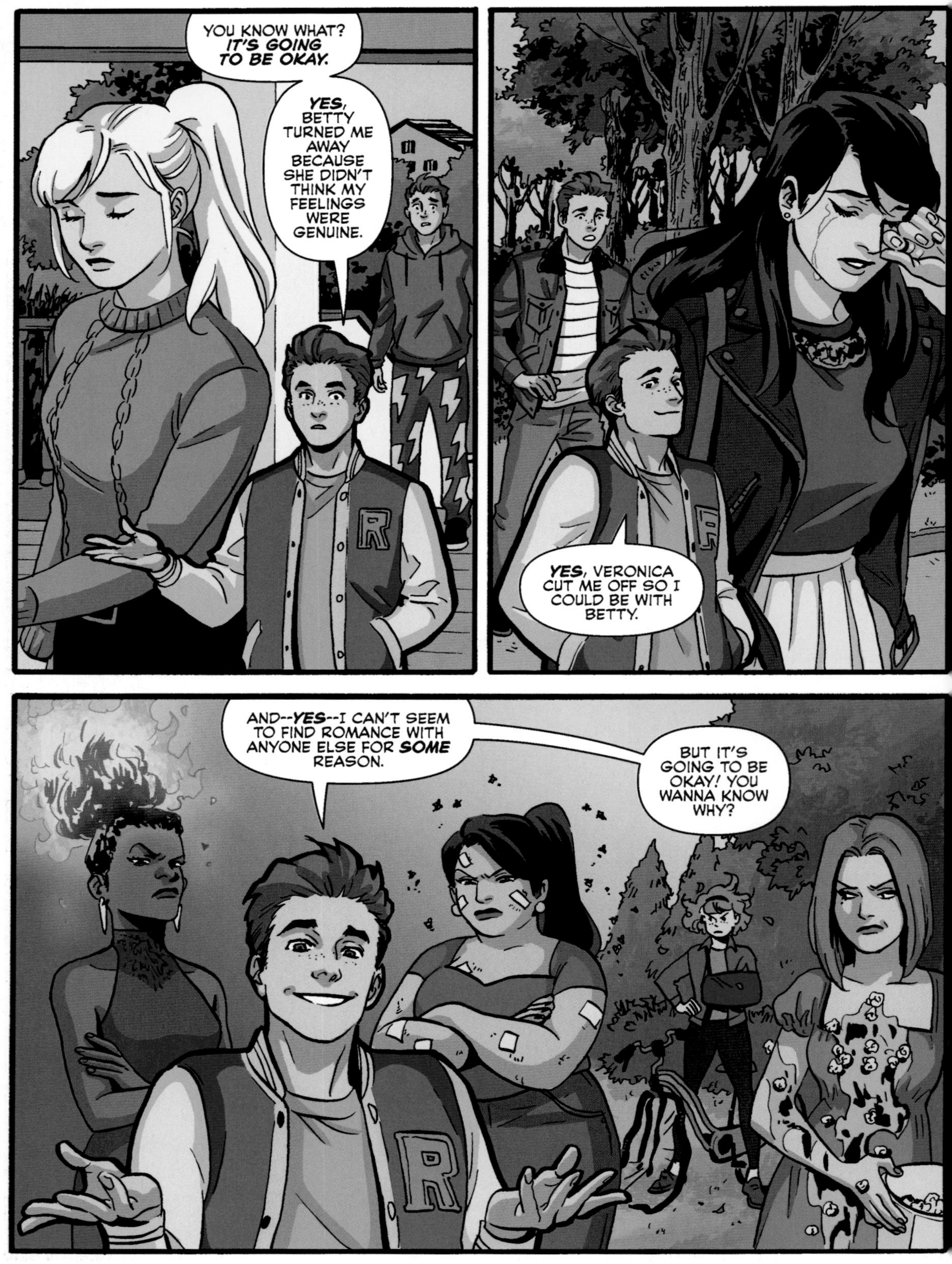

YOU KNOW WHAT? IT'S GOING TO BE OKAY.
YES, BETTY TURNED ME AWAY BECAUSE SHE DIDN'T THINK MY FEELINGS WERE GENUINE.
YES, VERONICA CUT ME OFF SO I COULD BE WITH BETTY.
AND--YES--I CAN'T SEEM TO FIND ROMANCE WITH ANYONE ELSE FOR SOME REASON.
BUT IT'S GOING TO BE OKAY! YOU WANNA KNOW WHY?

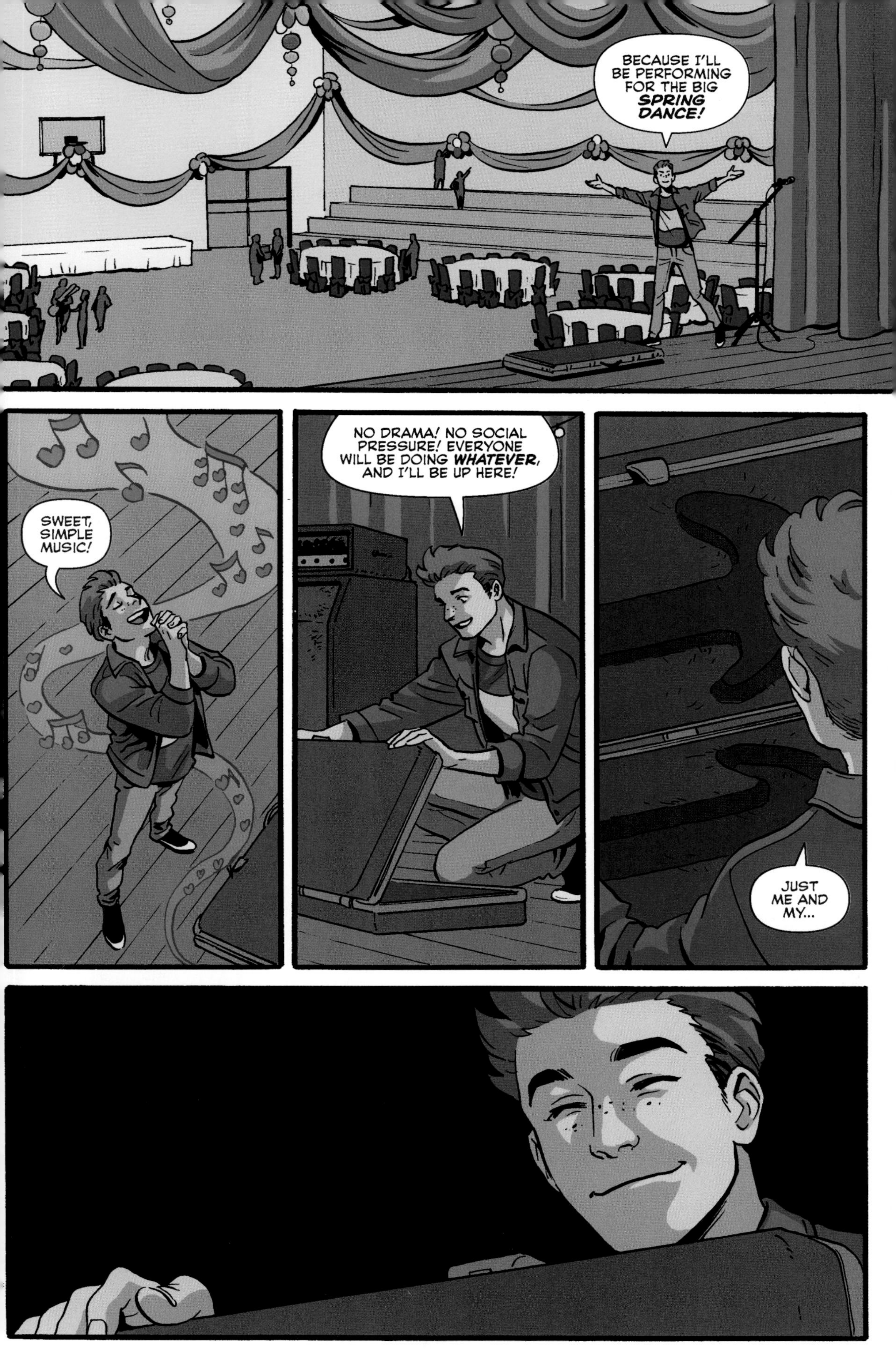
BECAUSE I'LL BE PERFORMING FOR THE BIG ***SPRING DANCE!***
SWEET, SIMPLE MUSIC!
NO DRAMA! NO SOCIAL PRESSURE! EVERYONE WILL BE DOING ***WHATEVER***, AND I'LL BE UP HERE!
JUST ME AND MY...

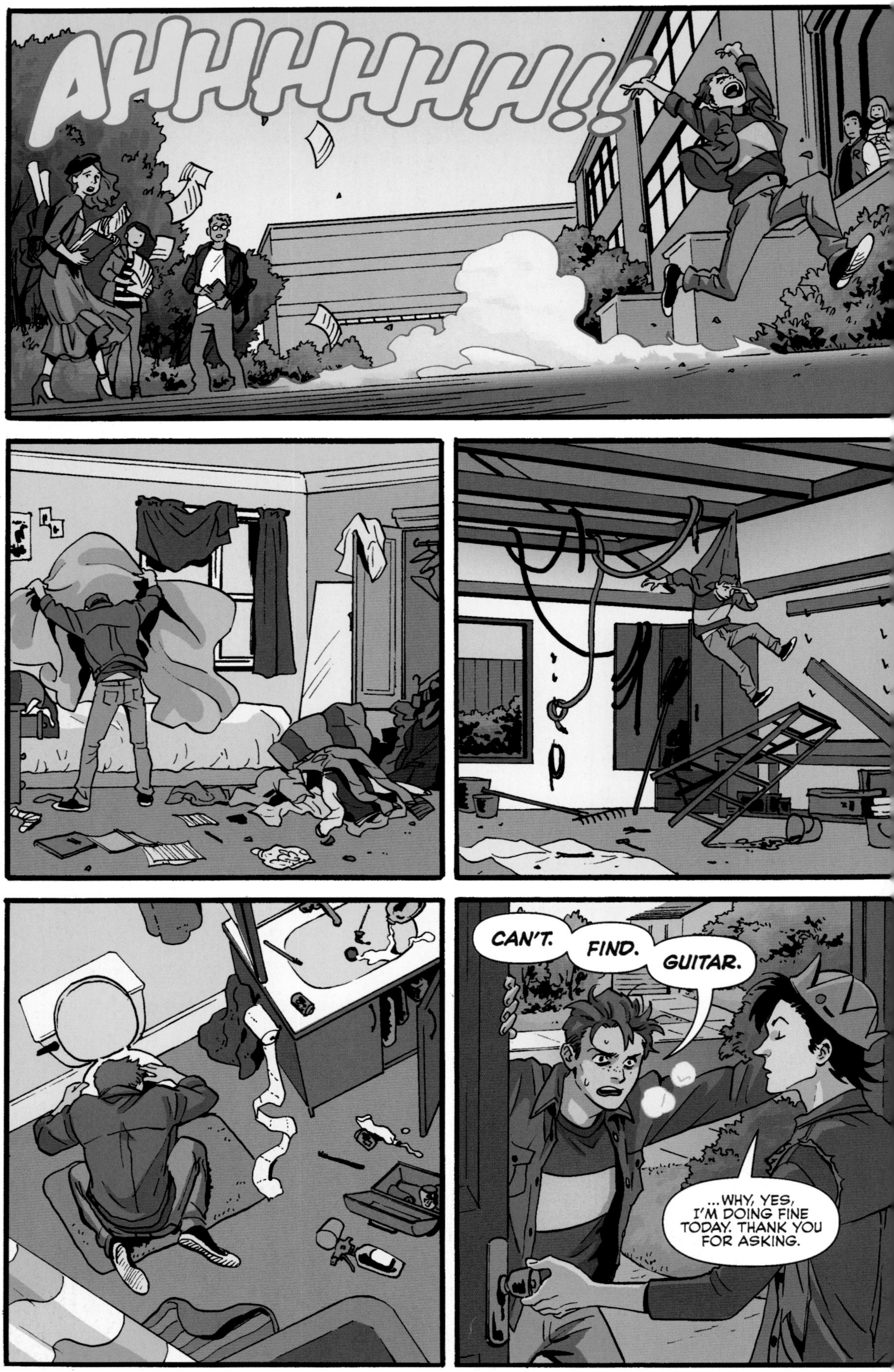
AHHHHHHH!!
CAN'T.
FIND.
GUITAR.
...WHY, YES, I'M DOING FINE TODAY. THANK YOU FOR ASKING.

CHAPTER TWO: REGGIE CHANGES HIS TUNE

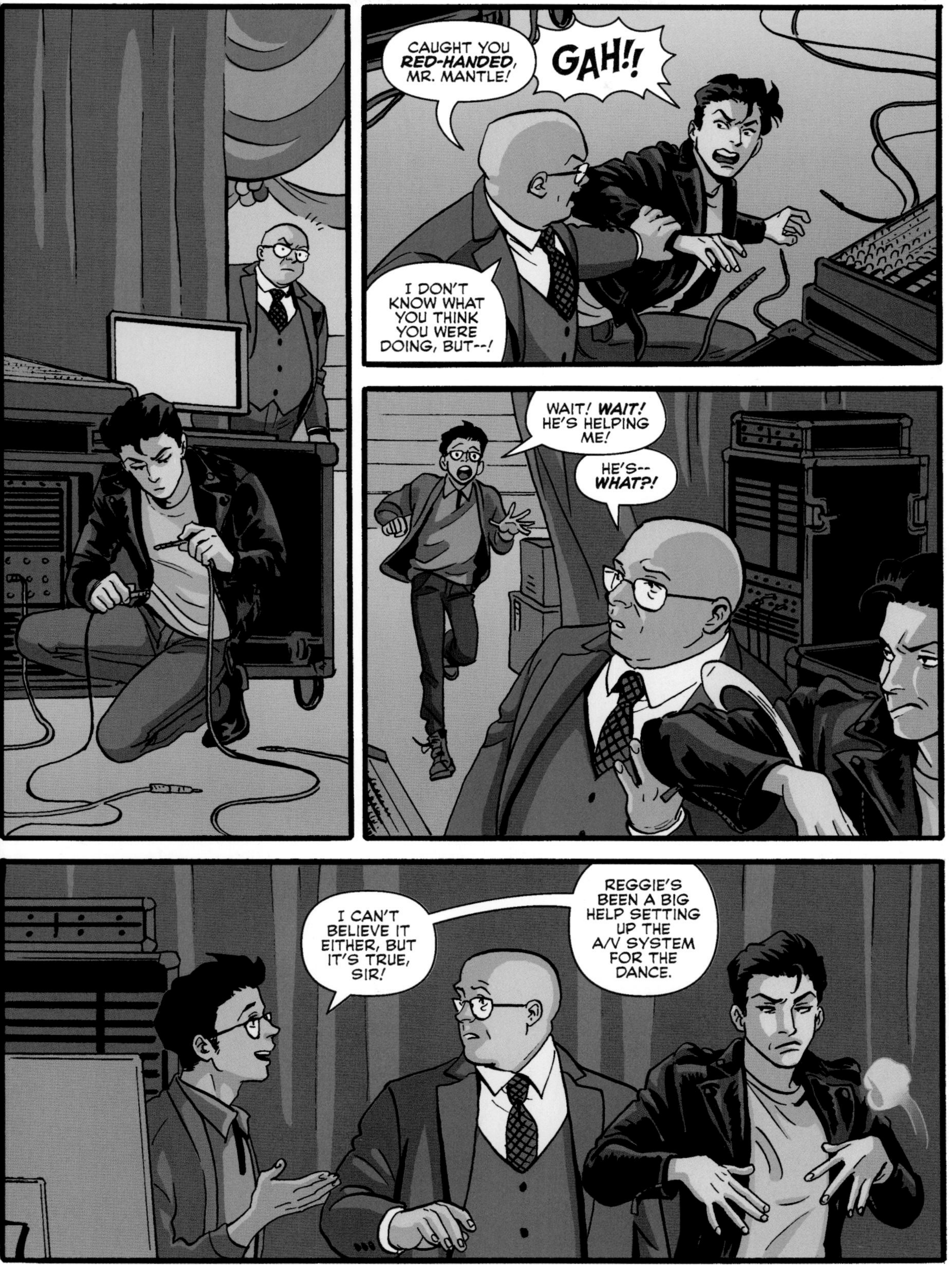
CAUGHT YOU RED-HANDED, MR. MANTLE!
GAH!!
I DON'T KNOW WHAT YOU THINK YOU WERE DOING, BUT--!
WAIT! WAIT! HE'S HELPING ME!
HE'S-- WHAT?!
I CAN'T BELIEVE IT EITHER, BUT IT'S TRUE, SIR!
REGGIE'S BEEN A BIG HELP SETTING UP THE A/V SYSTEM FOR THE DANCE.

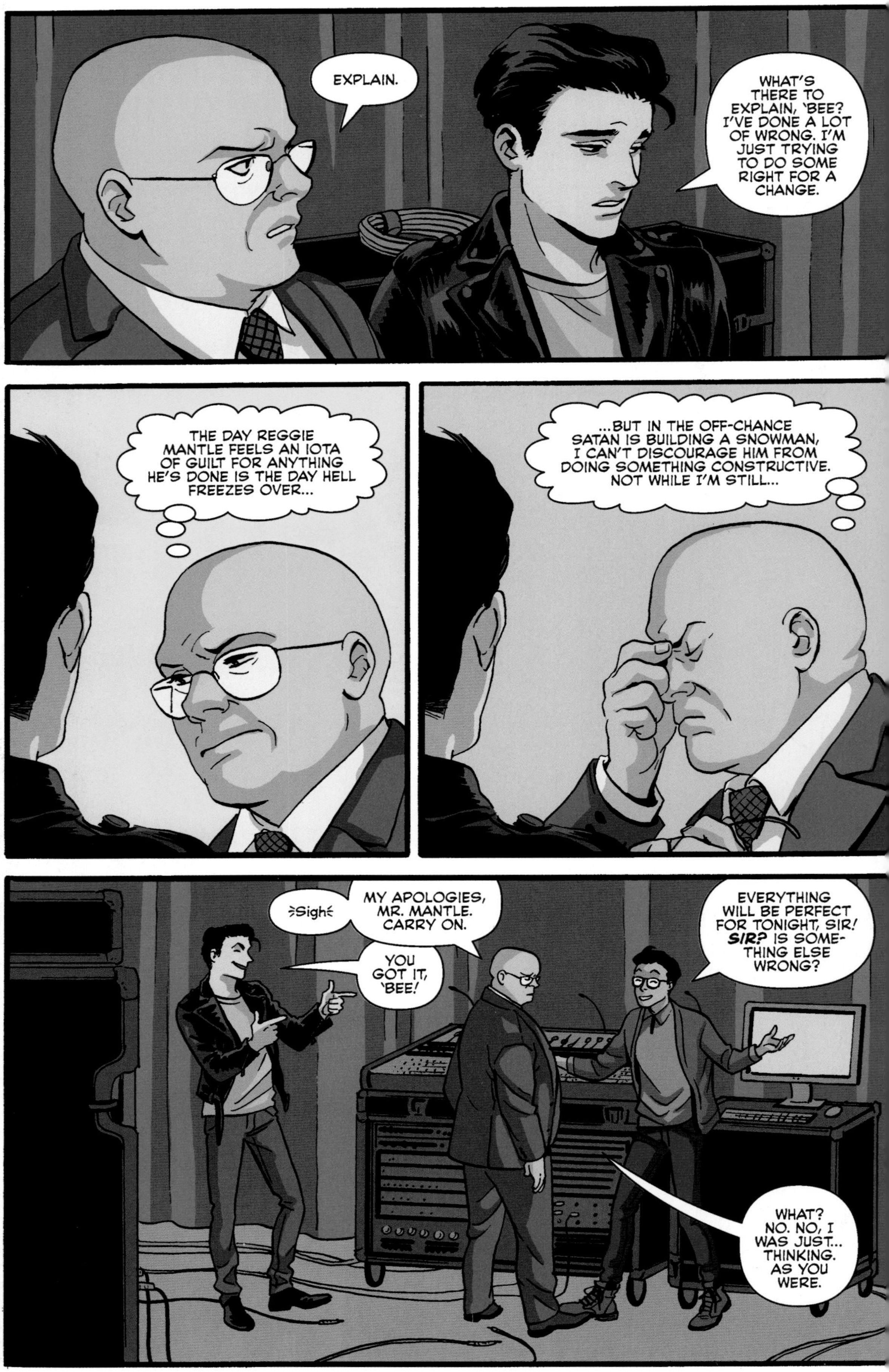
EXPLAIN.
WHAT'S THERE TO EXPLAIN, 'BEE? I'VE DONE A LOT OF WRONG. I'M JUST TRYING TO DO SOME RIGHT FOR A CHANGE.
THE DAY REGGIE MANTLE FEELS AN IOTA OF GUILT FOR ANYTHING HE'S DONE IS THE DAY HELL FREEZES OVER...
...BUT IN THE OFF-CHANCE SATAN IS BUILDING A SNOWMAN, I CAN'T DISCOURAGE HIM FROM DOING SOMETHING CONSTRUCTIVE. NOT WHILE I'M STILL...
Sigh
MY APOLOGIES, MR. MANTLE. CARRY ON.
YOU GOT IT, 'BEE!
EVERYTHING WILL BE PERFECT FOR TONIGHT, SIR! SIR? IS SOMETHING ELSE WRONG?
WHAT? NO. NO, I WAS JUST... THINKING. AS YOU WERE.

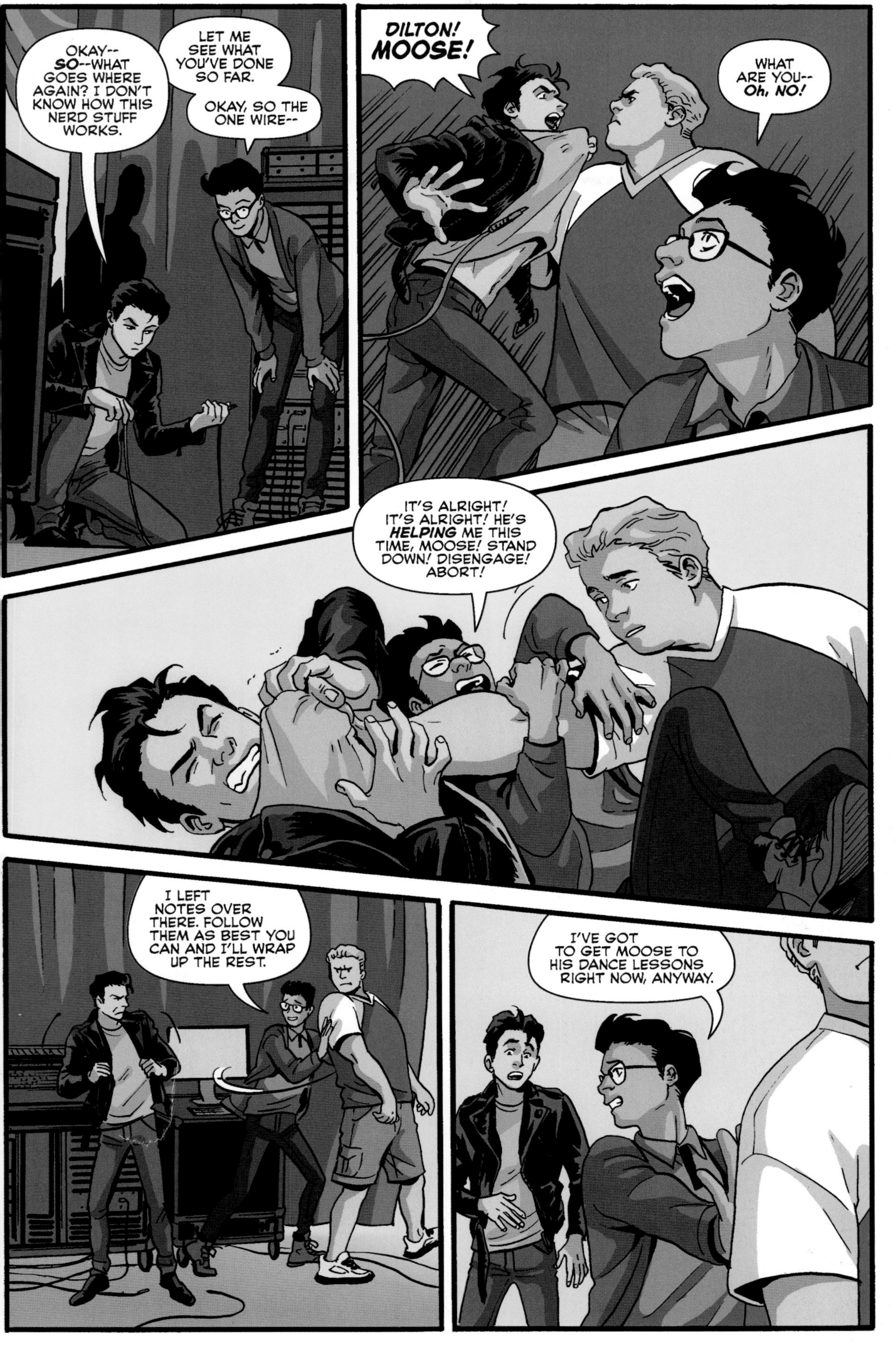
OKAY-- SO--WHAT GOES WHERE AGAIN? I DON'T KNOW HOW THIS NERD STUFF WORKS.
LET ME SEE WHAT YOU'VE DONE SO FAR.
OKAY, SO THE ONE WIRE--
DILTON! MOOSE!
WHAT ARE YOU-- Oh, NO!
IT'S ALRIGHT! IT'S ALRIGHT! HE'S HELPING ME THIS TIME, MOOSE! STAND DOWN! DISENGAGE! ABORT!
I LEFT NOTES OVER THERE. FOLLOW THEM AS BEST YOU CAN AND I'LL WRAP UP THE REST.
I'VE GOT TO GET MOOSE TO HIS DANCE LESSONS RIGHT NOW, ANYWAY.

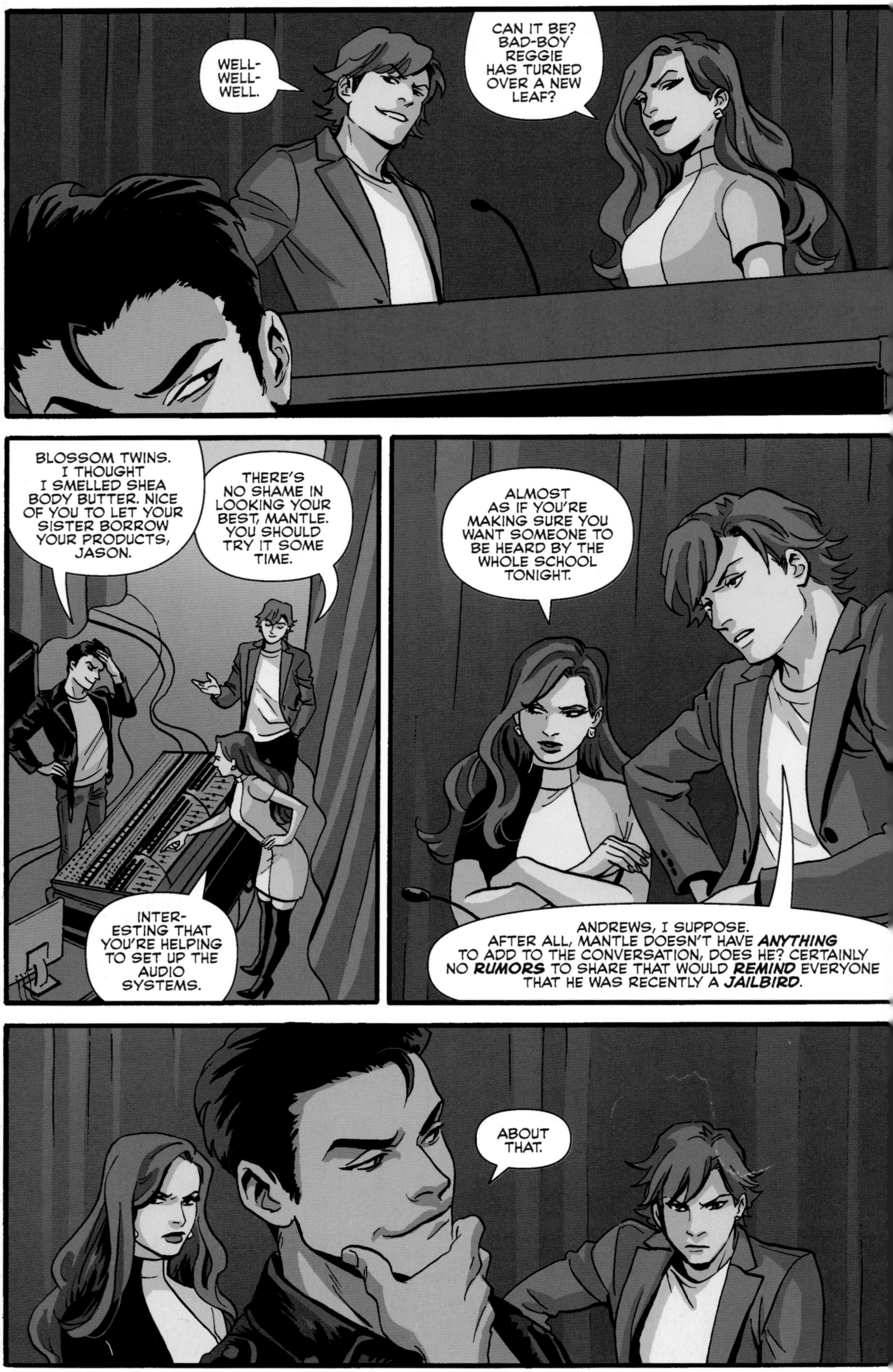
WELL-WELL-WELL.
CAN IT BE? BAD-BOY REGGIE HAS TURNED OVER A NEW LEAF?
BLOSSOM TWINS. I THOUGHT I SMELLED SHEA BODY BUTTER. NICE OF YOU TO LET YOUR SISTER BORROW YOUR PRODUCTS, JASON.
THERE'S NO SHAME IN LOOKING YOUR BEST, MANTLE. YOU SHOULD TRY IT SOME TIME.
INTERESTING THAT YOU'RE HELPING TO SET UP THE AUDIO SYSTEMS.
ALMOST AS IF YOU'RE MAKING SURE YOU WANT SOMEONE TO BE HEARD BY THE WHOLE SCHOOL TONIGHT.
ANDREWS, I SUPPOSE. AFTER ALL, MANTLE DOESN'T HAVE ***ANYTHING*** TO ADD TO THE CONVERSATION, DOES HE? CERTAINLY NO ***RUMORS*** TO SHARE THAT WOULD ***REMIND*** EVERYONE THAT HE WAS RECENTLY A ***JAILBIRD***.
ABOUT THAT.

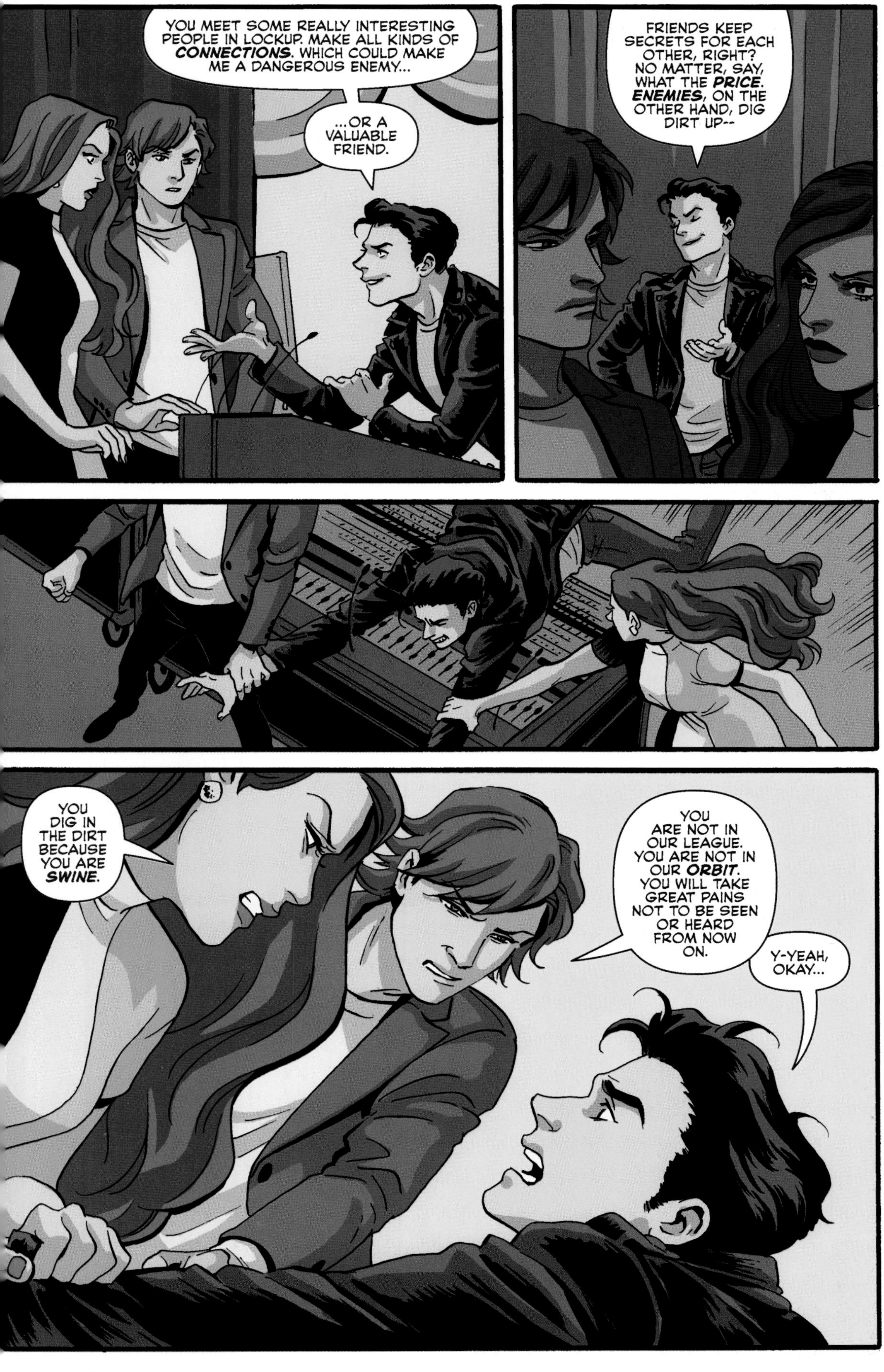
YOU MEET SOME REALLY INTERESTING PEOPLE IN LOCKUP. MAKE ALL KINDS OF **CONNECTIONS**. WHICH COULD MAKE ME A DANGEROUS ENEMY...
...OR A VALUABLE FRIEND.
FRIENDS KEEP SECRETS FOR EACH OTHER, RIGHT? NO MATTER, SAY, WHAT THE **PRICE**. **ENEMIES**, ON THE OTHER HAND, DIG DIRT UP--
YOU DIG IN THE DIRT BECAUSE YOU ARE **SWINE**.
YOU ARE NOT IN OUR LEAGUE. YOU ARE NOT IN OUR **ORBIT**. YOU WILL TAKE GREAT PAINS NOT TO BE SEEN OR HEARD FROM NOW ON.
Y-YEAH, OKAY...

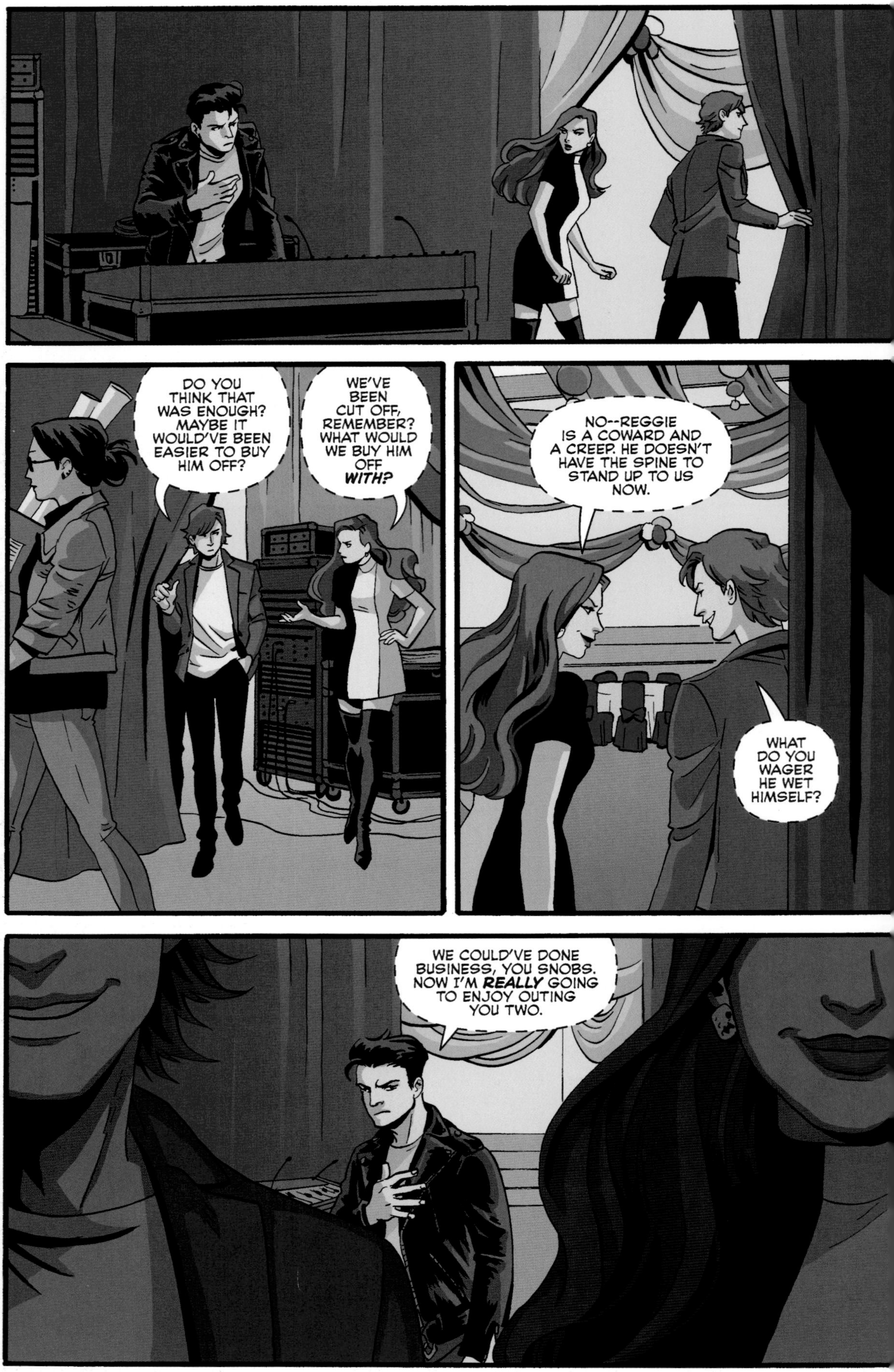

DO YOU THINK THAT WAS ENOUGH? MAYBE IT WOULD'VE BEEN EASIER TO BUY HIM OFF?
WE'VE BEEN CUT OFF, REMEMBER? WHAT WOULD WE BUY HIM OFF *WITH?*
NO--REGGIE IS A COWARD AND A CREEP. HE DOESN'T HAVE THE SPINE TO STAND UP TO US NOW.
WHAT DO YOU WAGER HE WET HIMSELF?
WE COULD'VE DONE BUSINESS, YOU SNOBS. NOW I'M ***REALLY*** GOING TO ENJOY OUTING YOU TWO.

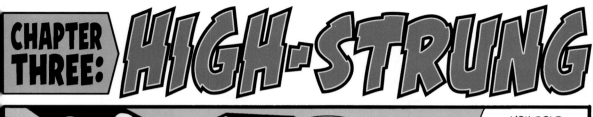

CHAPTER THREE: HIGH-STRUNG

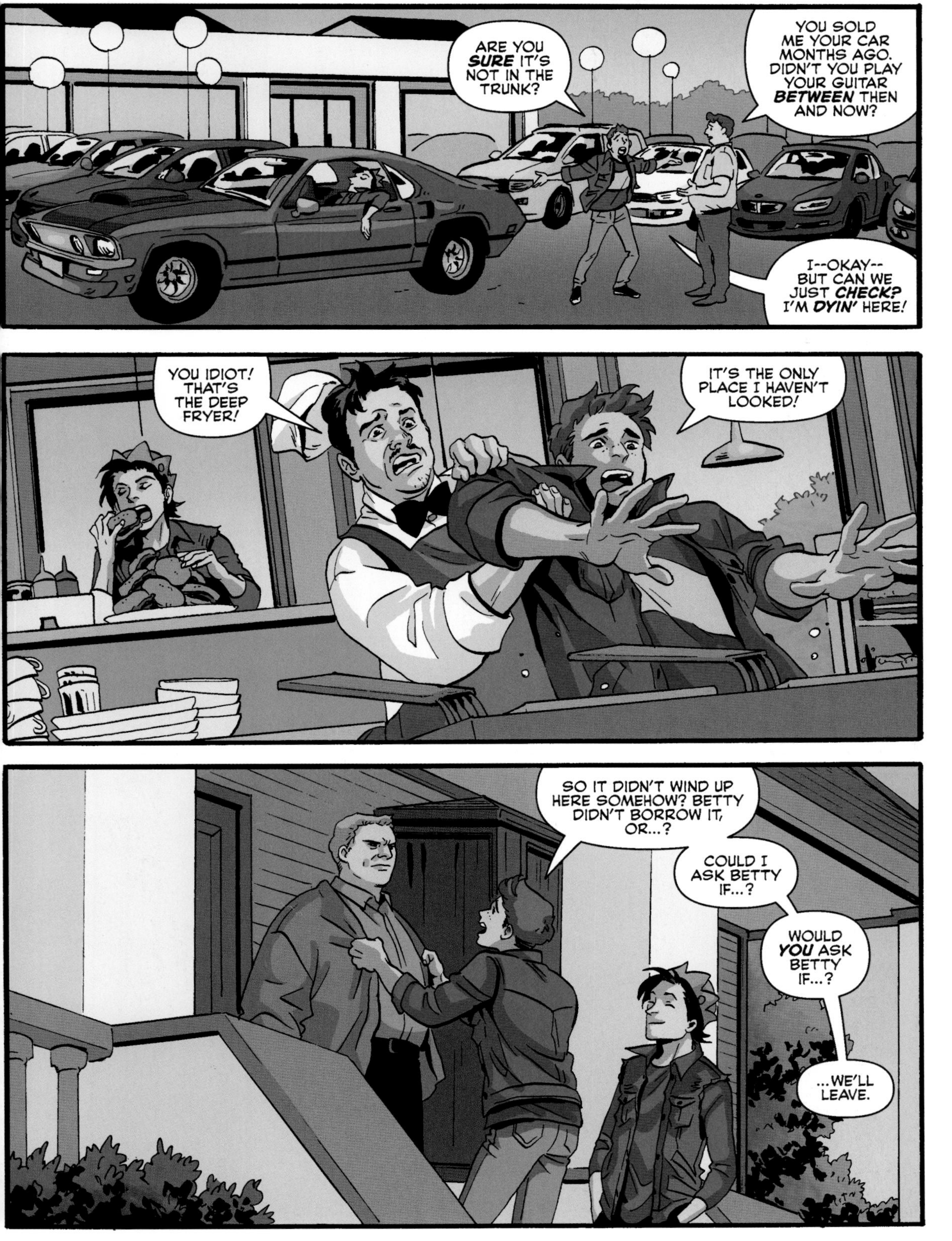
ARE YOU SURE IT'S NOT IN THE TRUNK?
YOU SOLD ME YOUR CAR MONTHS AGO. DIDN'T YOU PLAY YOUR GUITAR BETWEEN THEN AND NOW?
I--OKAY-- BUT CAN WE JUST CHECK? I'M DYIN' HERE!
YOU IDIOT! THAT'S THE DEEP FRYER!
IT'S THE ONLY PLACE I HAVEN'T LOOKED!
SO IT DIDN'T WIND UP HERE SOMEHOW? BETTY DIDN'T BORROW IT, OR...?
COULD I ASK BETTY IF...?
WOULD YOU ASK BETTY IF...?
...WE'LL LEAVE.

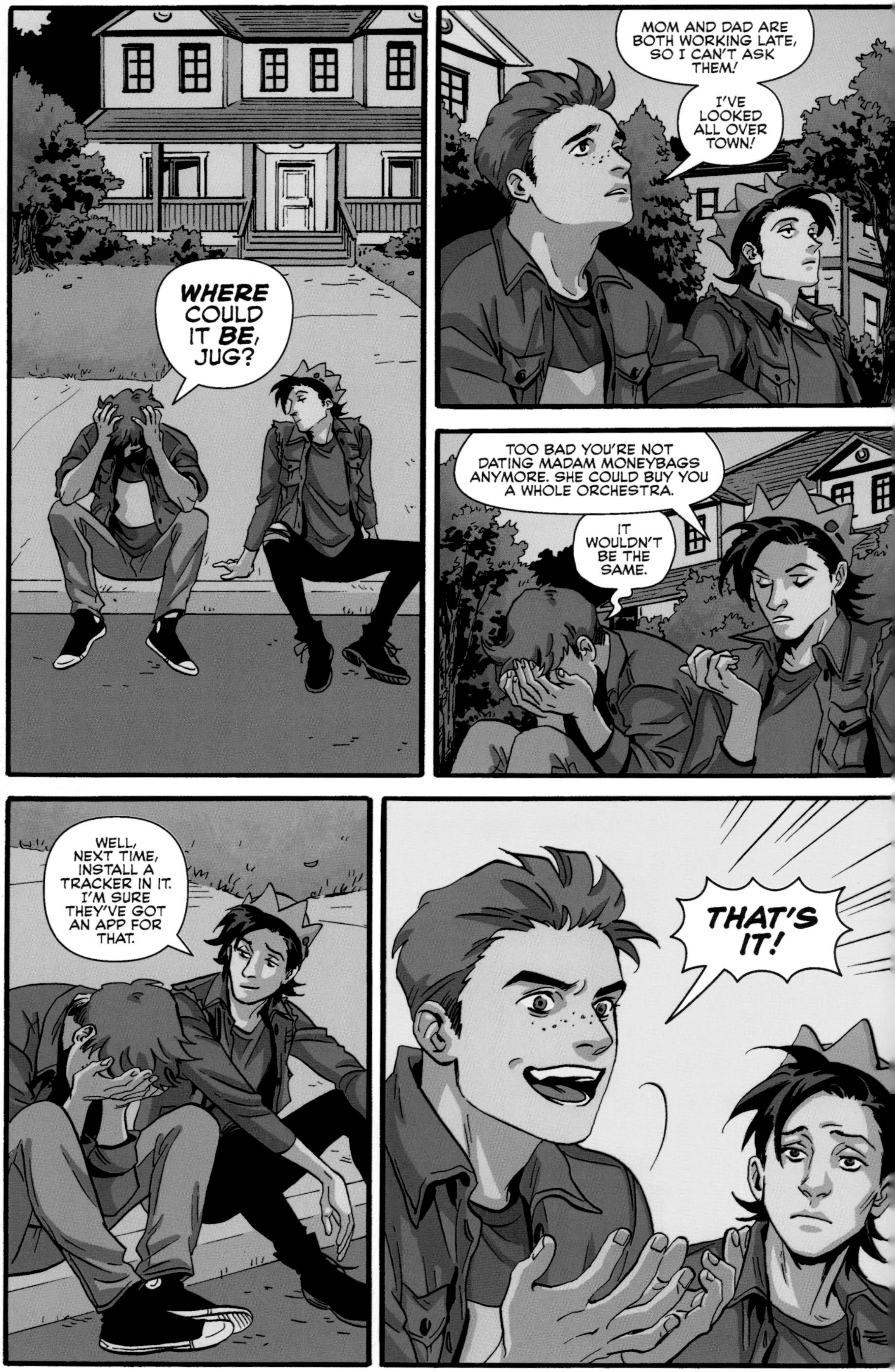
WHERE COULD IT BE, JUG?
MOM AND DAD ARE BOTH WORKING LATE, SO I CAN'T ASK THEM!
I'VE LOOKED ALL OVER TOWN!
TOO BAD YOU'RE NOT DATING MADAM MONEYBAGS ANYMORE. SHE COULD BUY YOU A WHOLE ORCHESTRA.
IT WOULDN'T BE THE SAME.
WELL, NEXT TIME, INSTALL A TRACKER IN IT. I'M SURE THEY'VE GOT AN APP FOR THAT.
THAT'S IT!

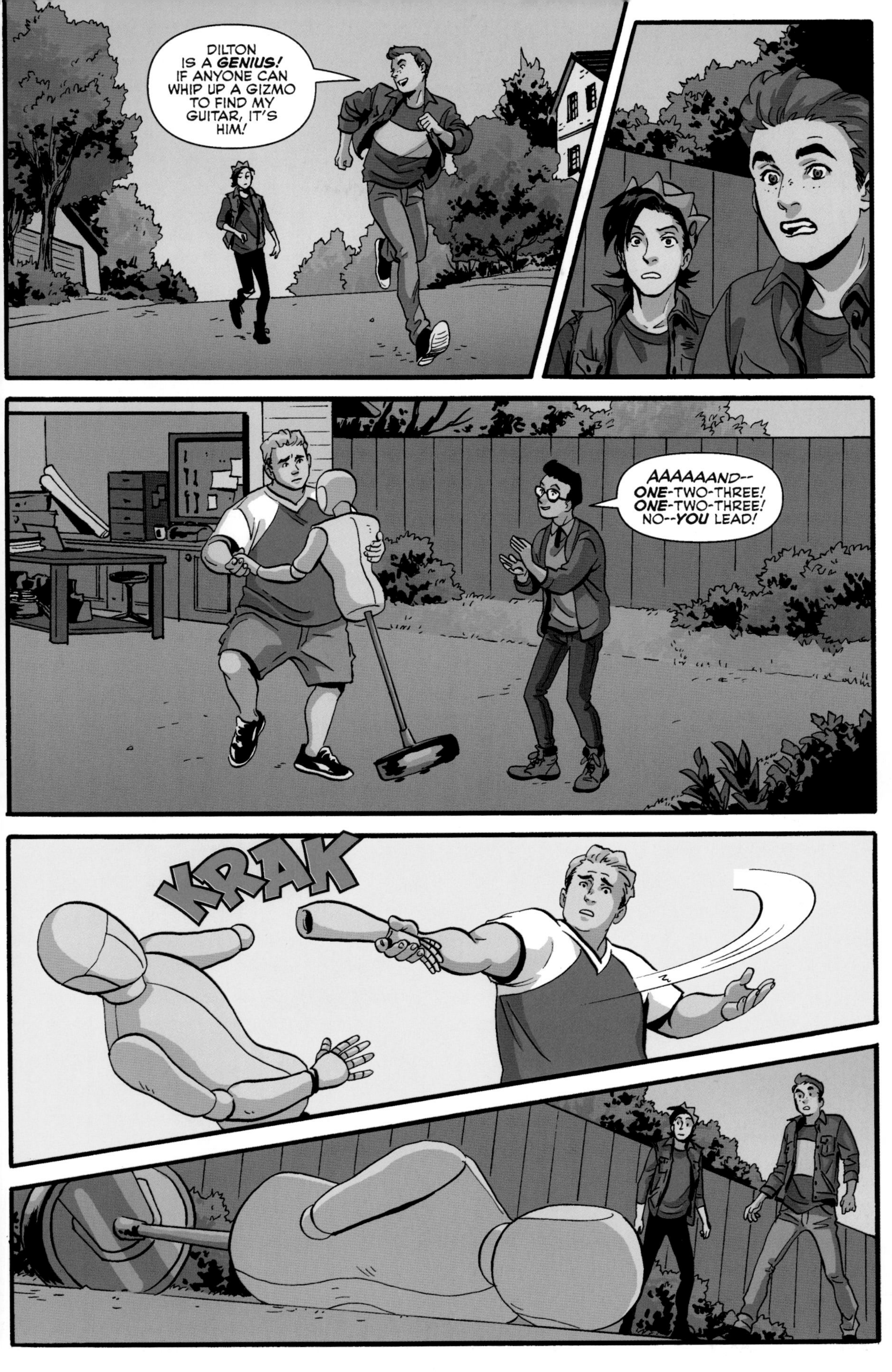
DILTON IS A **GENIUS!** IF ANYONE CAN WHIP UP A GIZMO TO FIND MY GUITAR, IT'S HIM!
AAAAAAND--
ONE-TWO-THREE! ***ONE***-TWO-THREE! NO--***YOU*** LEAD!
KRAK

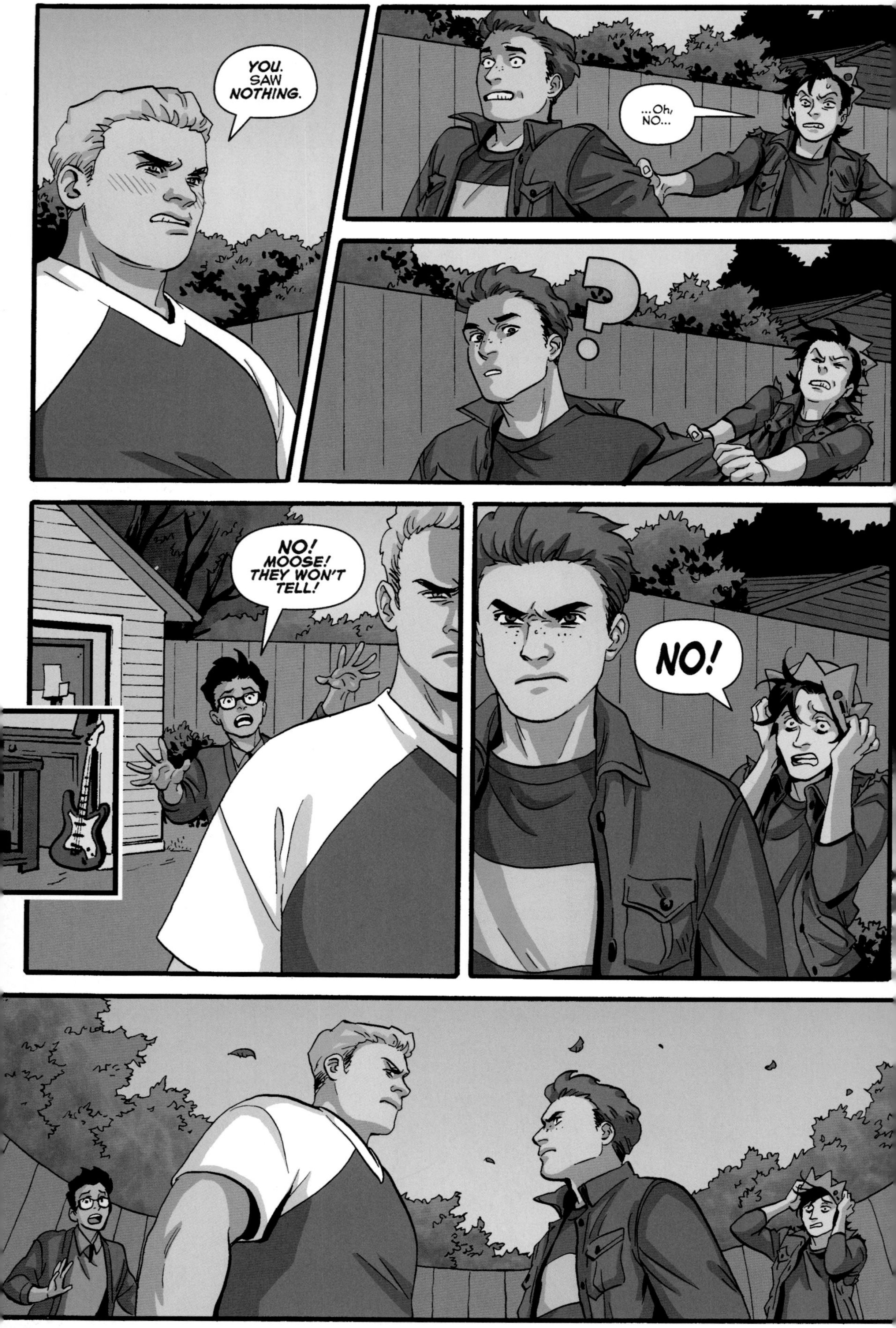
YOU. SAW NOTHING.
...Oh, NO...
?
NO! MOOSE! THEY WON'T TELL!
NO!

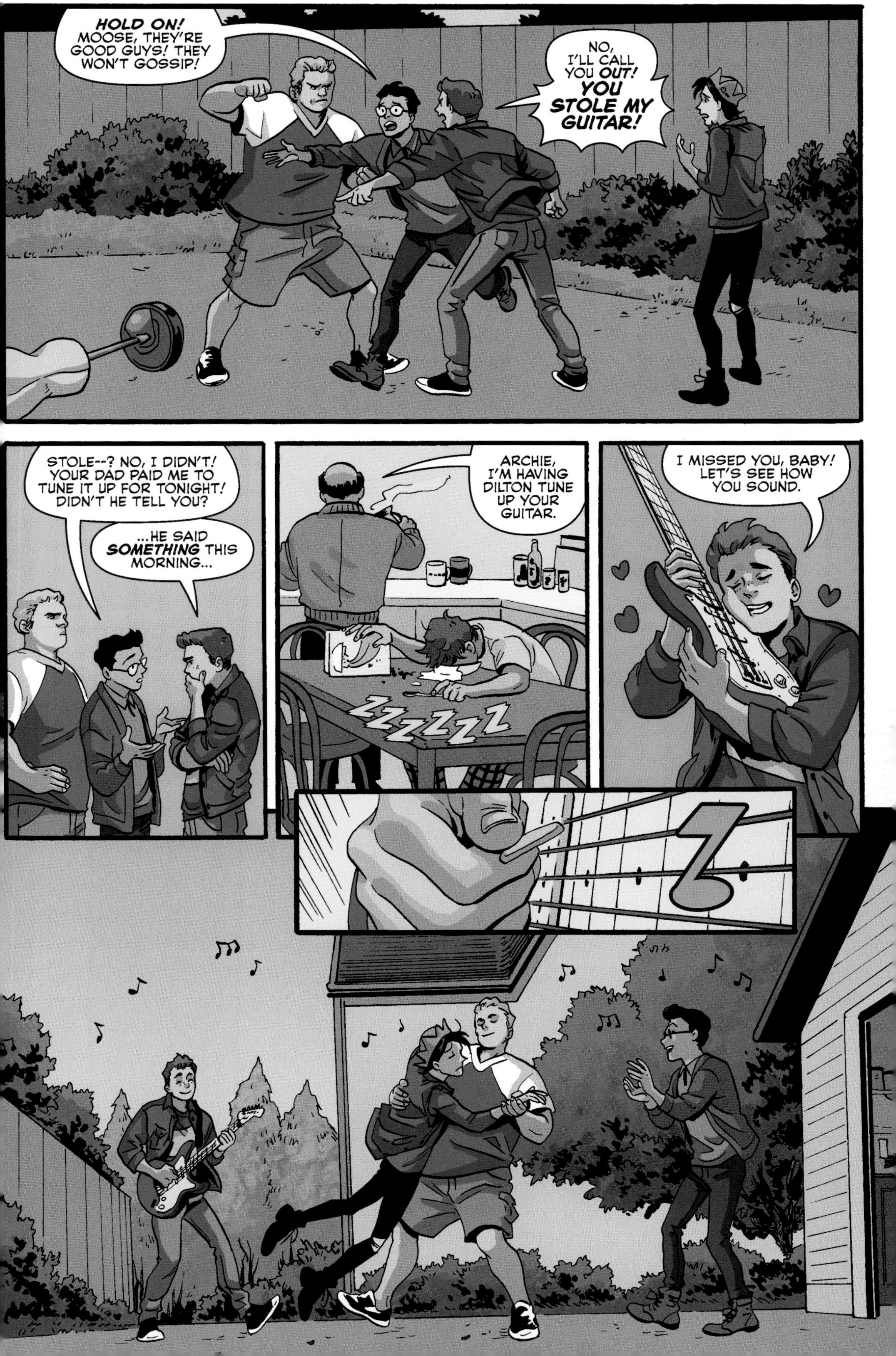

HOLD ON! MOOSE, THEY'RE GOOD GUYS! THEY WON'T GOSSIP!
NO, I'LL CALL YOU OUT! YOU STOLE MY GUITAR!
STOLE--? NO, I DIDN'T! YOUR DAD PAID ME TO TUNE IT UP FOR TONIGHT! DIDN'T HE TELL YOU?
...HE SAID SOMETHING THIS MORNING...
ARCHIE, I'M HAVING DILTON TUNE UP YOUR GUITAR.
ZZZZZZZ
I MISSED YOU, BABY! LET'S SEE HOW YOU SOUND.

CHAPTER FOUR: GARDEN OF LIES

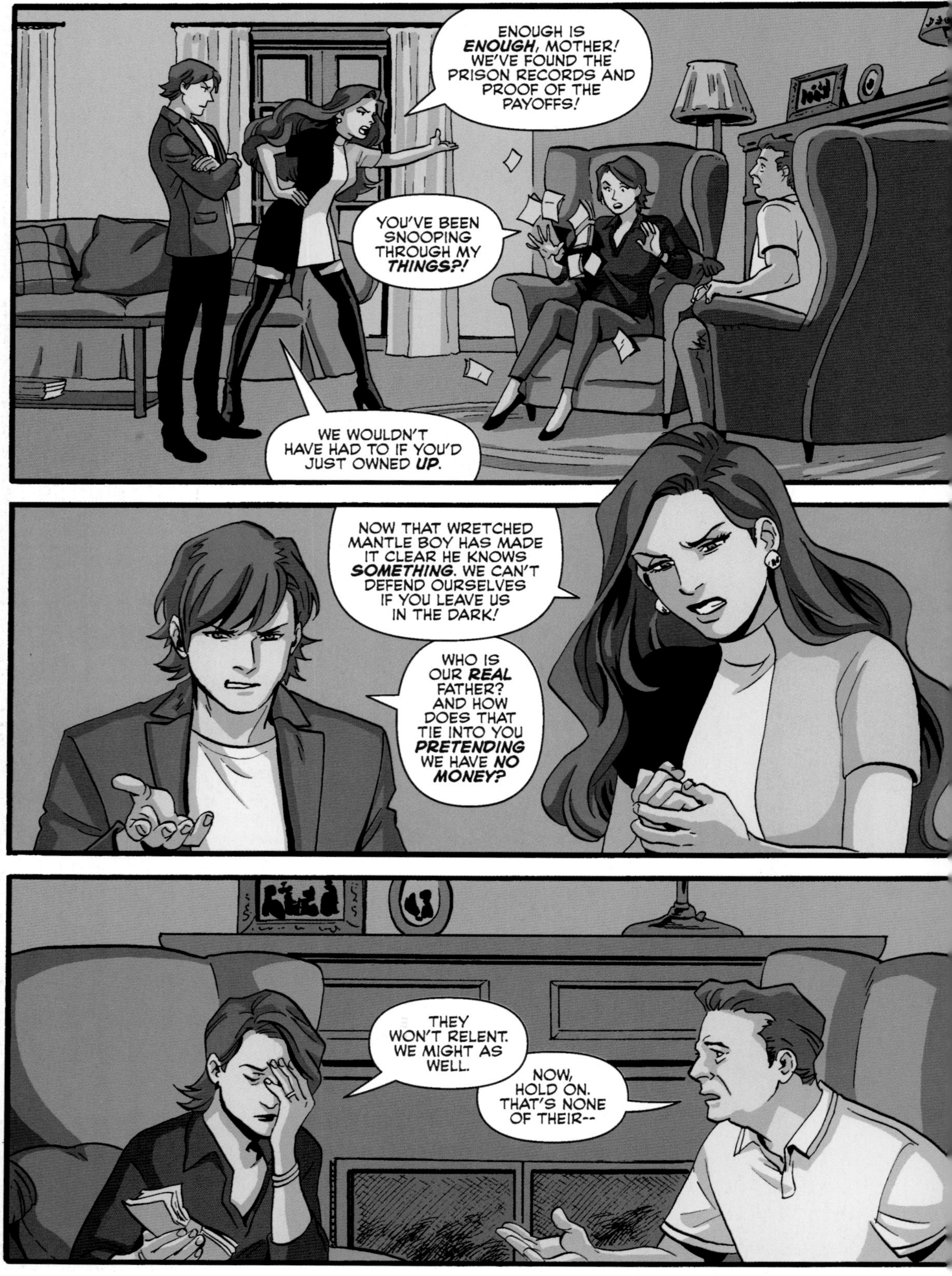
ENOUGH IS ENOUGH, MOTHER! WE'VE FOUND THE PRISON RECORDS AND PROOF OF THE PAYOFFS!
YOU'VE BEEN SNOOPING THROUGH MY THINGS?!
WE WOULDN'T HAVE HAD TO IF YOU'D JUST OWNED UP.
NOW THAT WRETCHED MANTLE BOY HAS MADE IT CLEAR HE KNOWS SOMETHING. WE CAN'T DEFEND OURSELVES IF YOU LEAVE US IN THE DARK!
WHO IS OUR REAL FATHER? AND HOW DOES THAT TIE INTO YOU PRETENDING WE HAVE NO MONEY?
THEY WON'T RELENT. WE MIGHT AS WELL.
NOW, HOLD ON. THAT'S NONE OF THEIR--

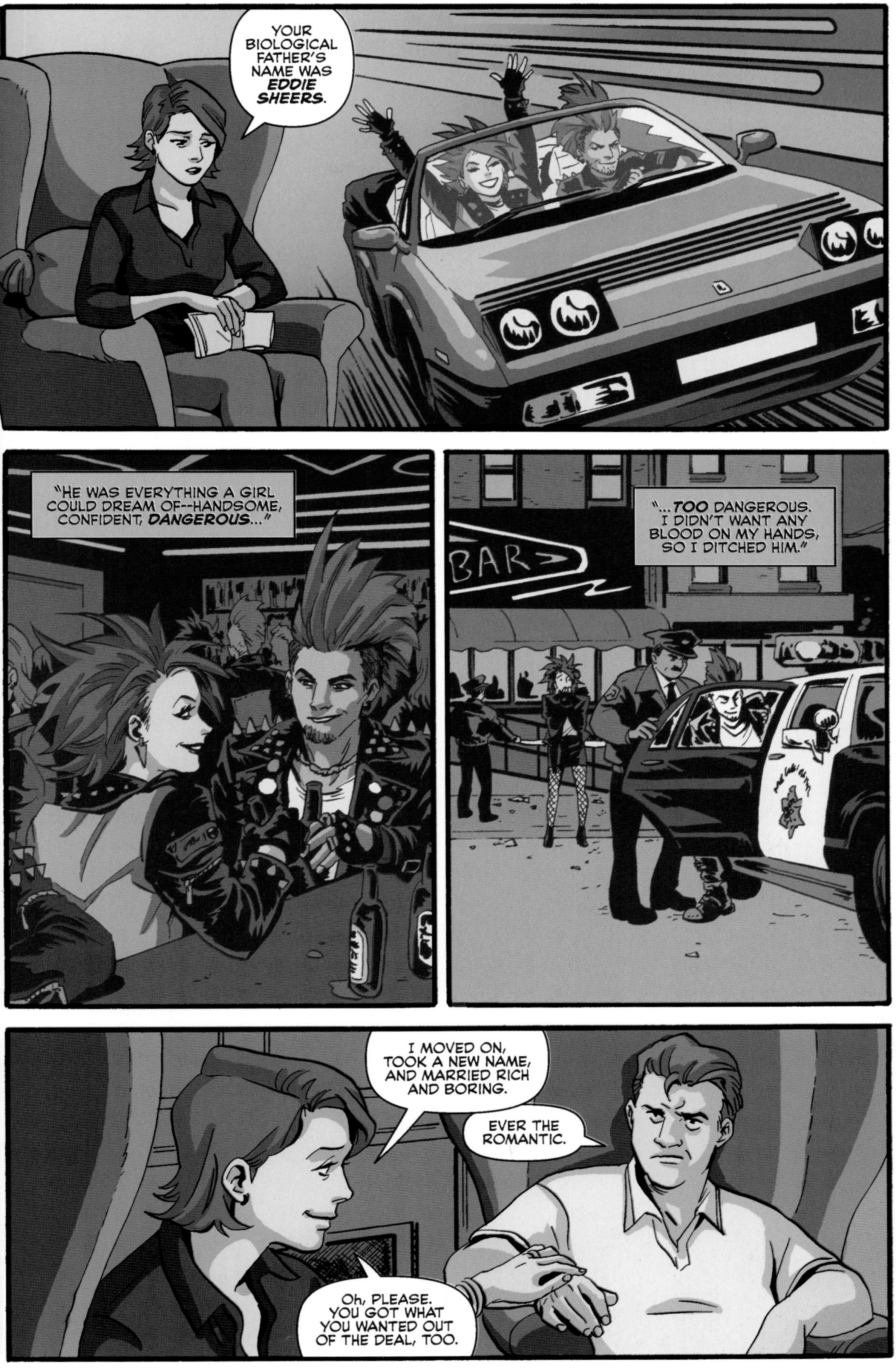
YOUR BIOLOGICAL FATHER'S NAME WAS EDDIE SHEERS.
"HE WAS EVERYTHING A GIRL COULD DREAM OF--HANDSOME, CONFIDENT, DANGEROUS..."
BAR
"...TOO DANGEROUS. I DIDN'T WANT ANY BLOOD ON MY HANDS, SO I DITCHED HIM."
I MOVED ON, TOOK A NEW NAME, AND MARRIED RICH AND BORING.
EVER THE ROMANTIC.
Oh, PLEASE. YOU GOT WHAT YOU WANTED OUT OF THE DEAL, TOO.

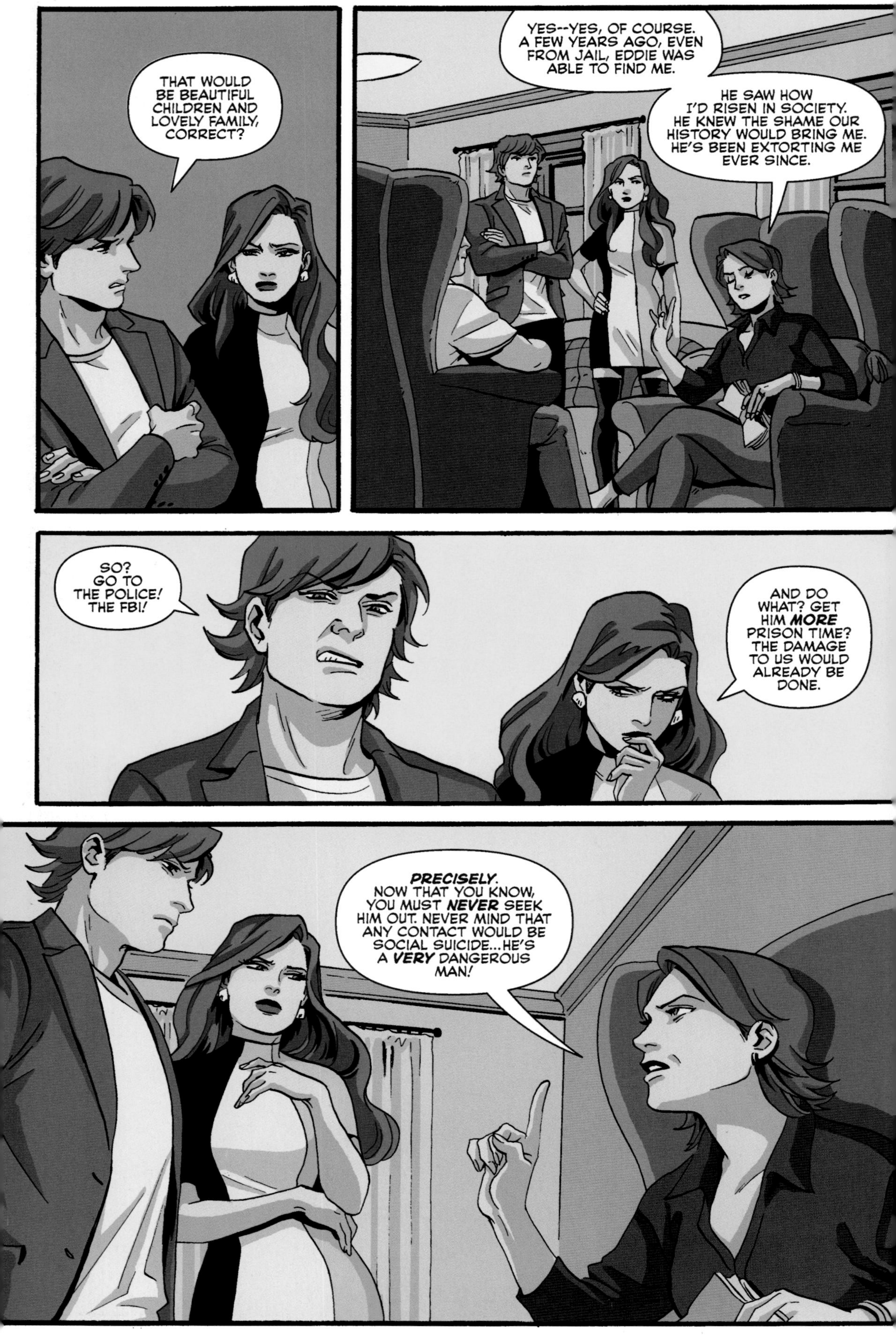
THAT WOULD BE BEAUTIFUL CHILDREN AND LOVELY FAMILY, CORRECT?
YES--YES, OF COURSE. A FEW YEARS AGO, EVEN FROM JAIL, EDDIE WAS ABLE TO FIND ME.
HE SAW HOW I'D RISEN IN SOCIETY. HE KNEW THE SHAME OUR HISTORY WOULD BRING ME. HE'S BEEN EXTORTING ME EVER SINCE.
SO? GO TO THE POLICE! THE FBI!
AND DO WHAT? GET HIM MORE PRISON TIME? THE DAMAGE TO US WOULD ALREADY BE DONE.
PRECISELY. NOW THAT YOU KNOW, YOU MUST NEVER SEEK HIM OUT. NEVER MIND THAT ANY CONTACT WOULD BE SOCIAL SUICIDE...HE'S A VERY DANGEROUS MAN!

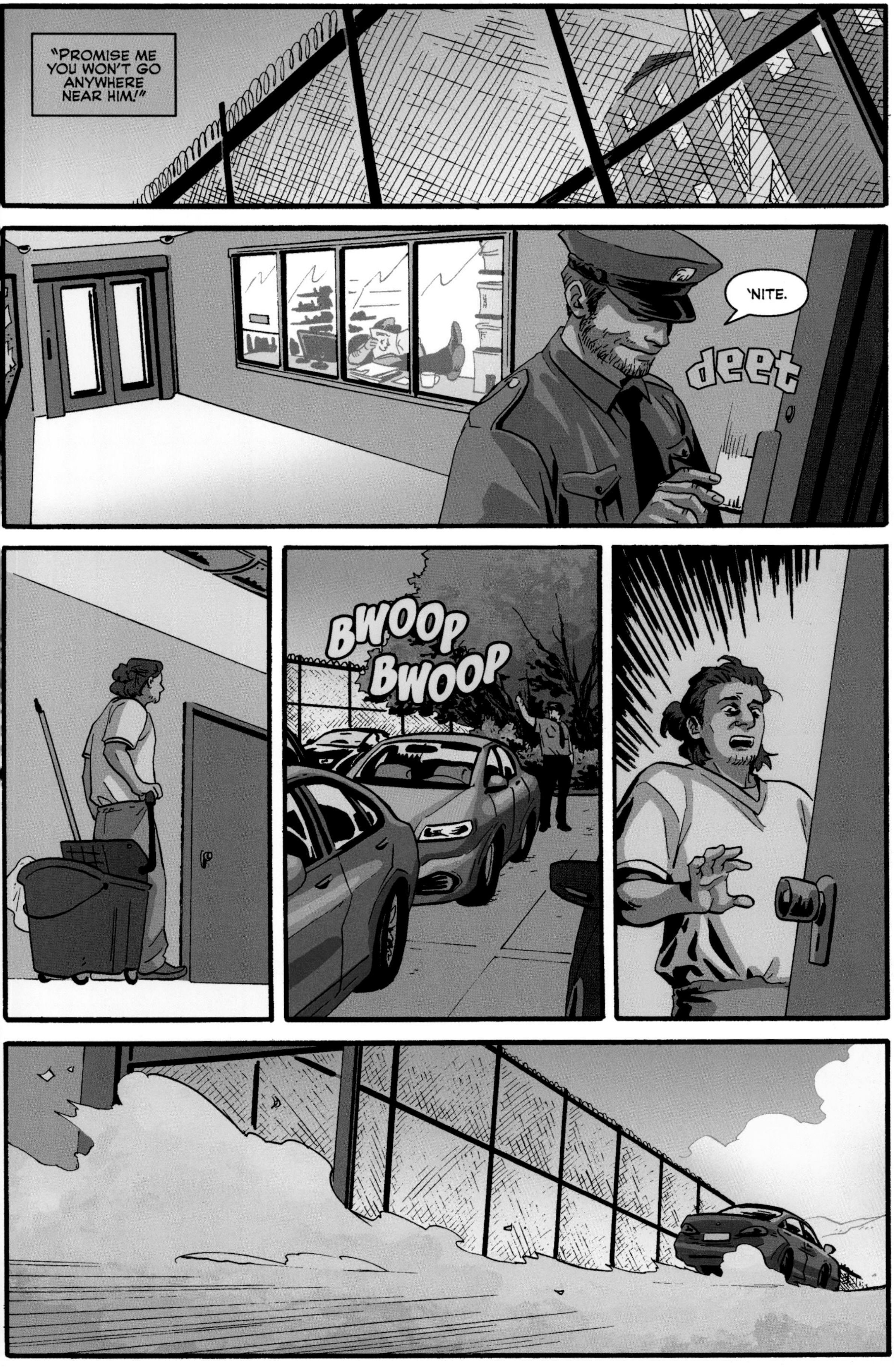
"PROMISE ME YOU WON'T GO ANYWHERE NEAR HIM!"
'NITE.
deet
BWOOP
BWOOP

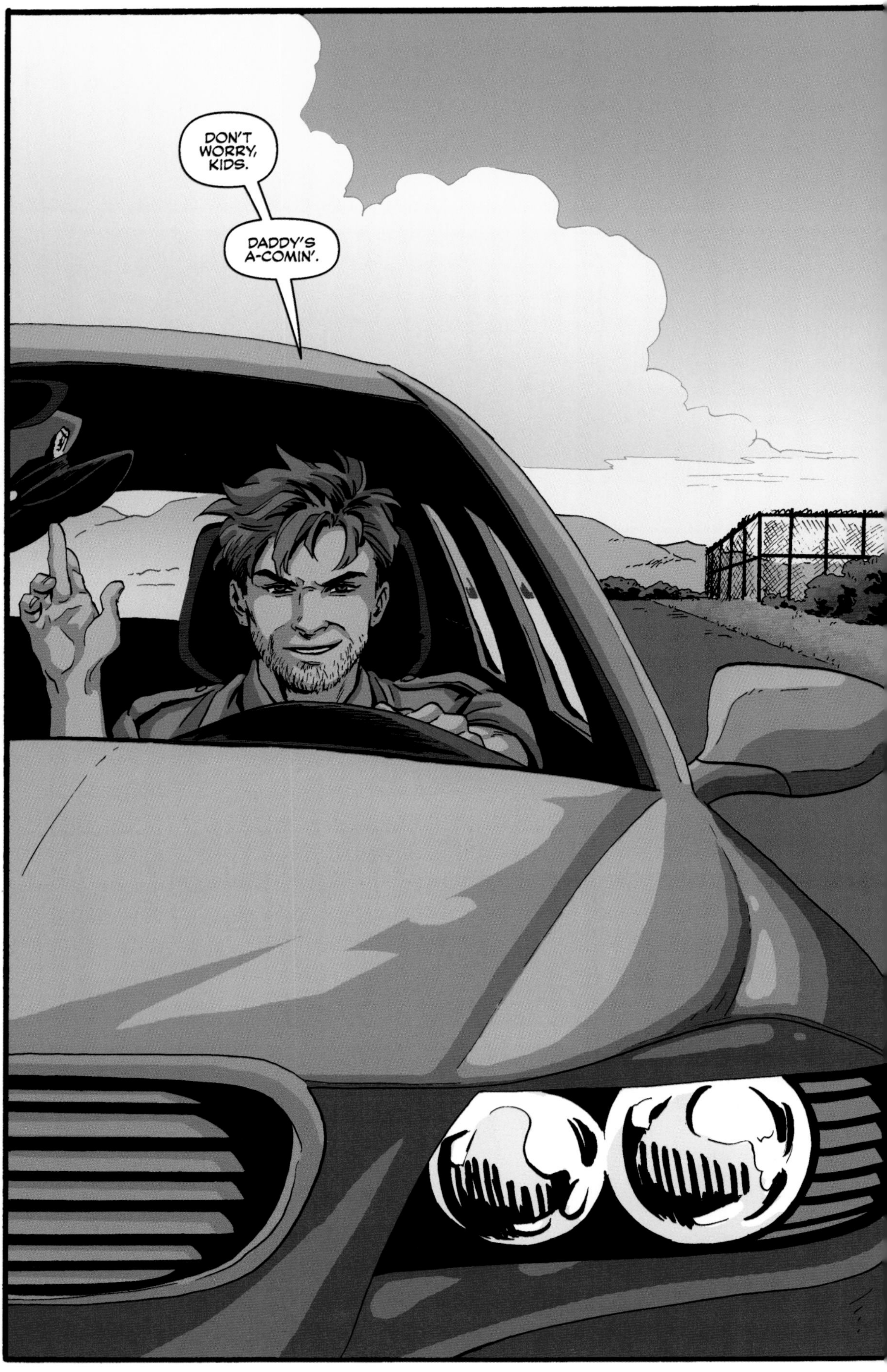
DON'T WORRY, KIDS.
DADDY'S A-COMIN'.

TO BE CONTINUED...

ISSUE THIRTY

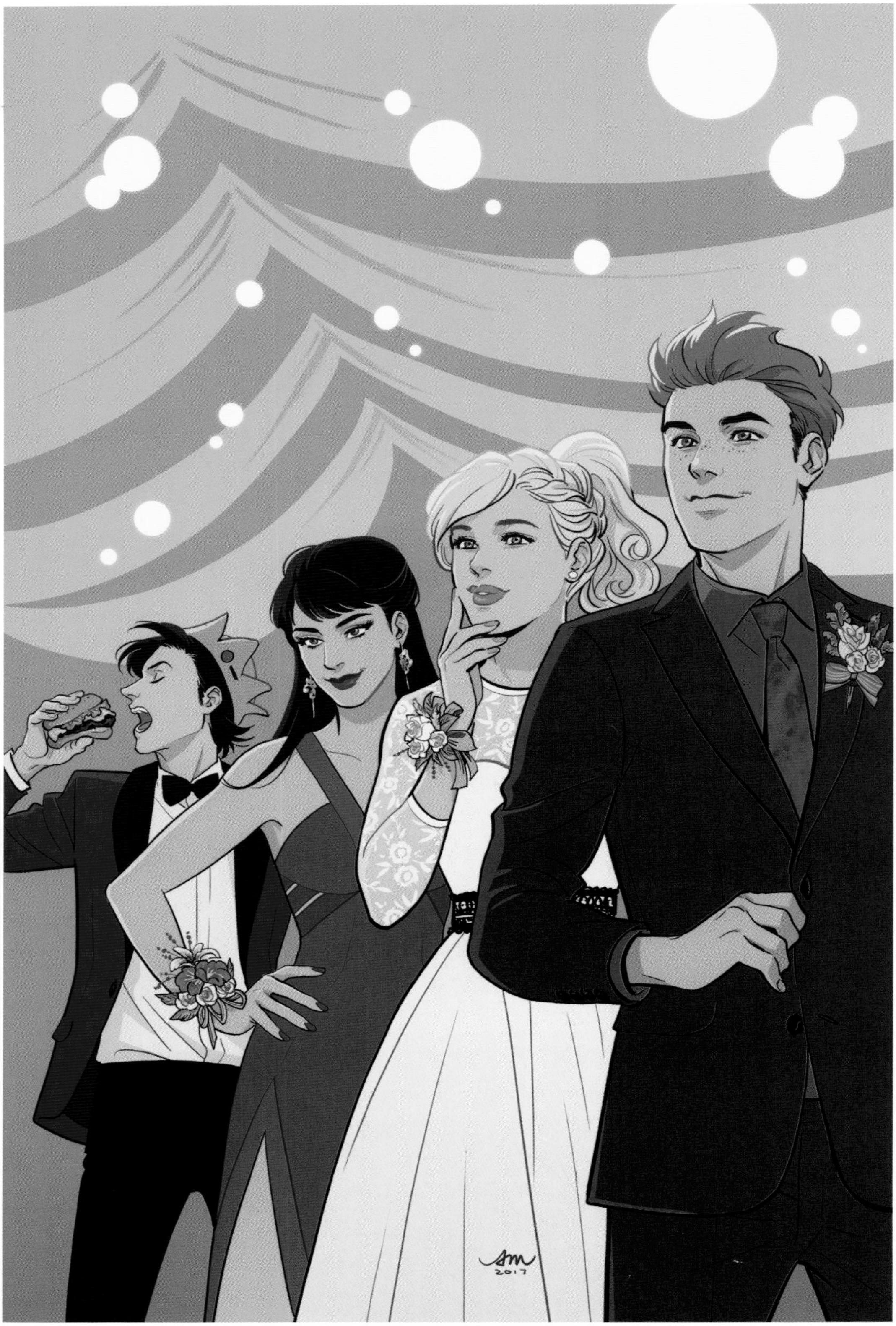
am
2017

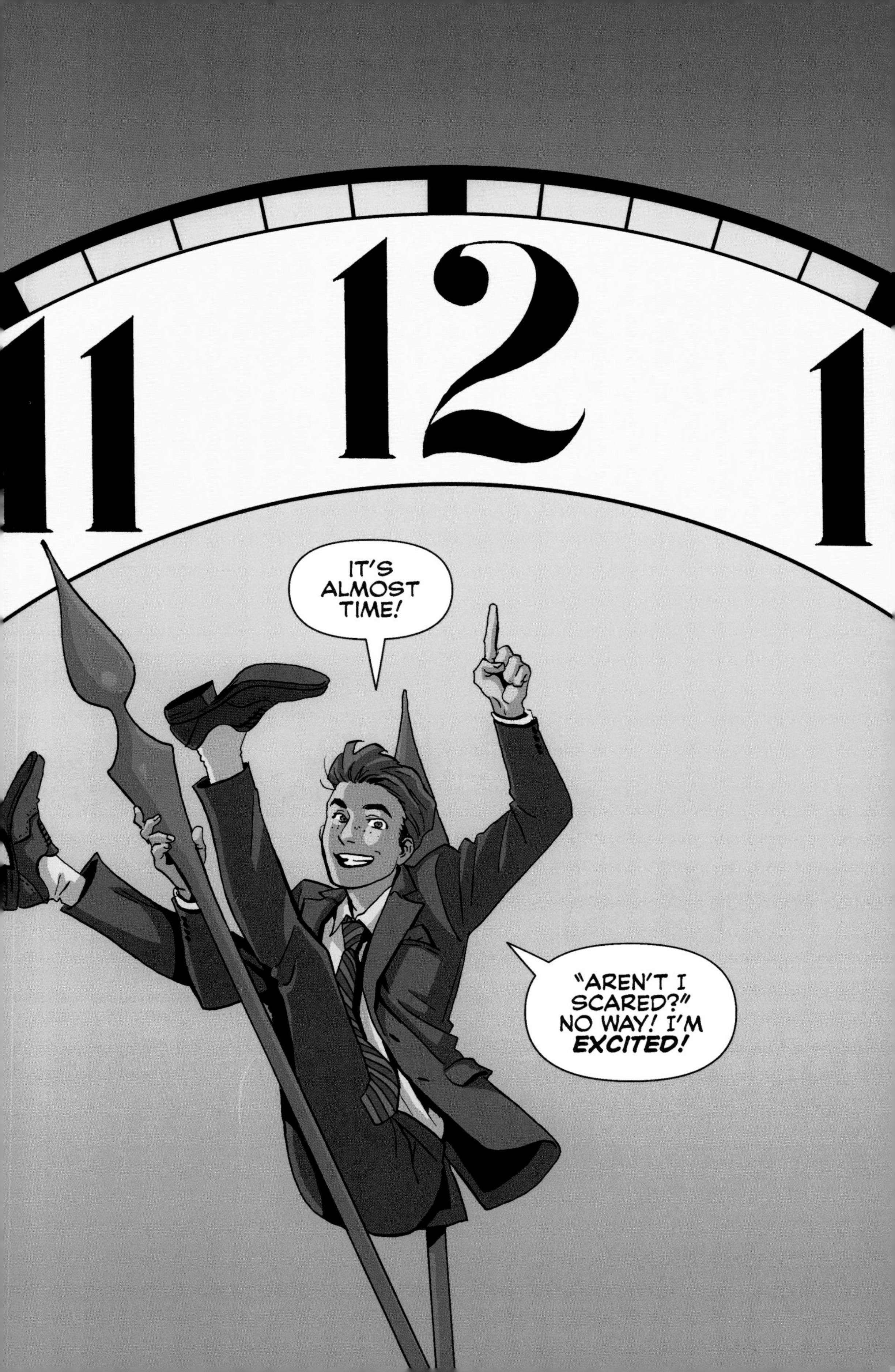
IT'S ALMOST TIME!
"AREN'T I SCARED?" NO WAY! I'M ***EXCITED!***

CHAPTER ONE: IT'S THE FINAL COUNTDOWN

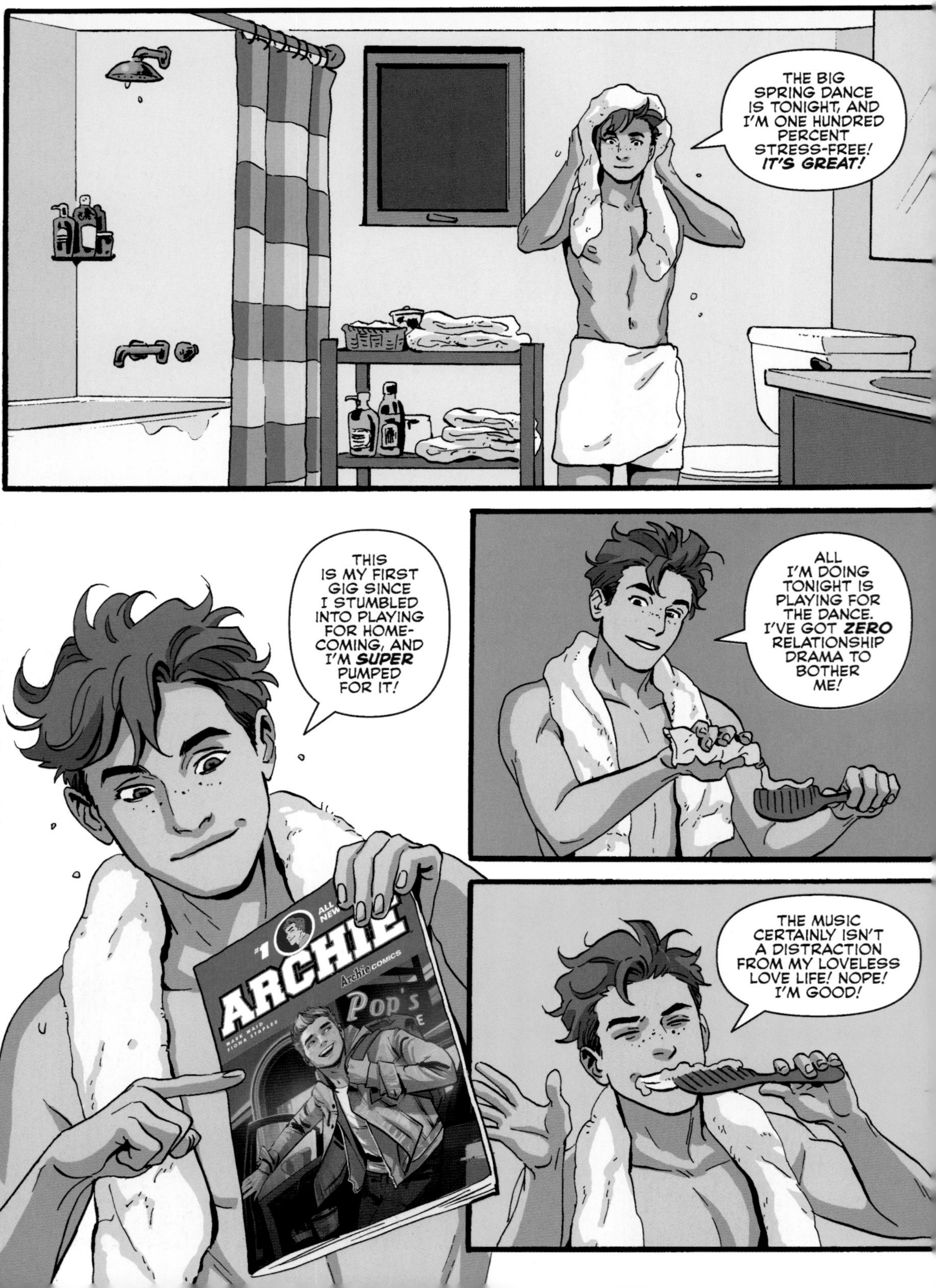
THE BIG SPRING DANCE IS TONIGHT, AND I'M ONE HUNDRED PERCENT STRESS-FREE! *IT'S GREAT!*
THIS IS MY FIRST GIG SINCE I STUMBLED INTO PLAYING FOR HOME-COMING, AND I'M *SUPER* PUMPED FOR IT!
#1
ALL NEW
ARCHIE
Archie COMICS
Pop's
MARK WAID
FIONA STAPLES
ALL I'M DOING TONIGHT IS PLAYING FOR THE DANCE. I'VE GOT *ZERO* RELATIONSHIP DRAMA TO BOTHER ME!
THE MUSIC CERTAINLY ISN'T A DISTRACTION FROM MY LOVELESS LOVE LIFE! NOPE! I'M GOOD!

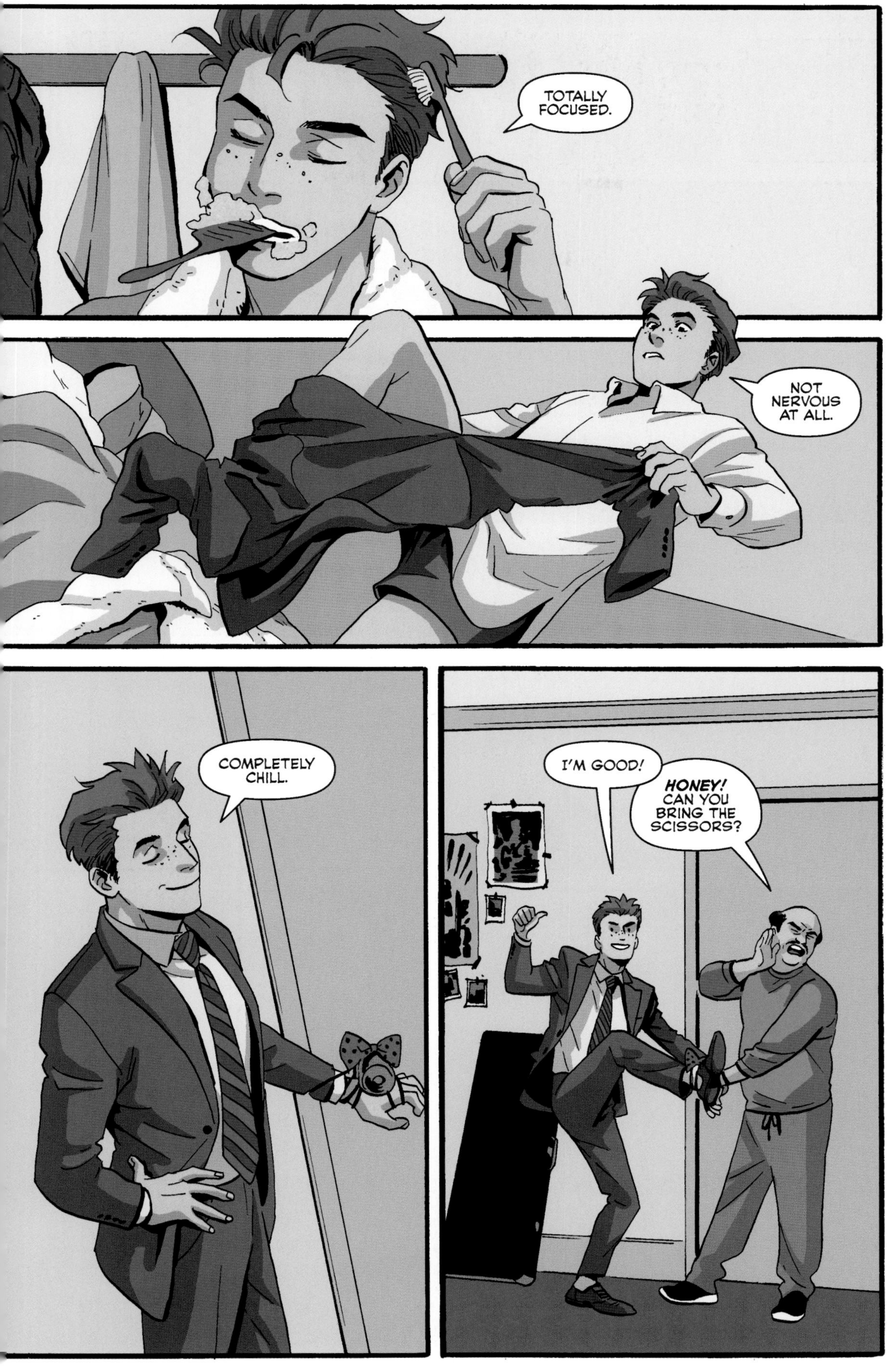
TOTALLY FOCUSED.
NOT NERVOUS AT ALL.
COMPLETELY CHILL.
I'M GOOD!
HONEY! CAN YOU BRING THE SCISSORS?

CHAPTER TWO: DATE FIGHT

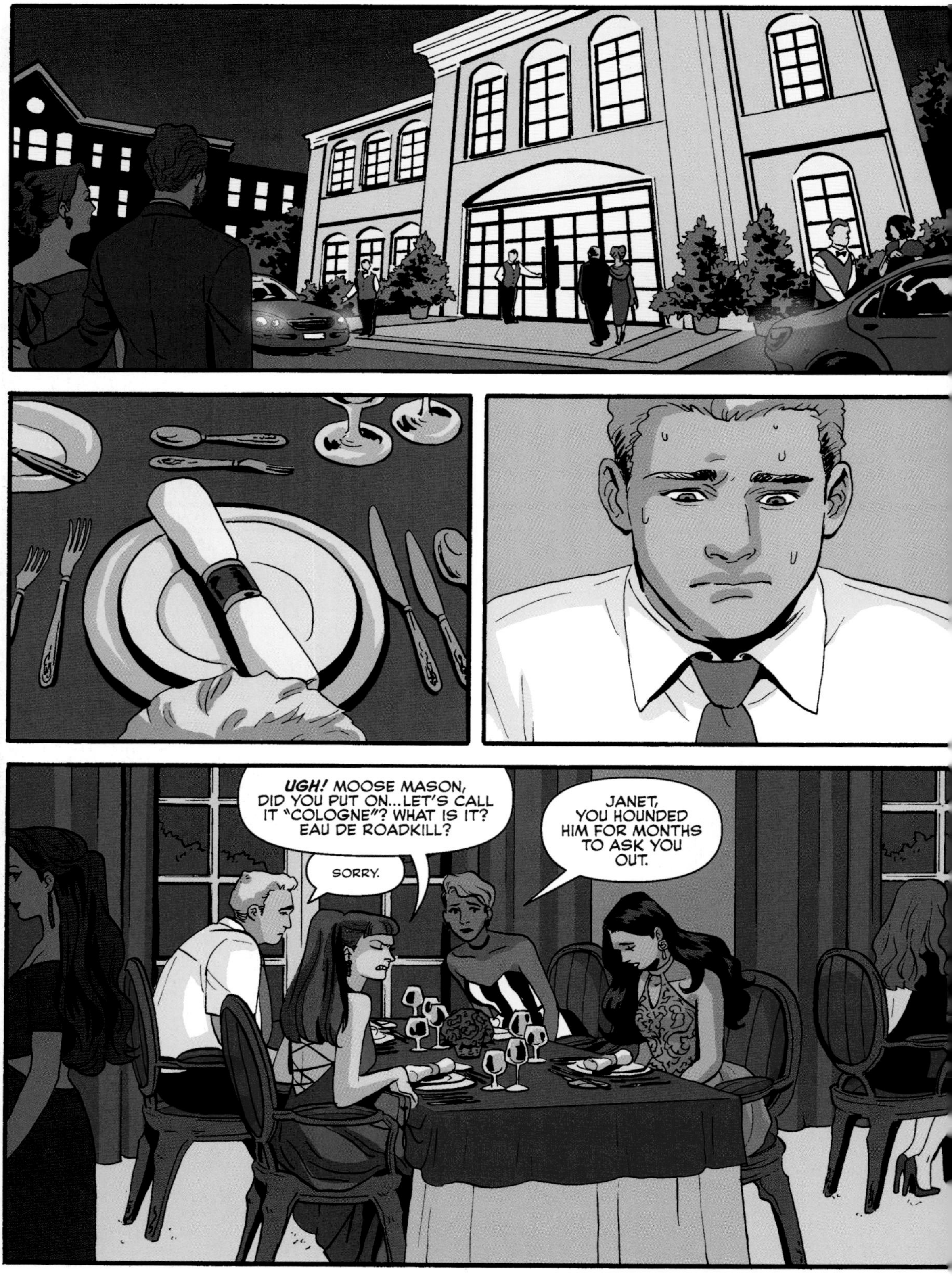

UGH! MOOSE MASON, DID YOU PUT ON...LET'S CALL IT "COLOGNE"? WHAT IS IT? EAU DE ROADKILL?
SORRY.
JANET, YOU HOUNDED HIM FOR MONTHS TO ASK YOU OUT.

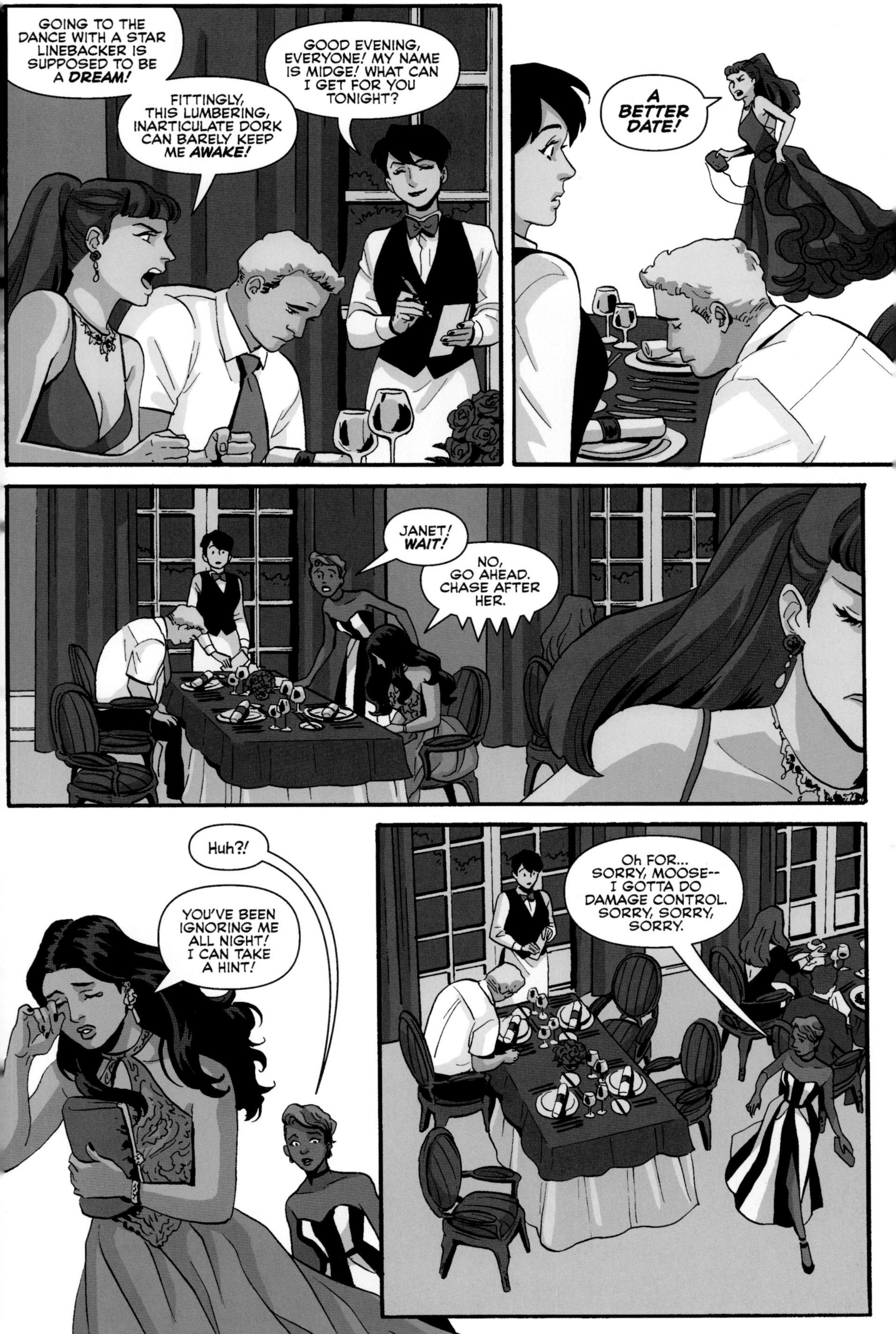
GOING TO THE DANCE WITH A STAR LINEBACKER IS SUPPOSED TO BE A DREAM!
FITTINGLY, THIS LUMBERING, INARTICULATE DORK CAN BARELY KEEP ME AWAKE!
GOOD EVENING, EVERYONE! MY NAME IS MIDGE! WHAT CAN I GET FOR YOU TONIGHT?
A BETTER DATE!
JANET! WAIT!
NO, GO AHEAD. CHASE AFTER HER.
Huh?!
YOU'VE BEEN IGNORING ME ALL NIGHT! I CAN TAKE A HINT!
Oh FOR... SORRY, MOOSE-- I GOTTA DO DAMAGE CONTROL. SORRY, SORRY, SORRY.

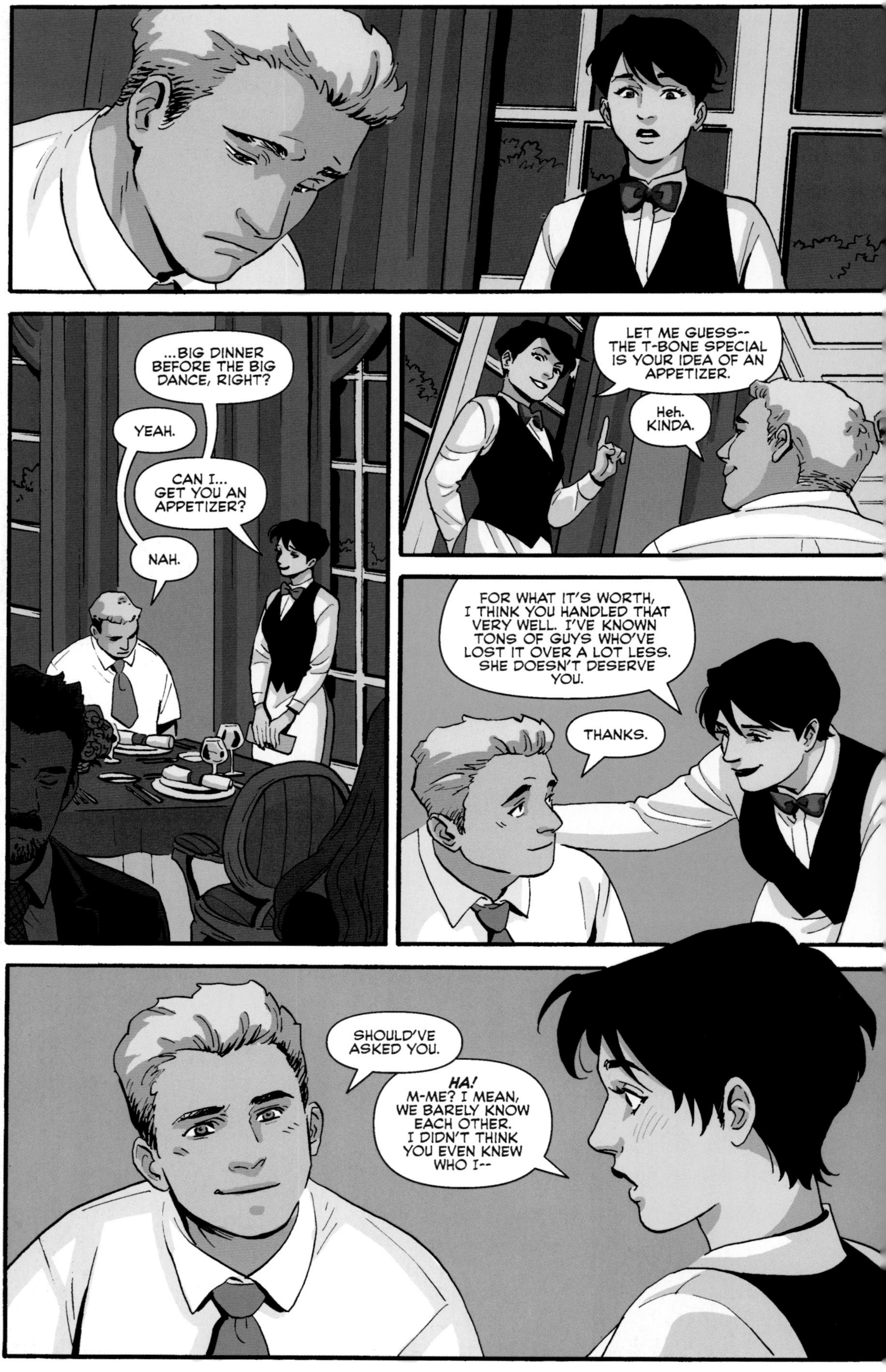
...BIG DINNER BEFORE THE BIG DANCE, RIGHT?
YEAH.
CAN I... GET YOU AN APPETIZER?
NAH.
LET ME GUESS-- THE T-BONE SPECIAL IS YOUR IDEA OF AN APPETIZER.
Heh. KINDA.
FOR WHAT IT'S WORTH, I THINK YOU HANDLED THAT VERY WELL. I'VE KNOWN TONS OF GUYS WHO'VE LOST IT OVER A LOT LESS. SHE DOESN'T DESERVE YOU.
THANKS.
SHOULD'VE ASKED YOU.
HA! M-ME? I MEAN, WE BARELY KNOW EACH OTHER. I DIDN'T THINK YOU EVEN KNEW WHO I--

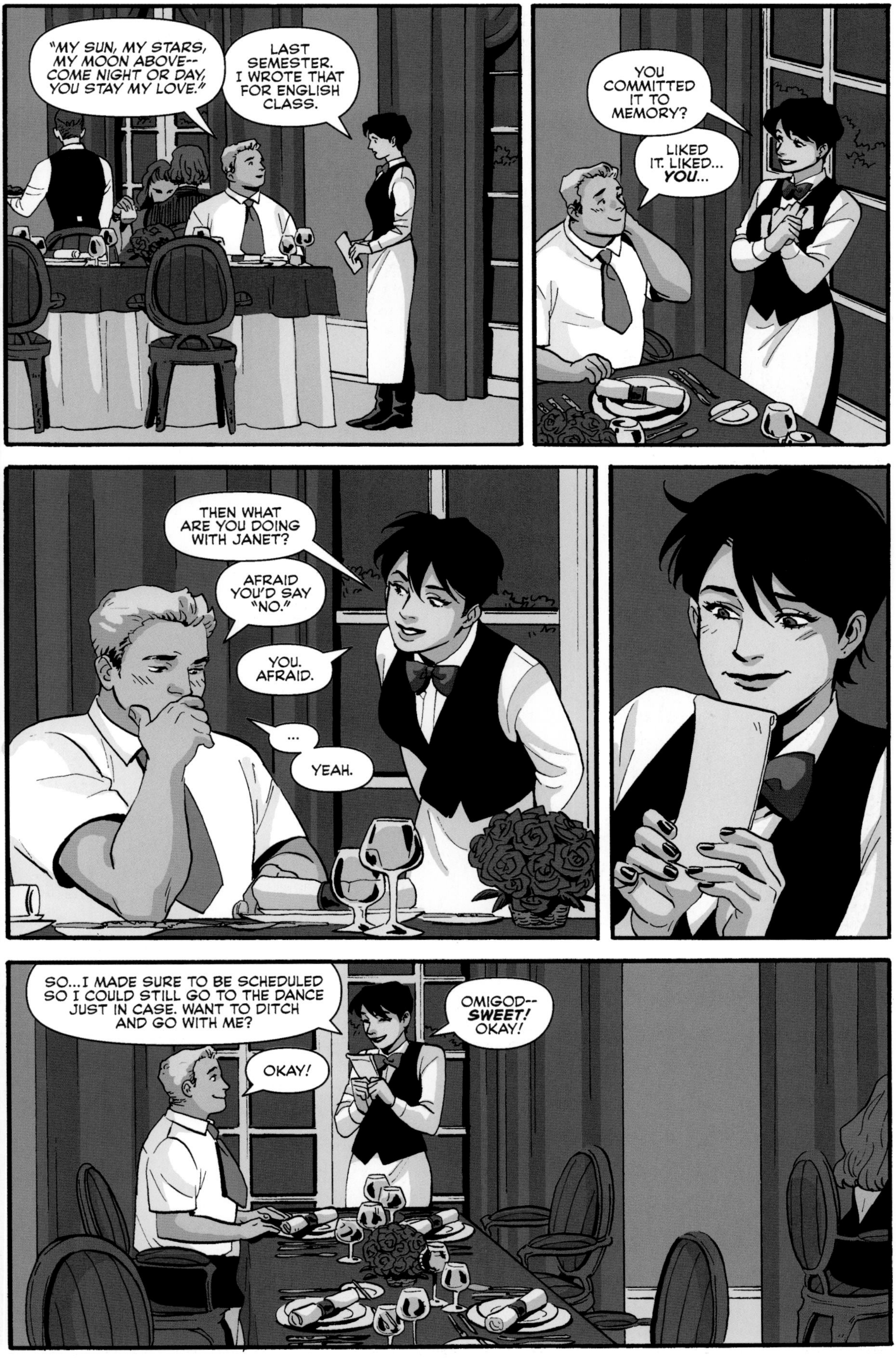
"MY SUN, MY STARS, MY MOON ABOVE-- COME NIGHT OR DAY, YOU STAY MY LOVE."
LAST SEMESTER. I WROTE THAT FOR ENGLISH CLASS.
YOU COMMITTED IT TO MEMORY?
LIKED IT. LIKED... *YOU*...
THEN WHAT ARE YOU DOING WITH JANET?
AFRAID YOU'D SAY "NO."
YOU. AFRAID.
...
YEAH.
SO...I MADE SURE TO BE SCHEDULED SO I COULD STILL GO TO THE DANCE JUST IN CASE. WANT TO DITCH AND GO WITH ME?
OKAY!
OMIGOD-- *SWEET!* OKAY!

CHAPTER THREE: LIKE FATHER, LIKE SON

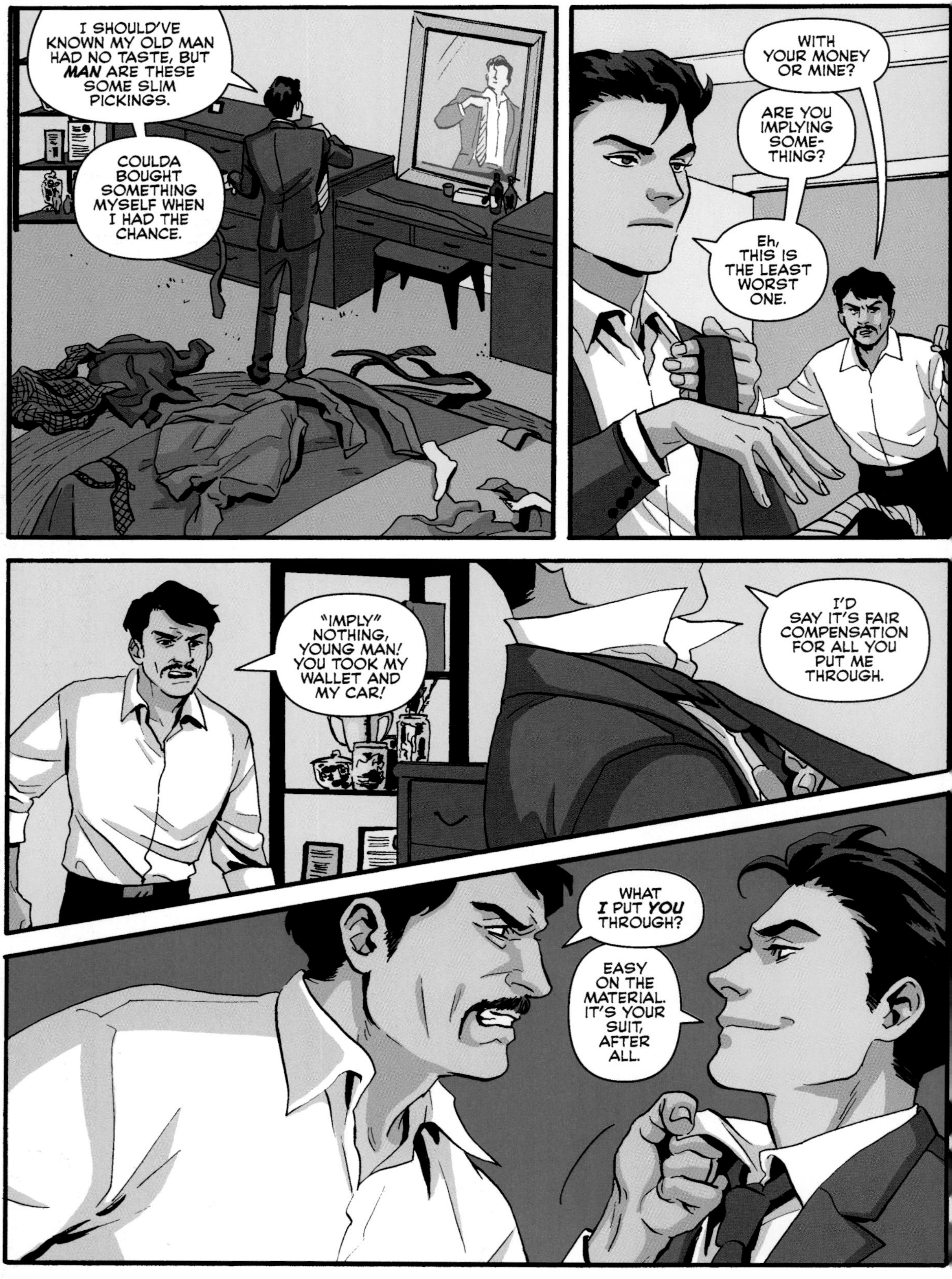
I SHOULD'VE KNOWN MY OLD MAN HAD NO TASTE, BUT *MAN* ARE THESE SOME SLIM PICKINGS.
COULDA BOUGHT SOMETHING MYSELF WHEN I HAD THE CHANCE.
WITH YOUR MONEY OR MINE?
ARE YOU IMPLYING SOME-THING?
Eh, THIS IS THE LEAST WORST ONE.
"IMPLY" NOTHING, YOUNG MAN! YOU TOOK MY WALLET AND MY CAR!
I'D SAY IT'S FAIR COMPENSATION FOR ALL YOU PUT ME THROUGH.
WHAT *I* PUT *YOU* THROUGH?
EASY ON THE MATERIAL. IT'S YOUR SUIT, AFTER ALL.

YOU... *YOU*...!

"PARASITE"?

"HE'S NOT MY EMPLOYEE, HE'S MY SON-- *UNFORTUNATELY*." --RICHARD MANTLE, 2018.

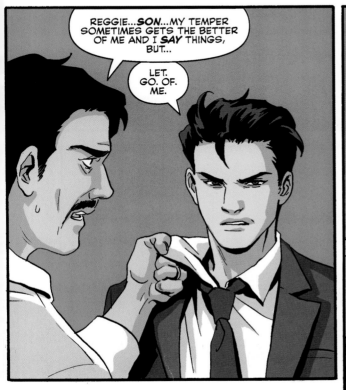

REGGIE...*SON*...MY TEMPER SOMETIMES GETS THE BETTER OF ME AND I *SAY* THINGS, BUT...

LET. GO. OF. ME.

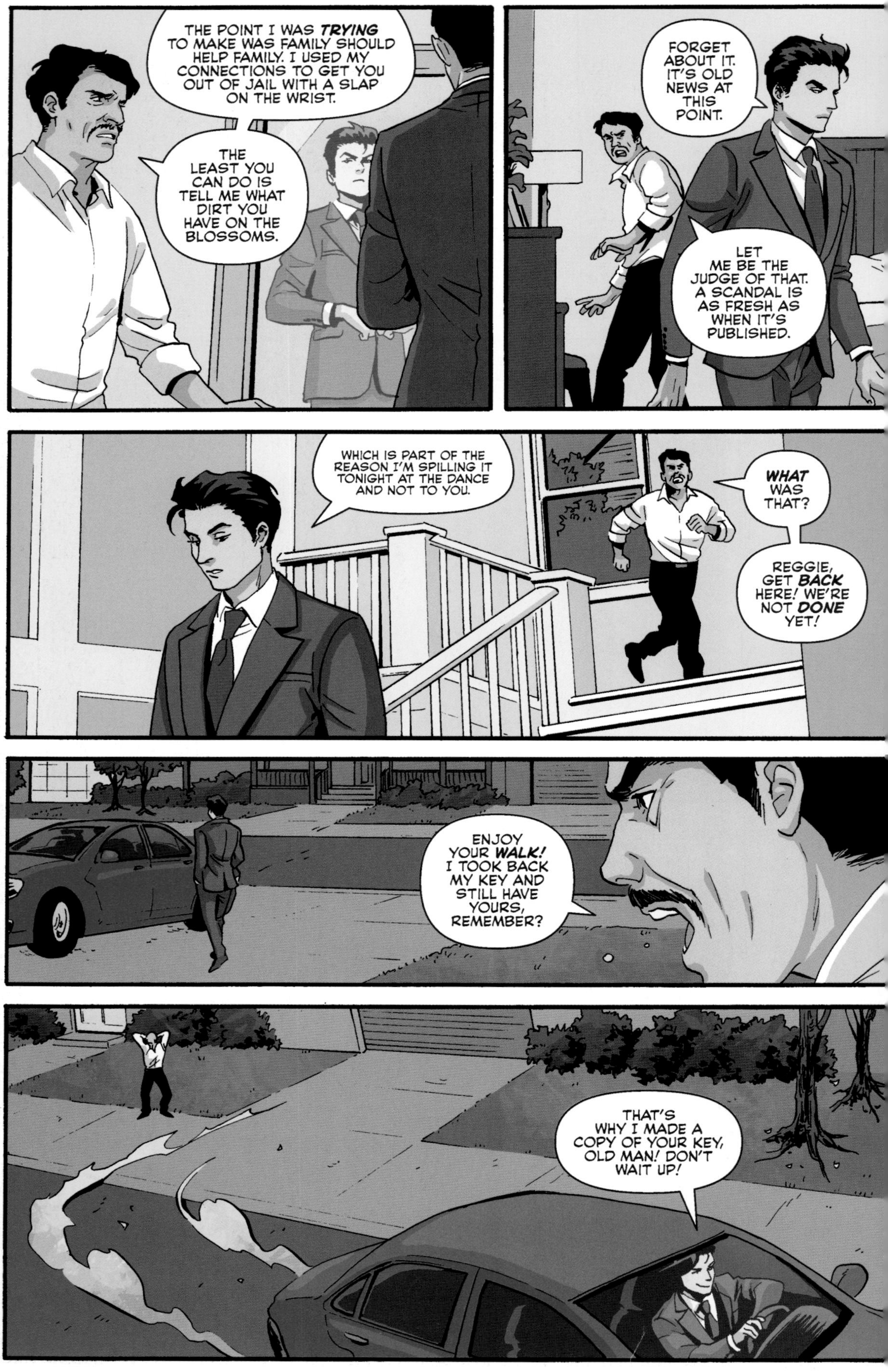
THE POINT I WAS TRYING TO MAKE WAS FAMILY SHOULD HELP FAMILY. I USED MY CONNECTIONS TO GET YOU OUT OF JAIL WITH A SLAP ON THE WRIST.
THE LEAST YOU CAN DO IS TELL ME WHAT DIRT YOU HAVE ON THE BLOSSOMS.
FORGET ABOUT IT. IT'S OLD NEWS AT THIS POINT.
LET ME BE THE JUDGE OF THAT. A SCANDAL IS AS FRESH AS WHEN IT'S PUBLISHED.
WHICH IS PART OF THE REASON I'M SPILLING IT TONIGHT AT THE DANCE AND NOT TO YOU.
WHAT WAS THAT?
REGGIE, GET BACK HERE! WE'RE NOT DONE YET!
ENJOY YOUR WALK! I TOOK BACK MY KEY AND STILL HAVE YOURS, REMEMBER?
THAT'S WHY I MADE A COPY OF YOUR KEY, OLD MAN! DON'T WAIT UP!

CHAPTER FOUR: MEMORY LANE

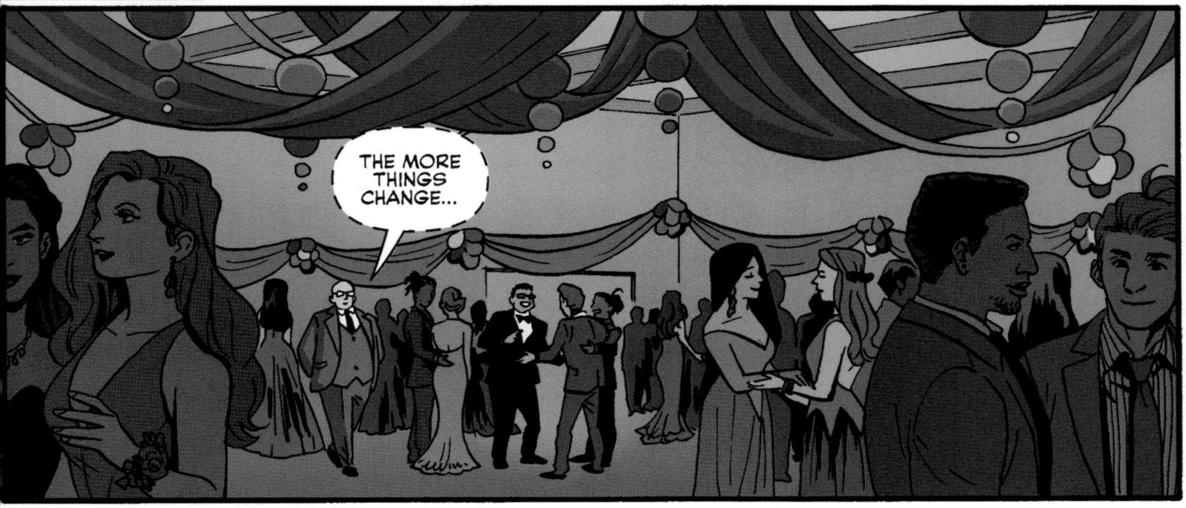
THE MORE THINGS CHANGE...

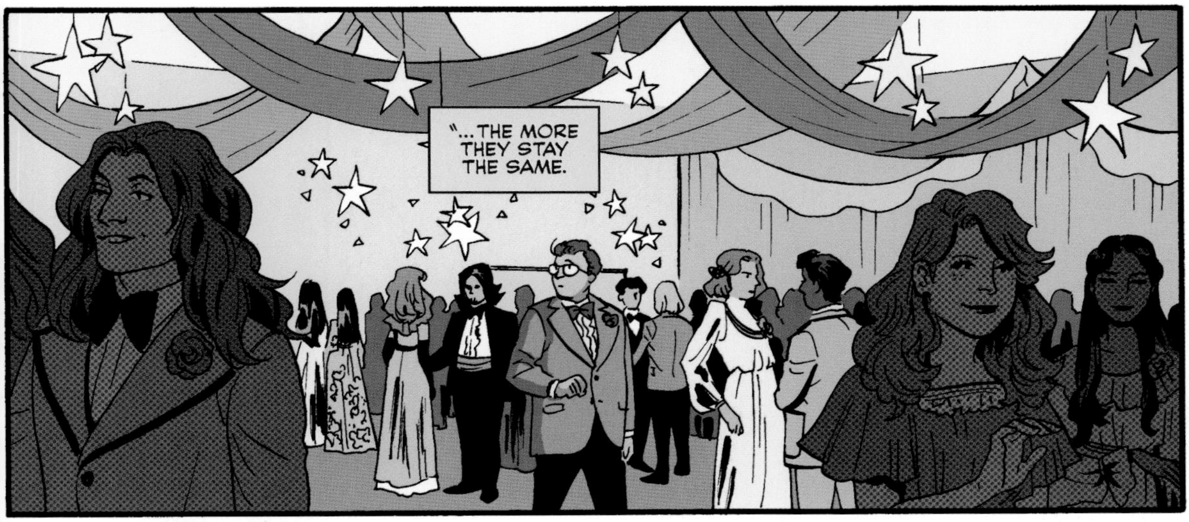
"...THE MORE THEY STAY THE SAME.

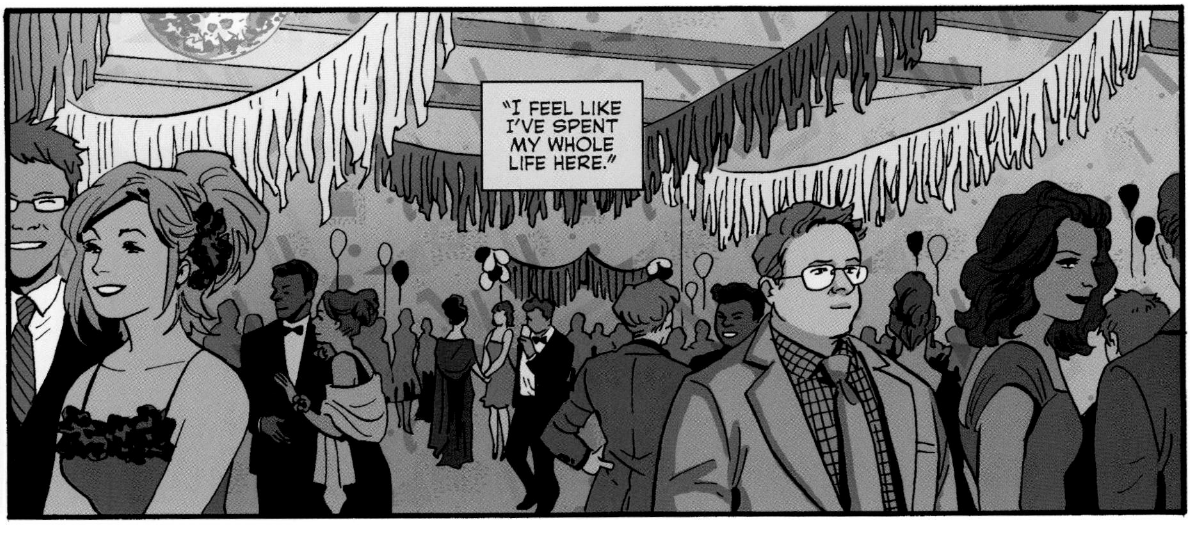
"I FEEL LIKE I'VE SPENT MY WHOLE LIFE HERE."

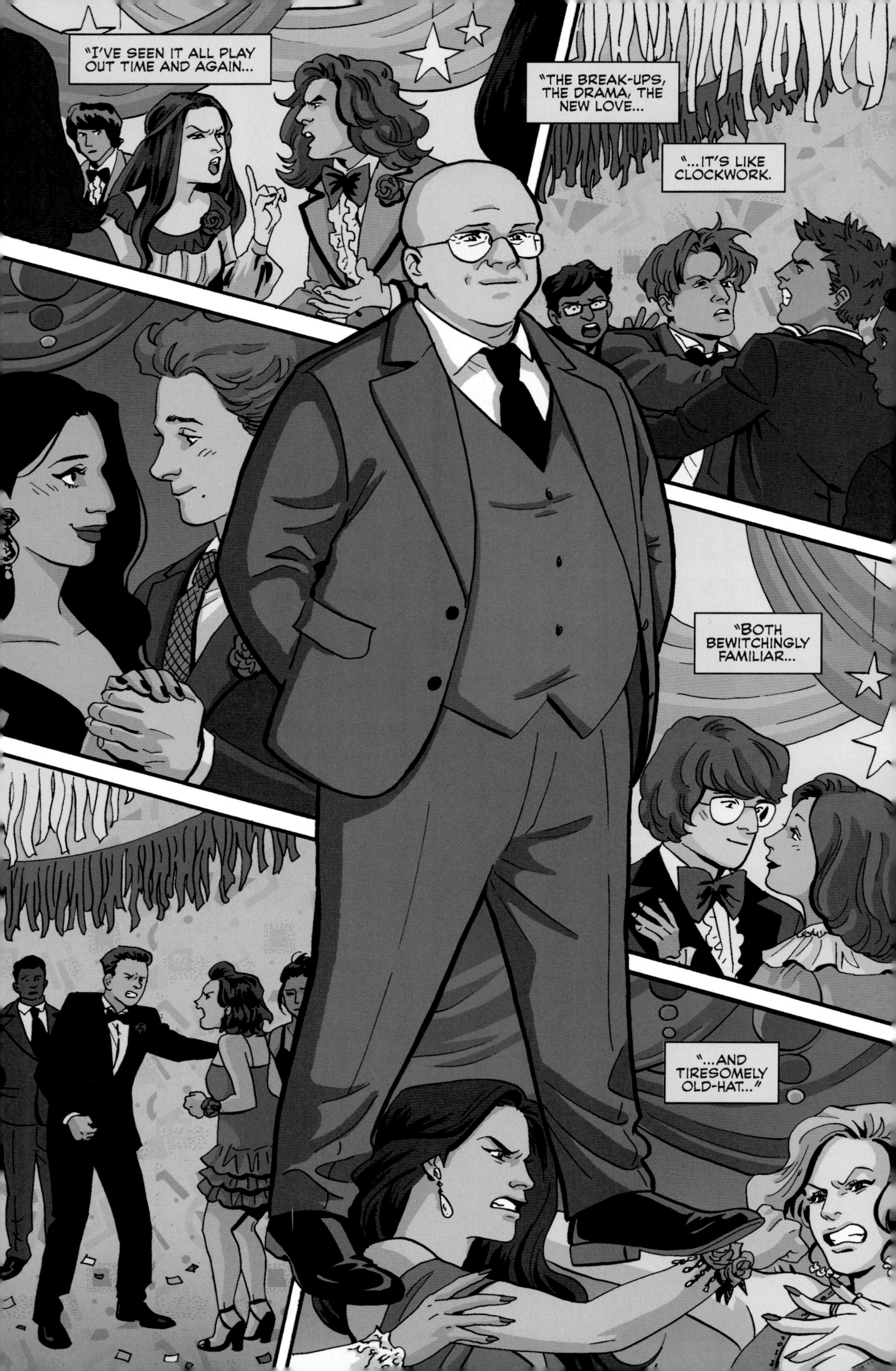
"I'VE SEEN IT ALL PLAY OUT TIME AND AGAIN...
"THE BREAK-UPS, THE DRAMA, THE NEW LOVE...
"...IT'S LIKE CLOCKWORK.
"BOTH BEWITCHINGLY FAMILIAR...
"...AND TIRESOMELY OLD-HAT..."

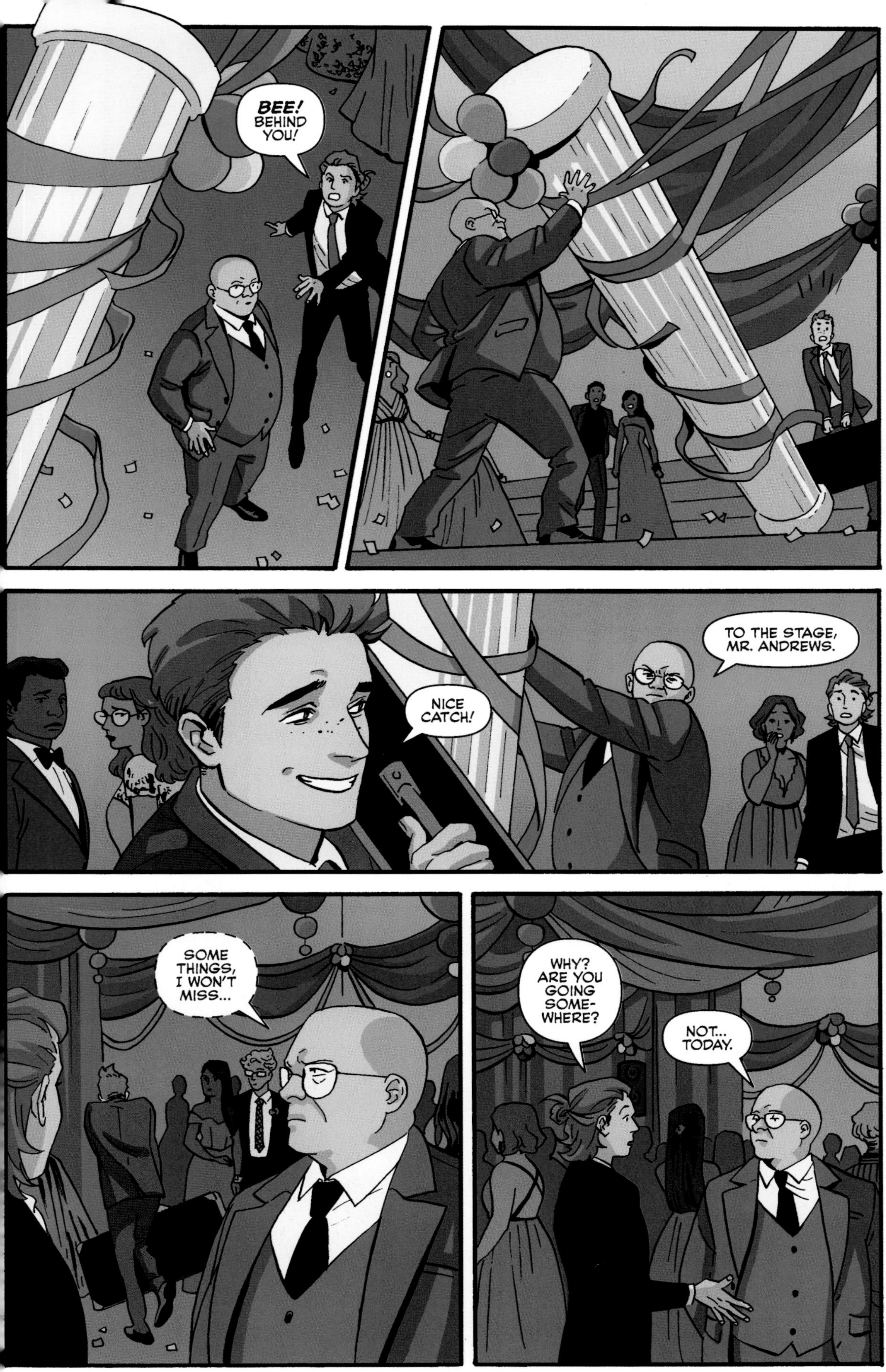
BEE! BEHIND YOU!
NICE CATCH!
TO THE STAGE, MR. ANDREWS.
SOME THINGS, I WON'T MISS...
WHY? ARE YOU GOING SOME-WHERE?
NOT... TODAY.

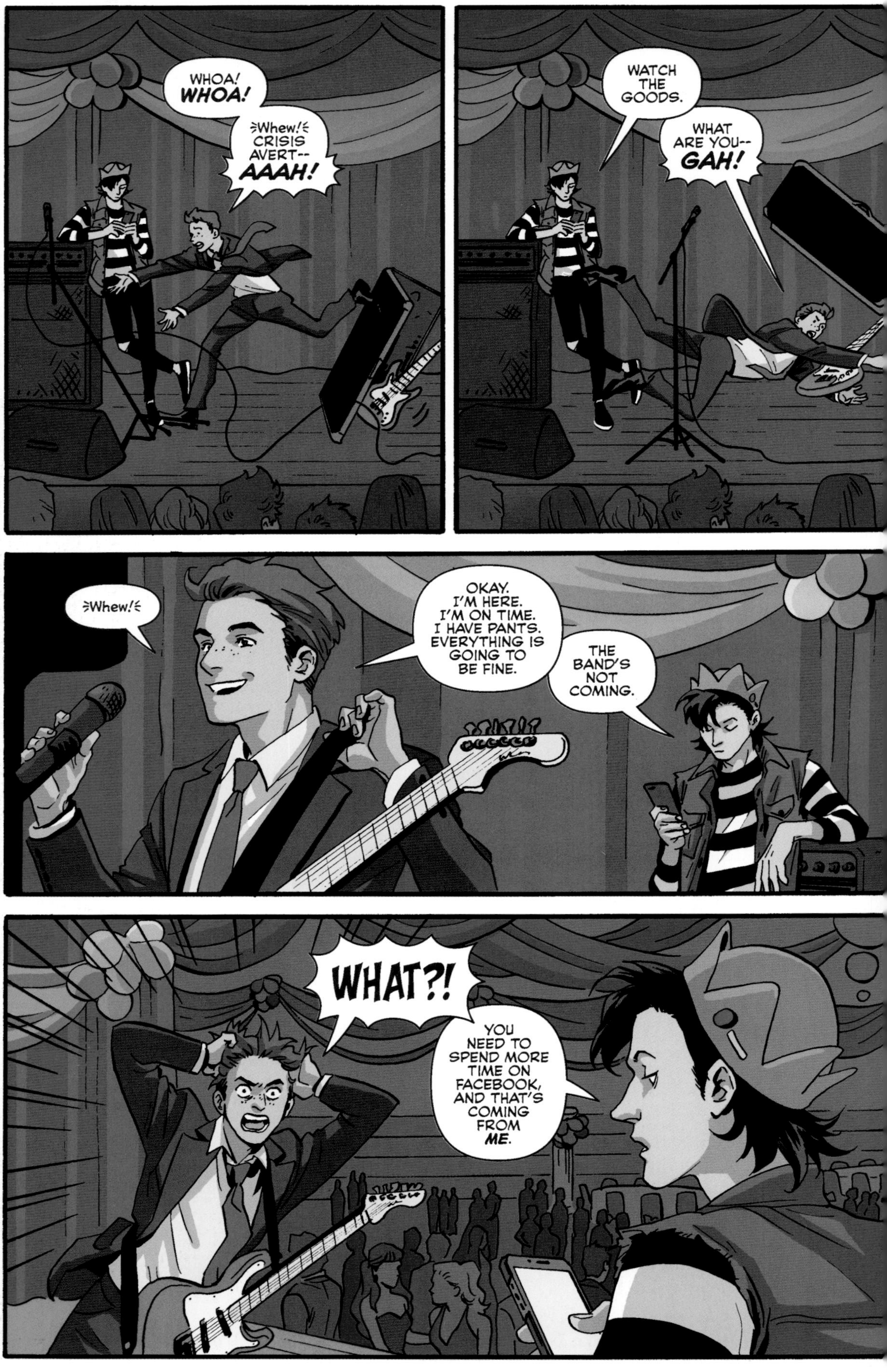
WHOA! WHOA!
Whew! CRISIS AVERT-- AAAH!
WATCH THE GOODS.
WHAT ARE YOU-- GAH!
Whew!
OKAY. I'M HERE. I'M ON TIME. I HAVE PANTS. EVERYTHING IS GOING TO BE FINE.
THE BAND'S NOT COMING.
WHAT?!
YOU NEED TO SPEND MORE TIME ON FACEBOOK, AND THAT'S COMING FROM ME.

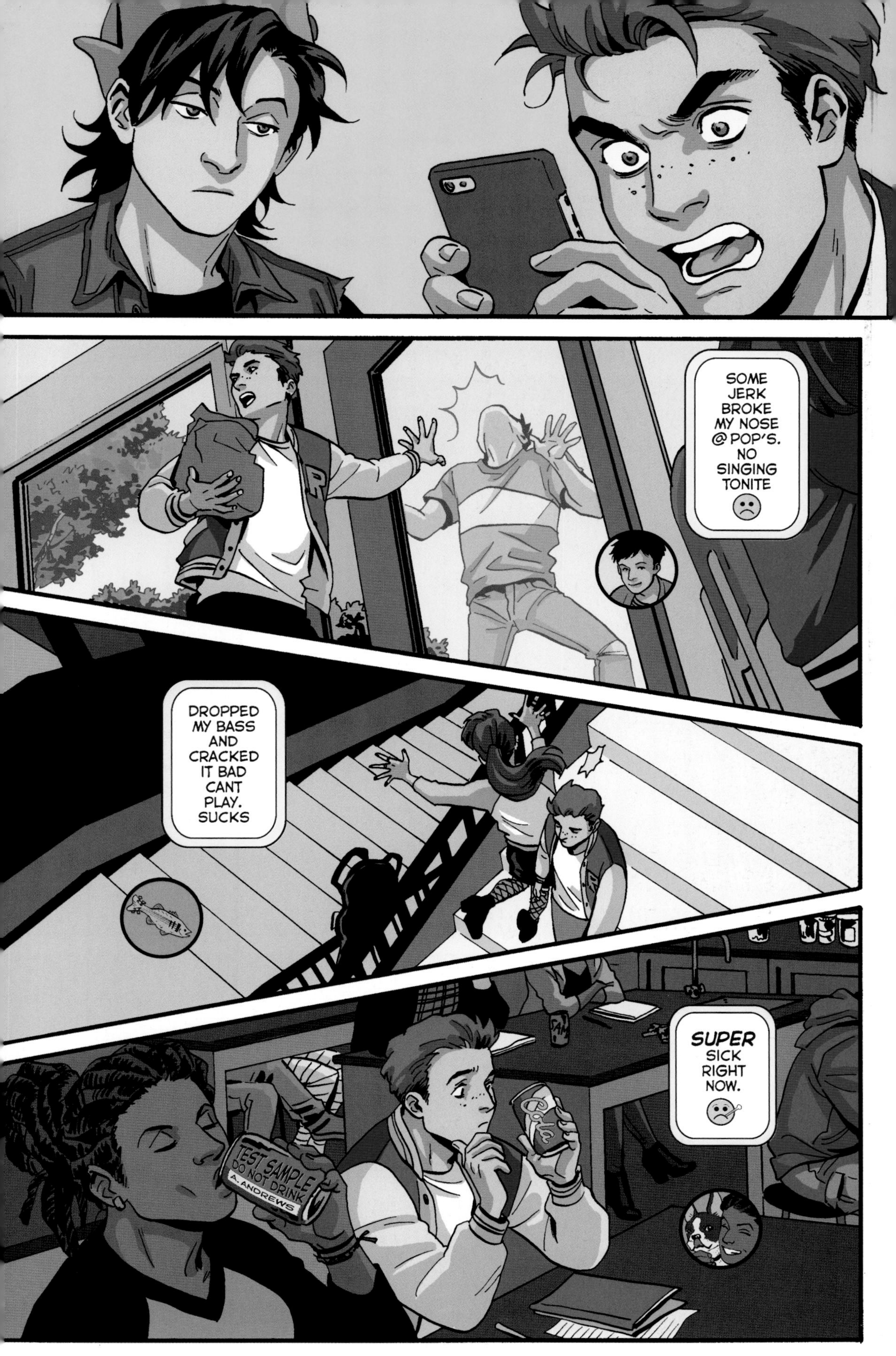
SOME JERK BROKE MY NOSE @POP'S. NO SINGING TONITE
DROPPED MY BASS AND CRACKED IT BAD CANT PLAY. SUCKS
SUPER SICK RIGHT NOW.
TEST SAMPLE DO NOT DRINK A. ANDREWS

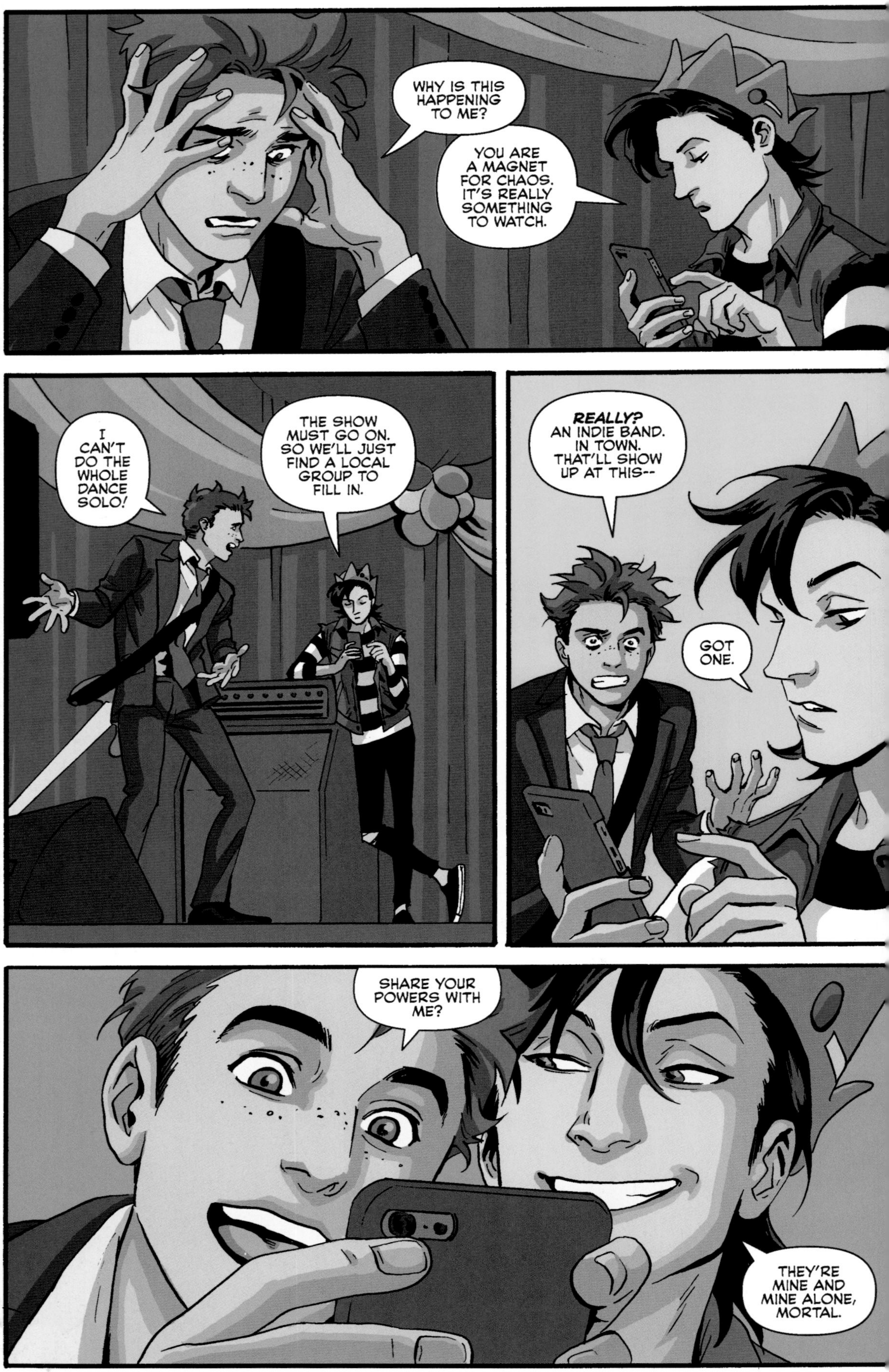
WHY IS THIS HAPPENING TO ME?
YOU ARE A MAGNET FOR CHAOS. IT'S REALLY SOMETHING TO WATCH.
I CAN'T DO THE WHOLE DANCE SOLO!
THE SHOW MUST GO ON. SO WE'LL JUST FIND A LOCAL GROUP TO FILL IN.
REALLY? AN INDIE BAND. IN TOWN. THAT'LL SHOW UP AT THIS--
GOT ONE.
SHARE YOUR POWERS WITH ME?
THEY'RE MINE AND MINE ALONE, MORTAL.

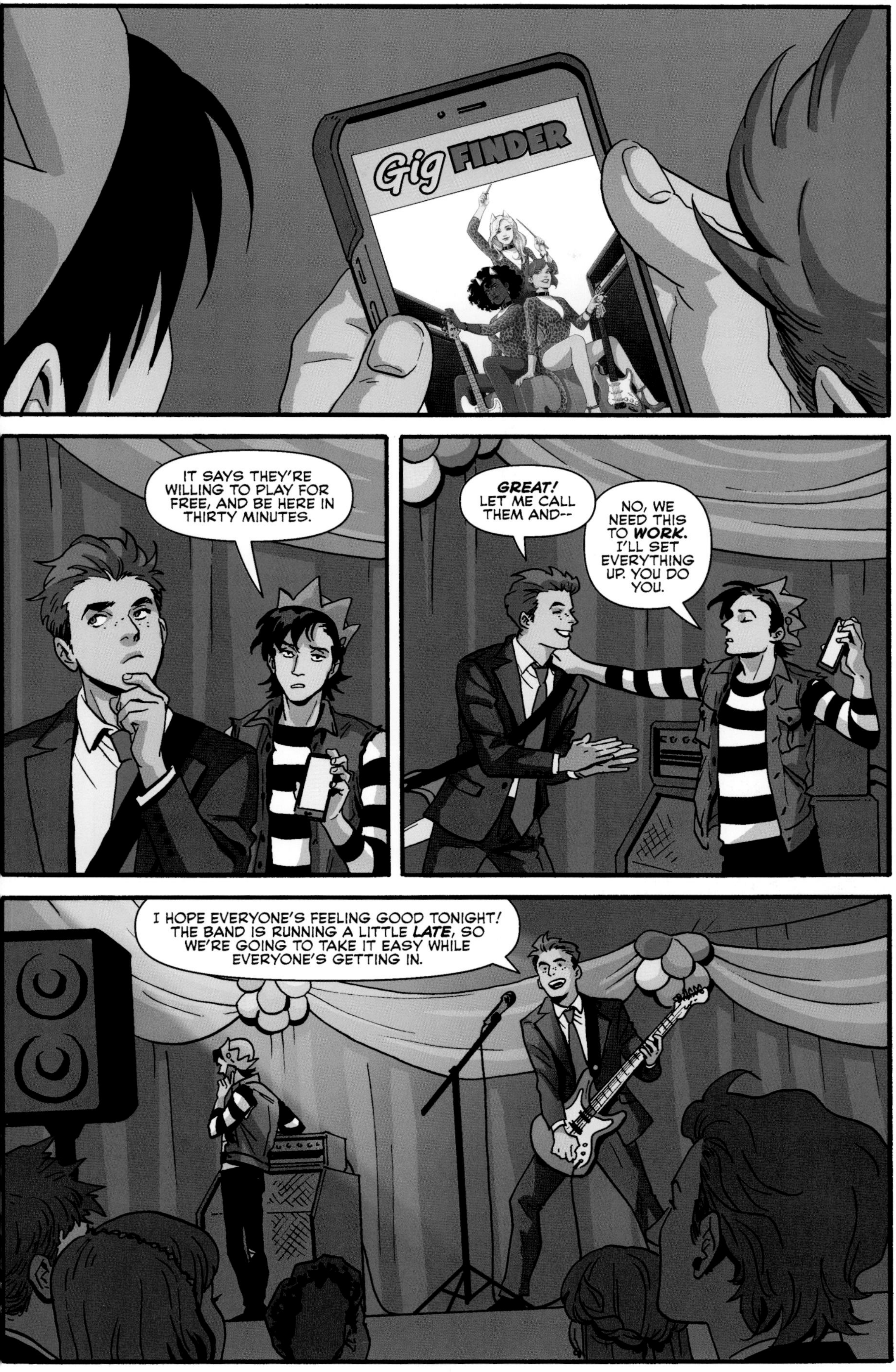
Gig FINDER
IT SAYS THEY'RE WILLING TO PLAY FOR FREE, AND BE HERE IN THIRTY MINUTES.
GREAT! LET ME CALL THEM AND--
NO, WE NEED THIS TO WORK. I'LL SET EVERYTHING UP. YOU DO YOU.
I HOPE EVERYONE'S FEELING GOOD TONIGHT! THE BAND IS RUNNING A LITTLE LATE, SO WE'RE GOING TO TAKE IT EASY WHILE EVERYONE'S GETTING IN.

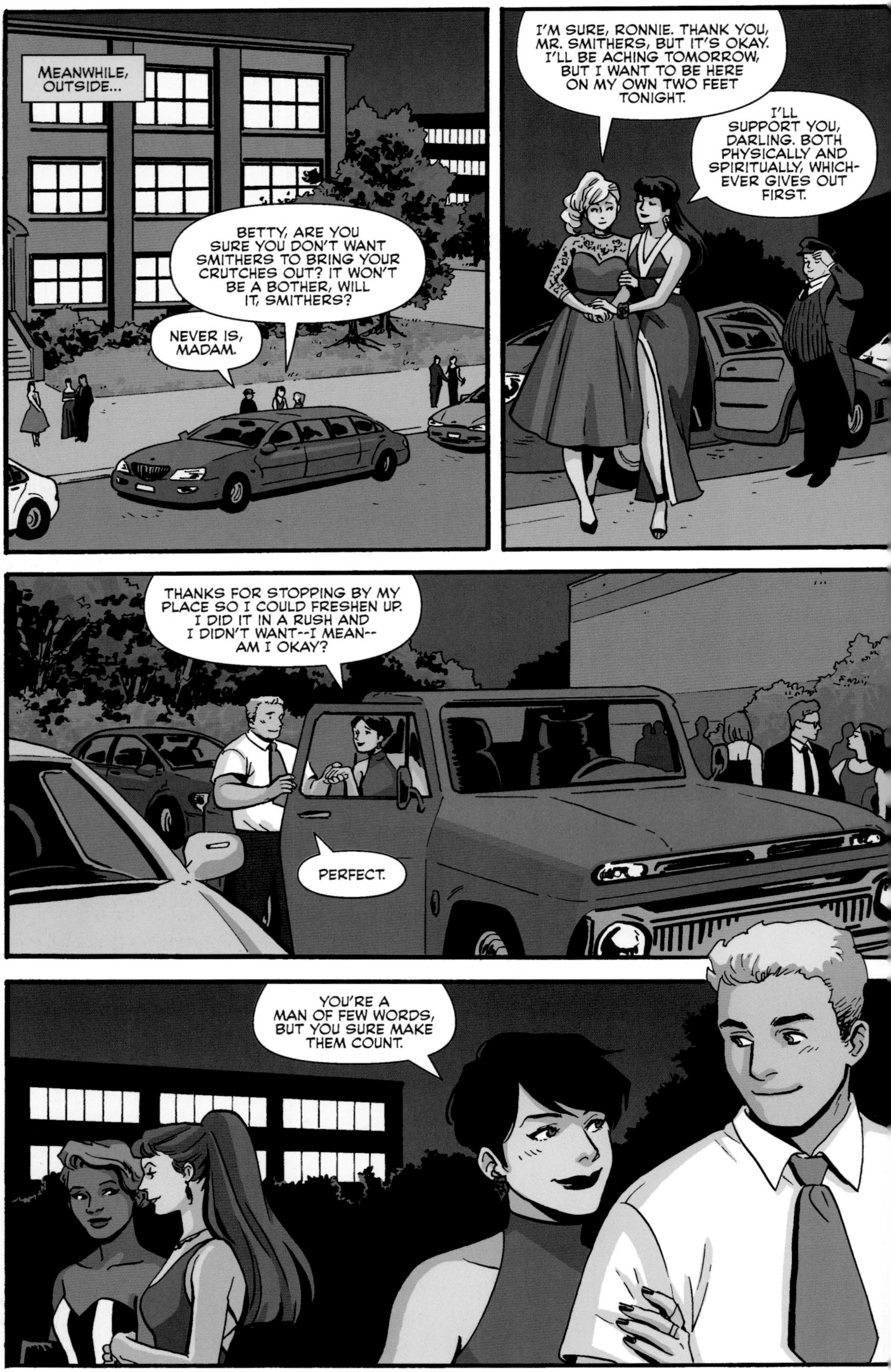

MEANWHILE, OUTSIDE...
BETTY, ARE YOU SURE YOU DON'T WANT SMITHERS TO BRING YOUR CRUTCHES OUT? IT WON'T BE A BOTHER, WILL IT, SMITHERS?
NEVER IS, MADAM.
I'M SURE, RONNIE. THANK YOU, MR. SMITHERS, BUT IT'S OKAY. I'LL BE ACHING TOMORROW, BUT I WANT TO BE HERE ON MY OWN TWO FEET TONIGHT.
I'LL SUPPORT YOU, DARLING. BOTH PHYSICALLY AND SPIRITUALLY, WHICH-EVER GIVES OUT FIRST.
THANKS FOR STOPPING BY MY PLACE SO I COULD FRESHEN UP. I DID IT IN A RUSH AND I DIDN'T WANT--I MEAN--AM I OKAY?
PERFECT.
YOU'RE A MAN OF FEW WORDS, BUT YOU SURE MAKE THEM COUNT.

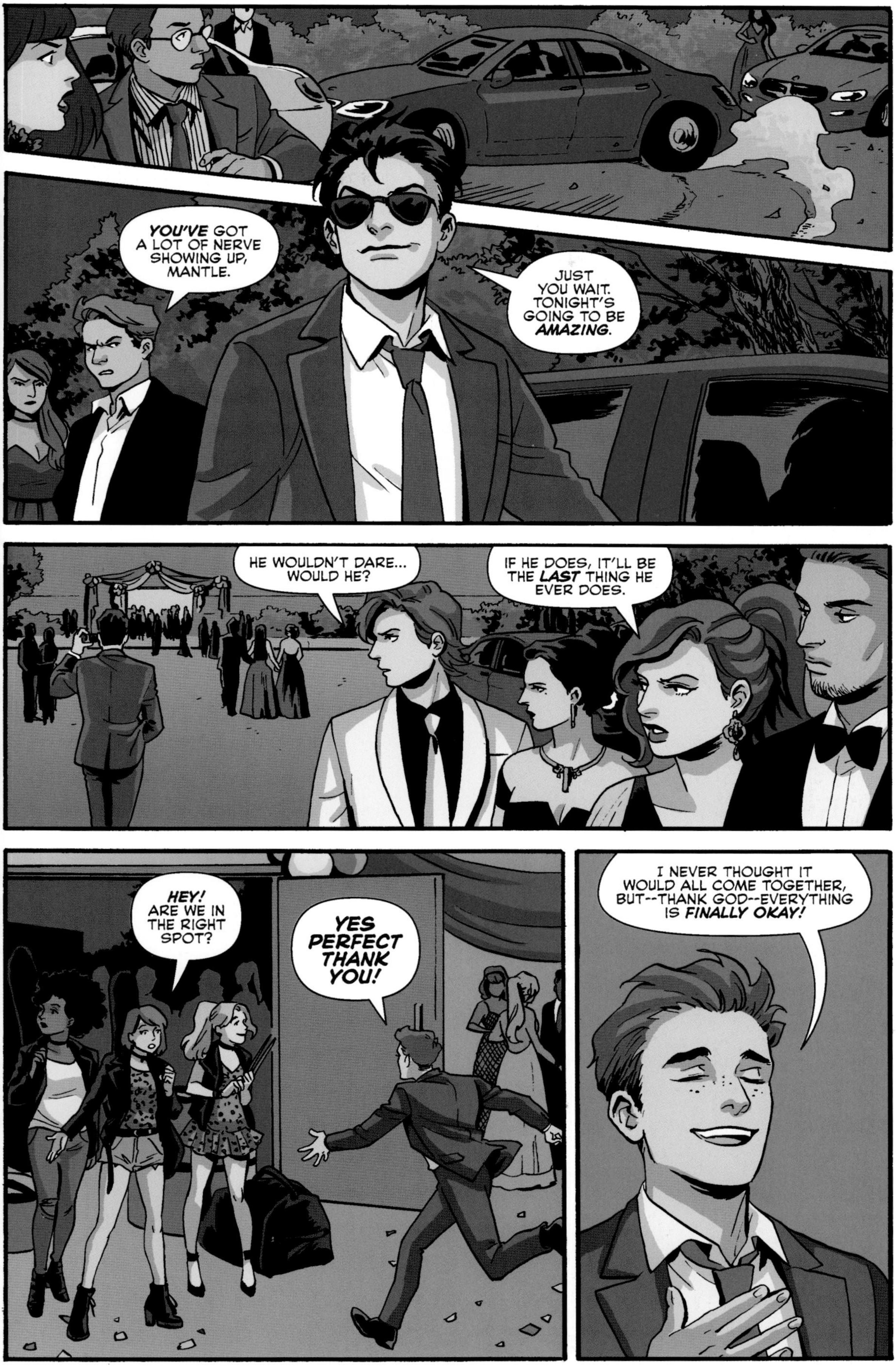
YOU'VE GOT A LOT OF NERVE SHOWING UP, MANTLE.
JUST YOU WAIT. TONIGHT'S GOING TO BE AMAZING.
HE WOULDN'T DARE... WOULD HE?
IF HE DOES, IT'LL BE THE LAST THING HE EVER DOES.
HEY! ARE WE IN THE RIGHT SPOT?
YES PERFECT THANK YOU!
I NEVER THOUGHT IT WOULD ALL COME TOGETHER, BUT--THANK GOD--EVERYTHING IS FINALLY OKAY!

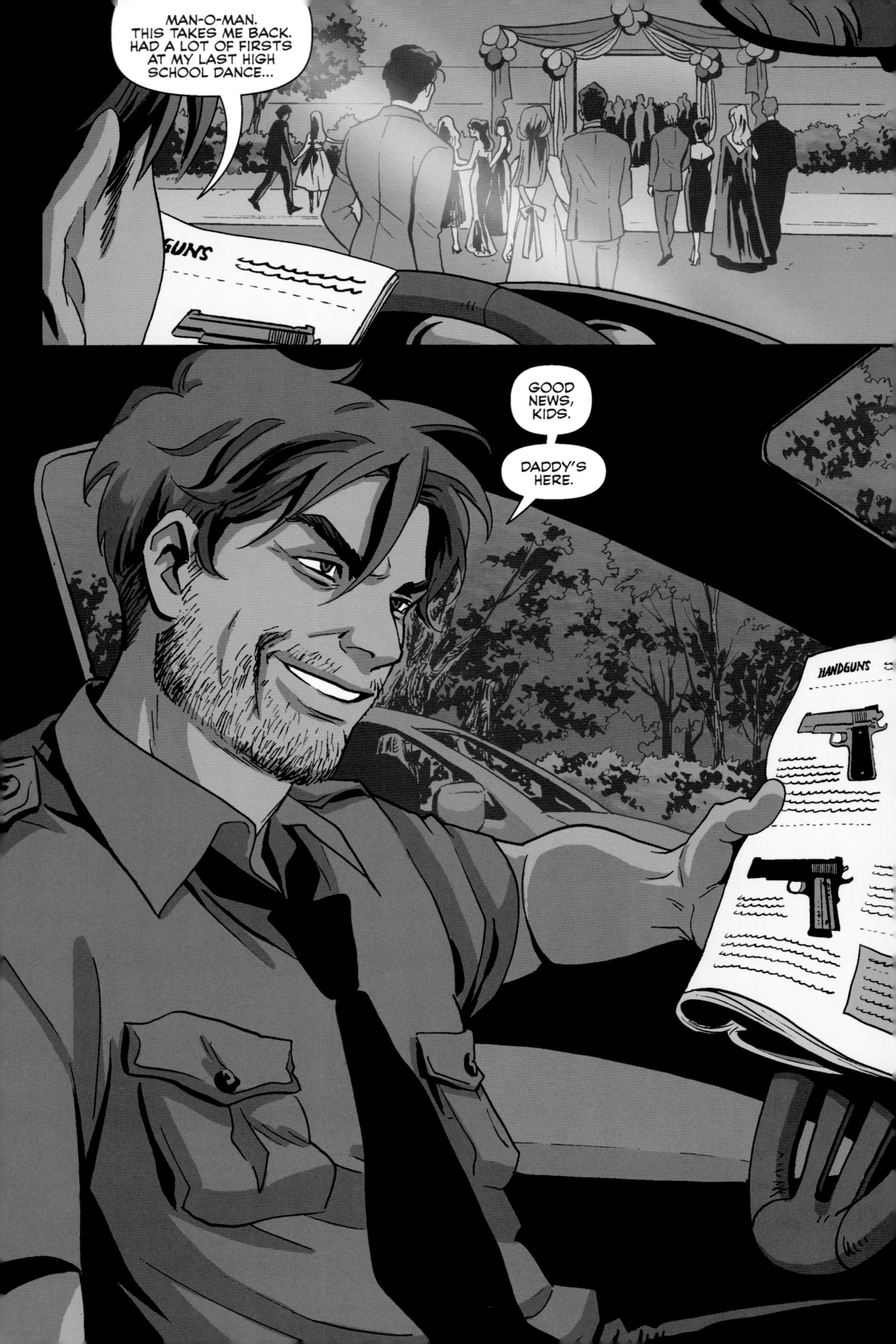
MAN-O-MAN. THIS TAKES ME BACK. HAD A LOT OF FIRSTS AT MY LAST HIGH SCHOOL DANCE...
GUNS
GOOD NEWS, KIDS.
DADDY'S HERE.
HANDGUNS

TO BE CONTINUED...

ISSUE THIRTY-ONE

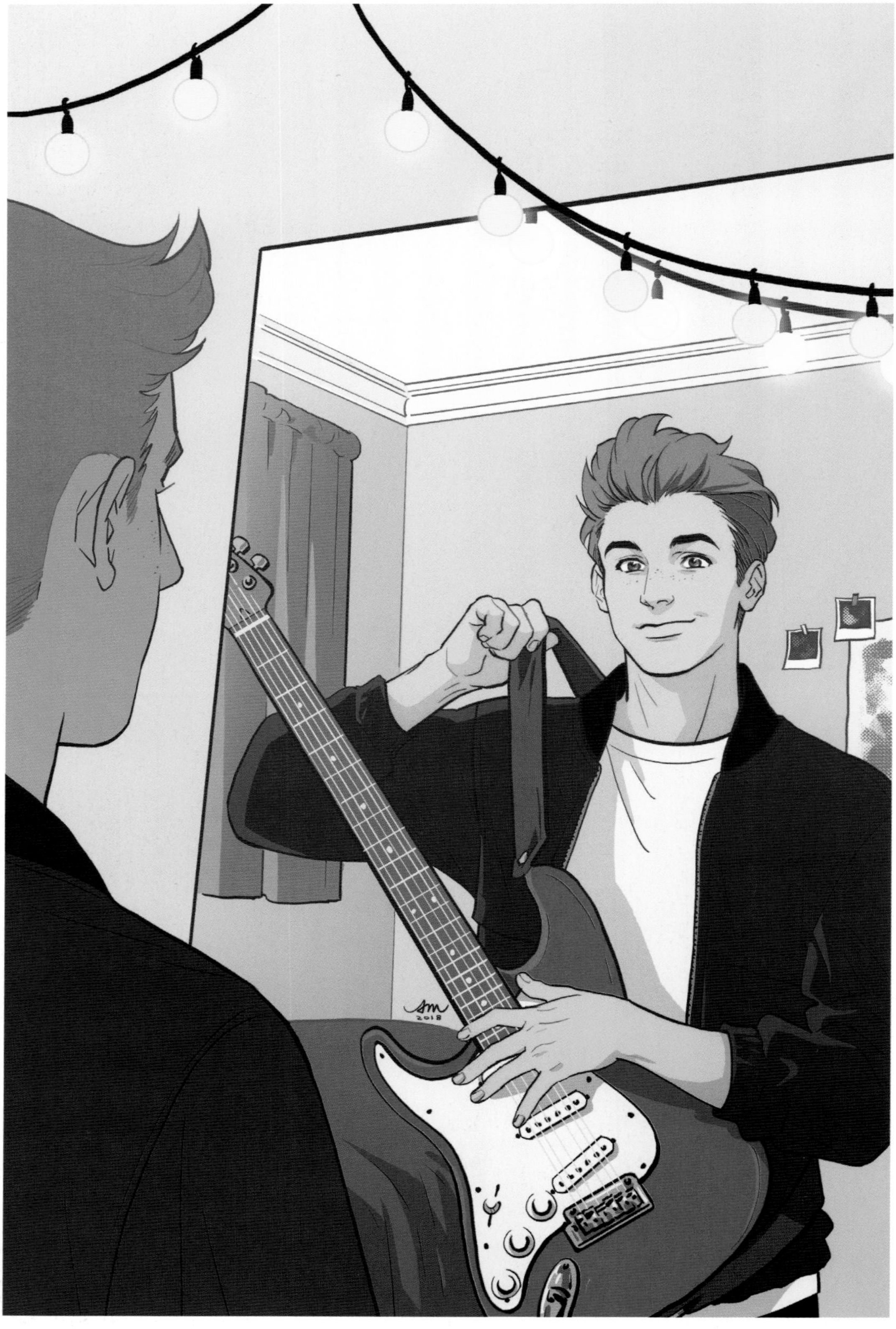

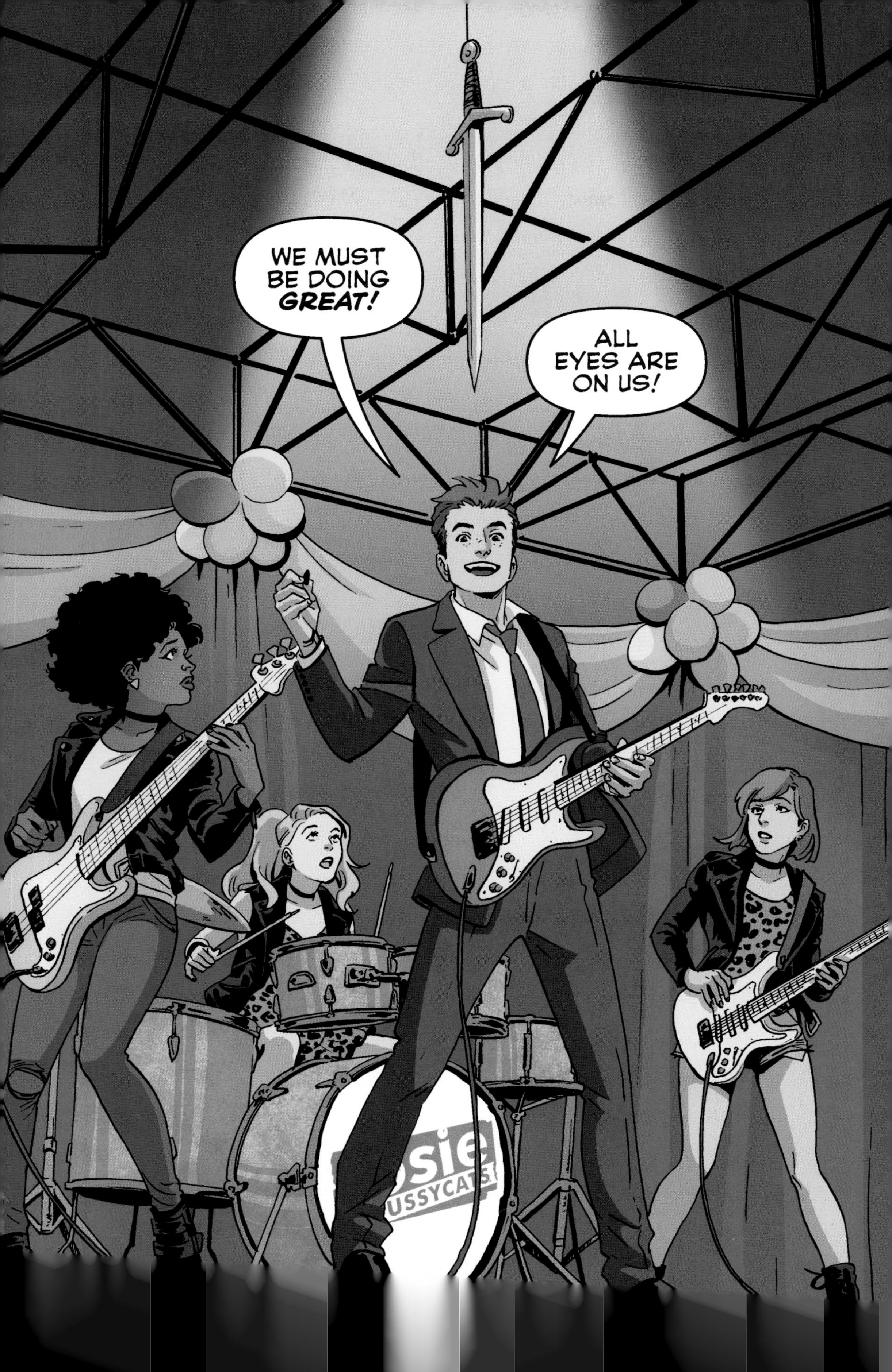
WE MUST BE DOING GREAT!
ALL EYES ARE ON US!

CHAPTER ONE: THE GANG'S ALL HERE

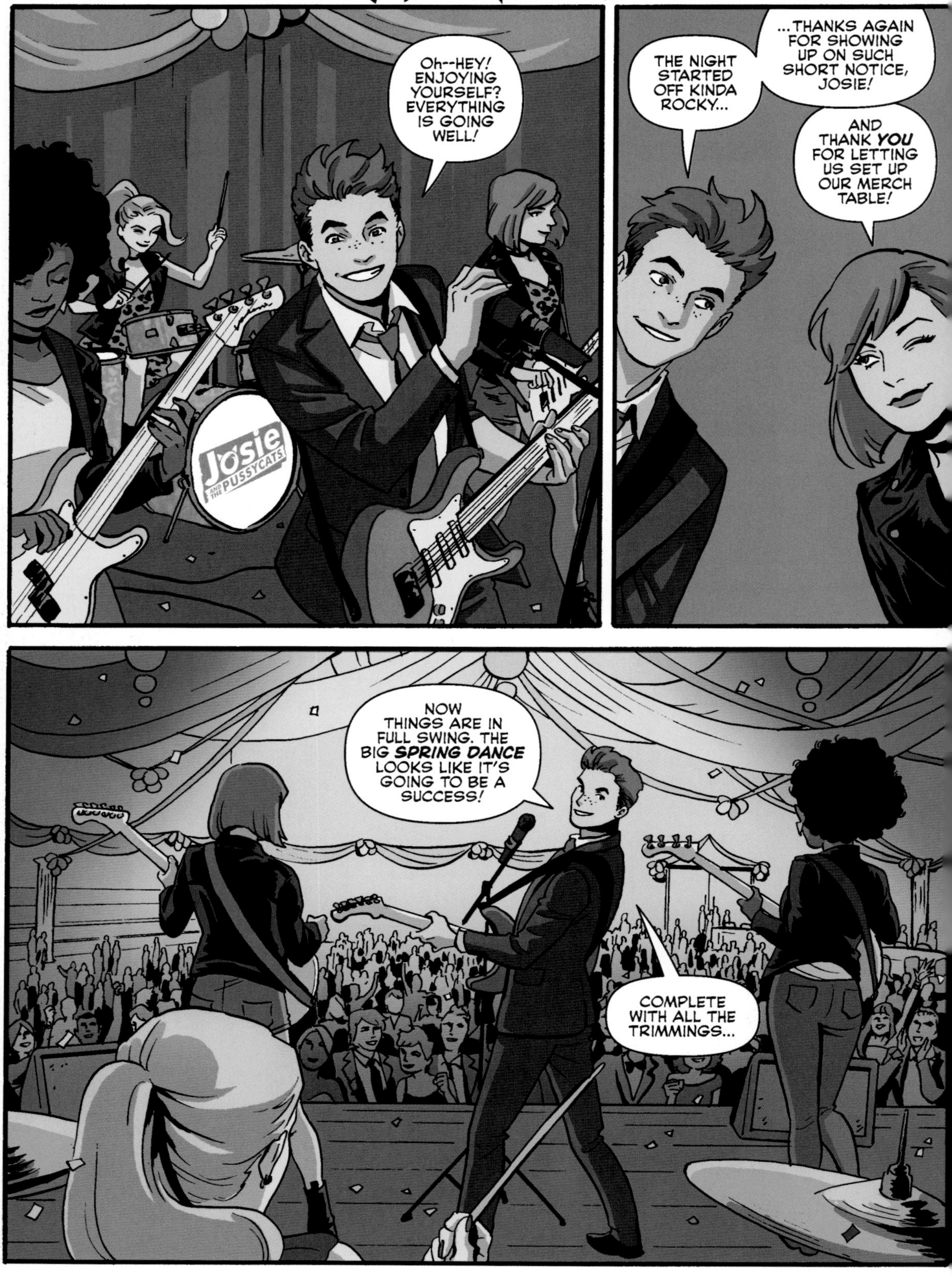
Oh--HEY! ENJOYING YOURSELF? EVERYTHING IS GOING WELL!
JOSIE AND THE PUSSYCATS
THE NIGHT STARTED OFF KINDA ROCKY...
...THANKS AGAIN FOR SHOWING UP ON SUCH SHORT NOTICE, JOSIE!
AND THANK *YOU* FOR LETTING US SET UP OUR MERCH TABLE!
NOW THINGS ARE IN FULL SWING. THE BIG *SPRING DANCE* LOOKS LIKE IT'S GOING TO BE A SUCCESS!
COMPLETE WITH ALL THE TRIMMINGS...

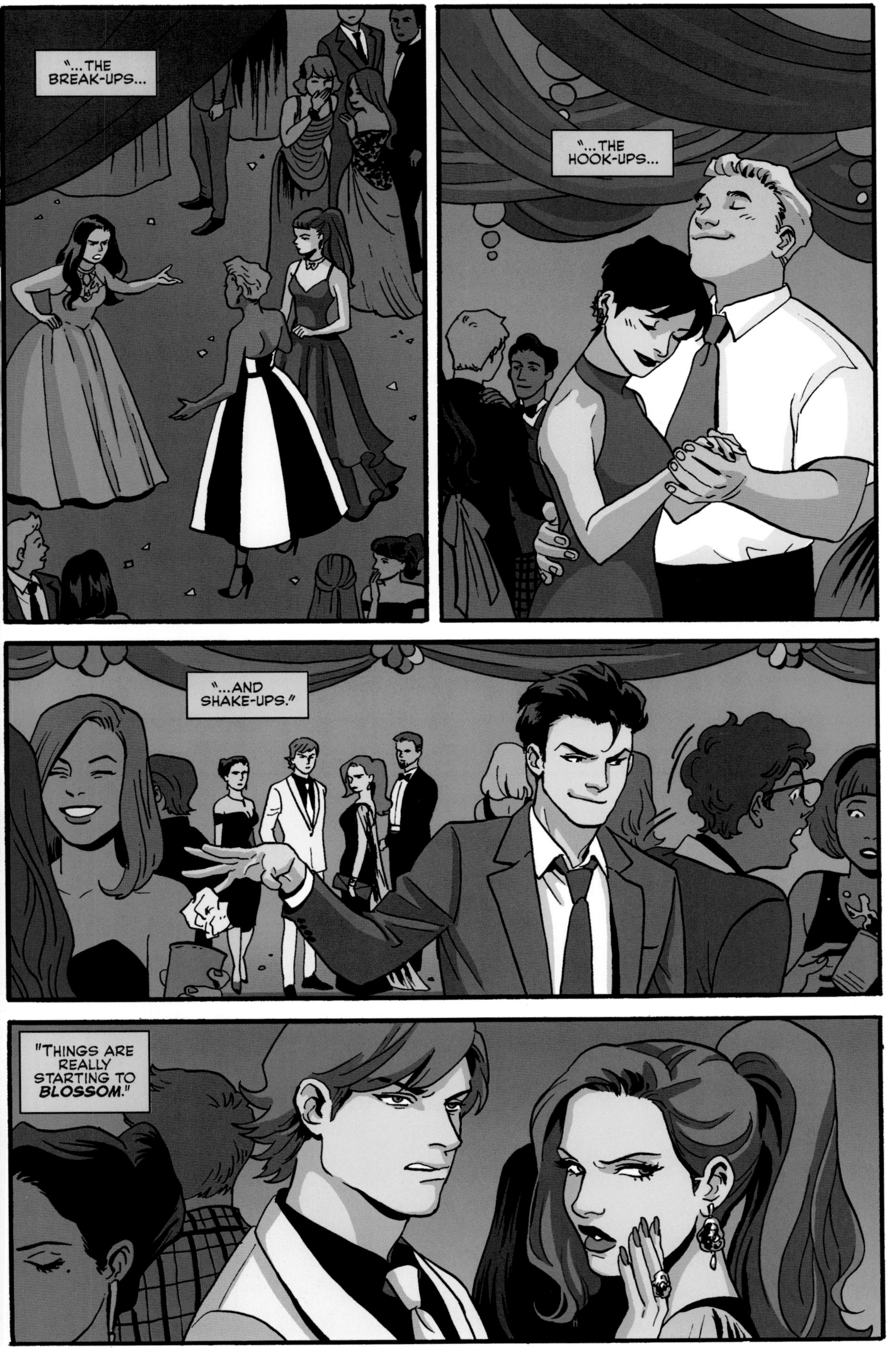
"...THE BREAK-UPS...
"...THE HOOK-UPS...
"...AND SHAKE-UPS."
"THINGS ARE REALLY STARTING TO BLOSSOM."

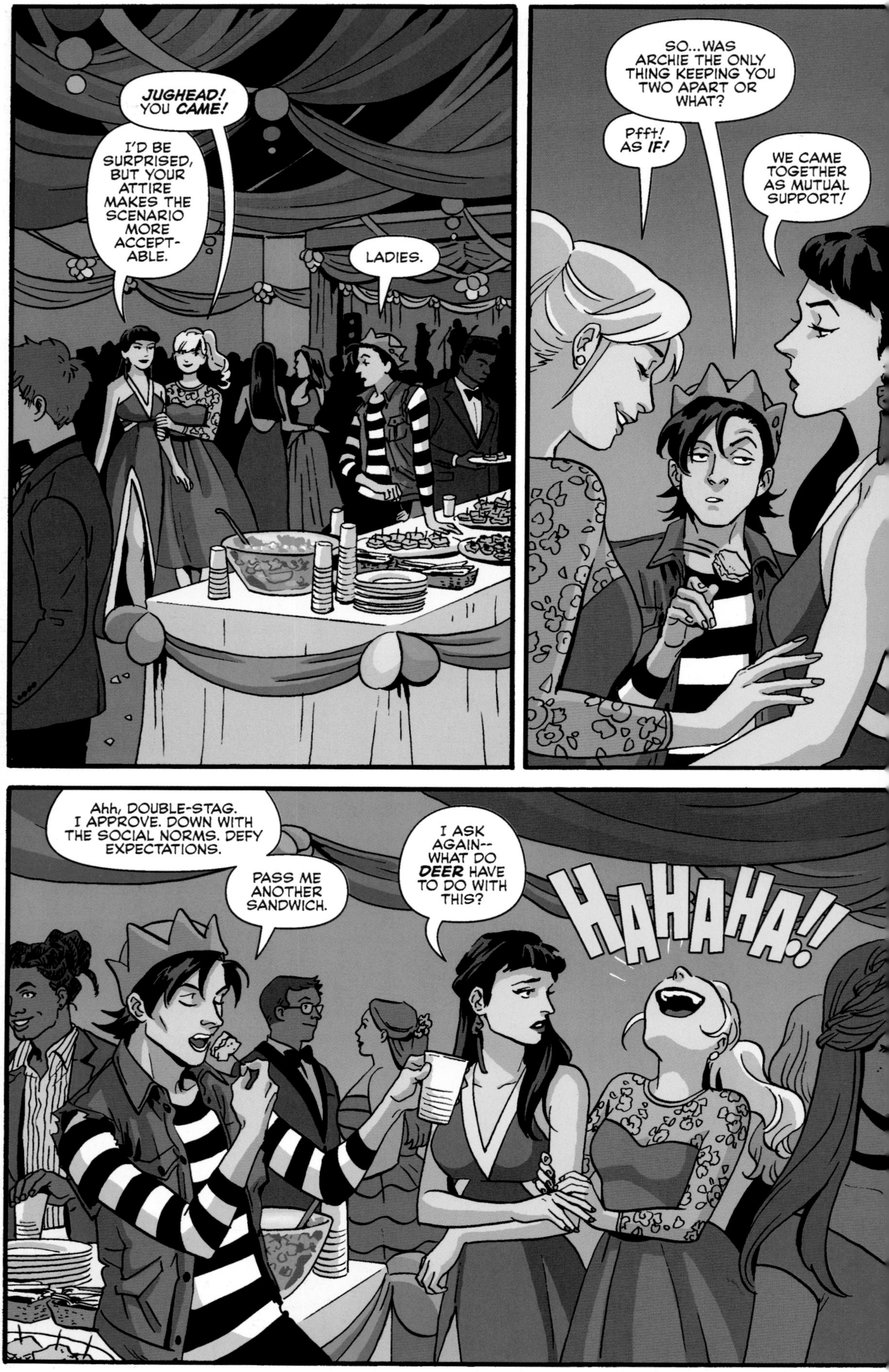
JUGHEAD! YOU CAME!
I'D BE SURPRISED, BUT YOUR ATTIRE MAKES THE SCENARIO MORE ACCEPT-ABLE.
LADIES.
SO...WAS ARCHIE THE ONLY THING KEEPING YOU TWO APART OR WHAT?
Pfft! AS IF!
WE CAME TOGETHER AS MUTUAL SUPPORT!
Ahh, DOUBLE-STAG. I APPROVE. DOWN WITH THE SOCIAL NORMS. DEFY EXPECTATIONS.
PASS ME ANOTHER SANDWICH.
I ASK AGAIN-- WHAT DO DEER HAVE TO DO WITH THIS?
HAHAHA!!

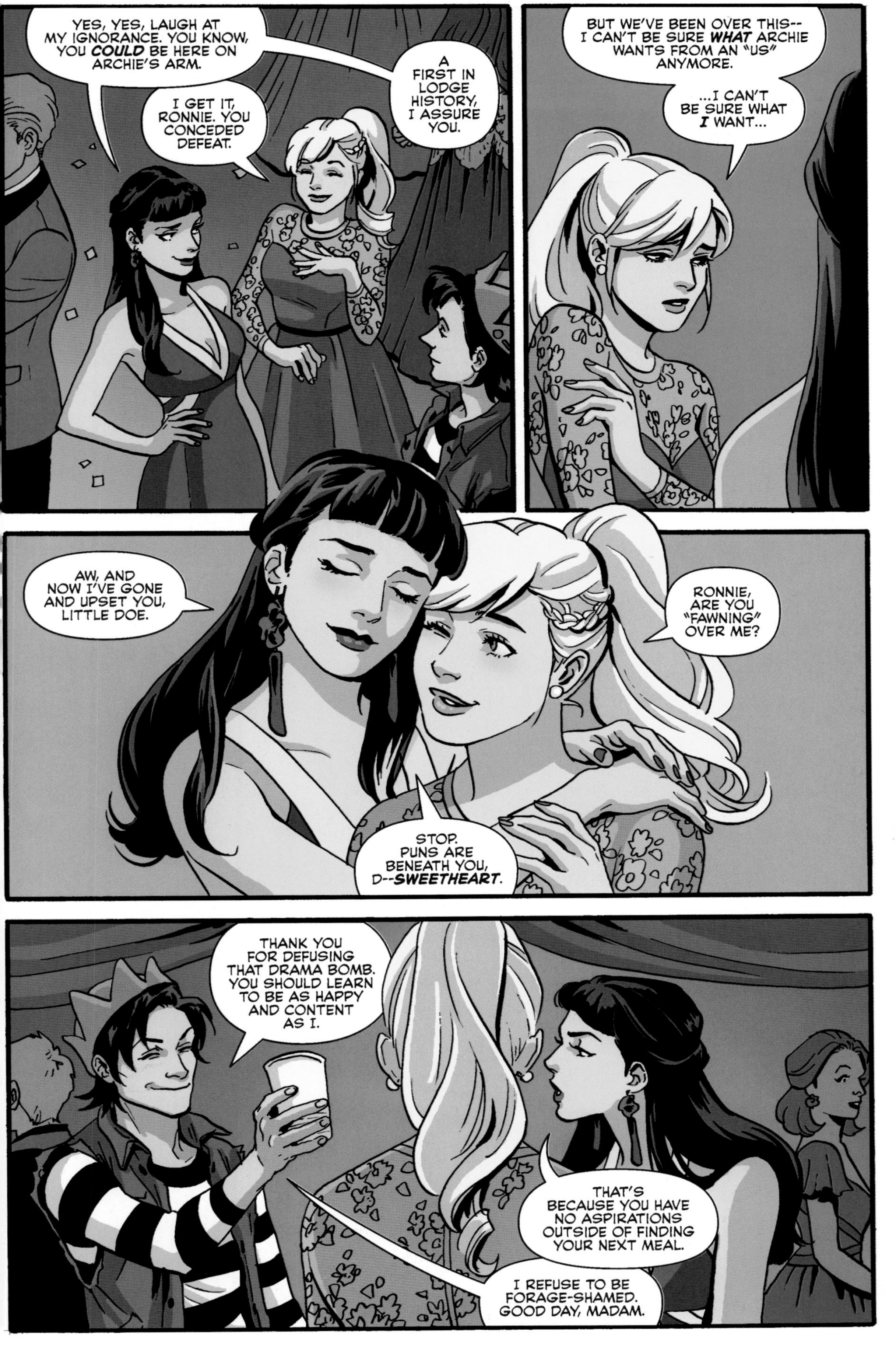

YES, YES, LAUGH AT MY IGNORANCE. YOU KNOW, YOU **COULD** BE HERE ON ARCHIE'S ARM.
I GET IT, RONNIE. YOU CONCEDED DEFEAT.
A FIRST IN LODGE HISTORY, I ASSURE YOU.
BUT WE'VE BEEN OVER THIS-- I CAN'T BE SURE **WHAT** ARCHIE WANTS FROM AN "US" ANYMORE.
...I CAN'T BE SURE WHAT **I** WANT...
AW, AND NOW I'VE GONE AND UPSET YOU, LITTLE DOE.
RONNIE, ARE YOU "FAWNING" OVER ME?
STOP. PUNS ARE BENEATH YOU, D--**SWEETHEART**.
THANK YOU FOR DEFUSING THAT DRAMA BOMB. YOU SHOULD LEARN TO BE AS HAPPY AND CONTENT AS I.
THAT'S BECAUSE YOU HAVE NO ASPIRATIONS OUTSIDE OF FINDING YOUR NEXT MEAL.
I REFUSE TO BE FORAGE-SHAMED. GOOD DAY, MADAM.

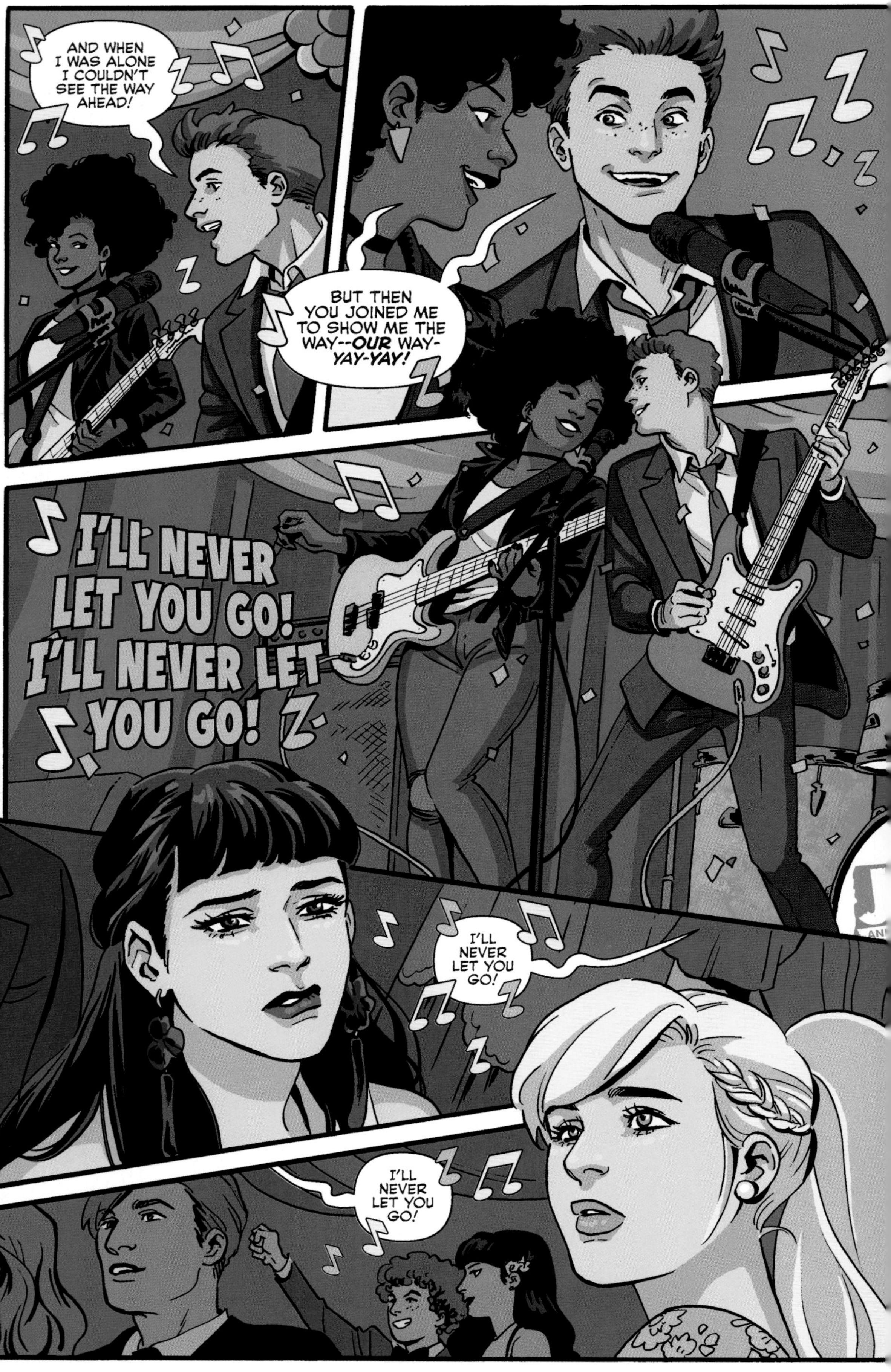
AND WHEN I WAS ALONE I COULDN'T SEE THE WAY AHEAD!
BUT THEN YOU JOINED ME TO SHOW ME THE WAY--OUR WAY-YAY-YAY!
I'LL NEVER LET YOU GO! I'LL NEVER LET YOU GO!
I'LL NEVER LET YOU GO!
I'LL NEVER LET YOU GO!

CHAPTER TWO: SHIFTING TIDES

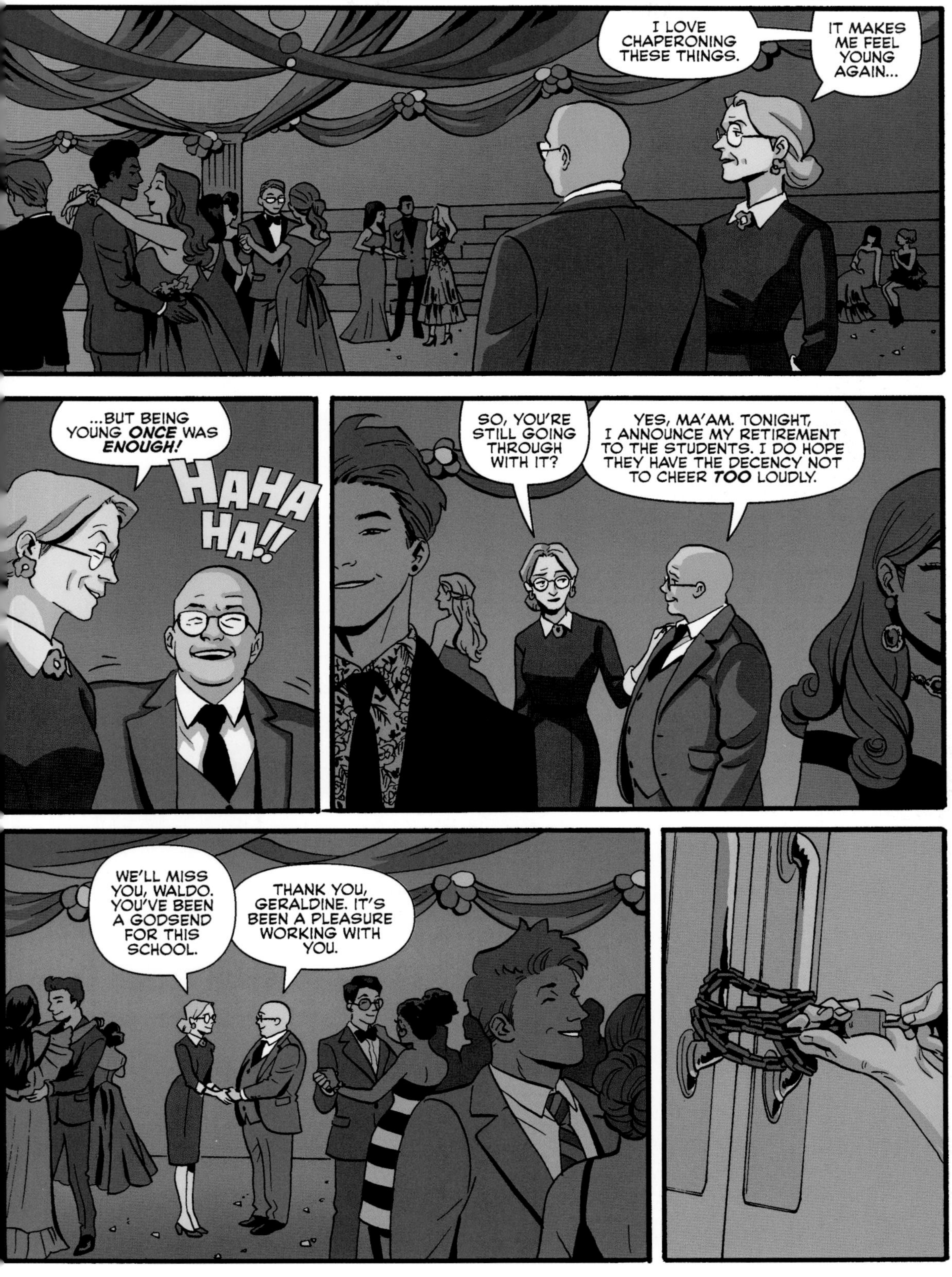
I LOVE CHAPERONING THESE THINGS.
IT MAKES ME FEEL YOUNG AGAIN...
...BUT BEING YOUNG ONCE WAS ENOUGH!
HAHAHA!!
SO, YOU'RE STILL GOING THROUGH WITH IT?
YES, MA'AM. TONIGHT, I ANNOUNCE MY RETIREMENT TO THE STUDENTS. I DO HOPE THEY HAVE THE DECENCY NOT TO CHEER TOO LOUDLY.
WE'LL MISS YOU, WALDO. YOU'VE BEEN A GODSEND FOR THIS SCHOOL.
THANK YOU, GERALDINE. IT'S BEEN A PLEASURE WORKING WITH YOU.

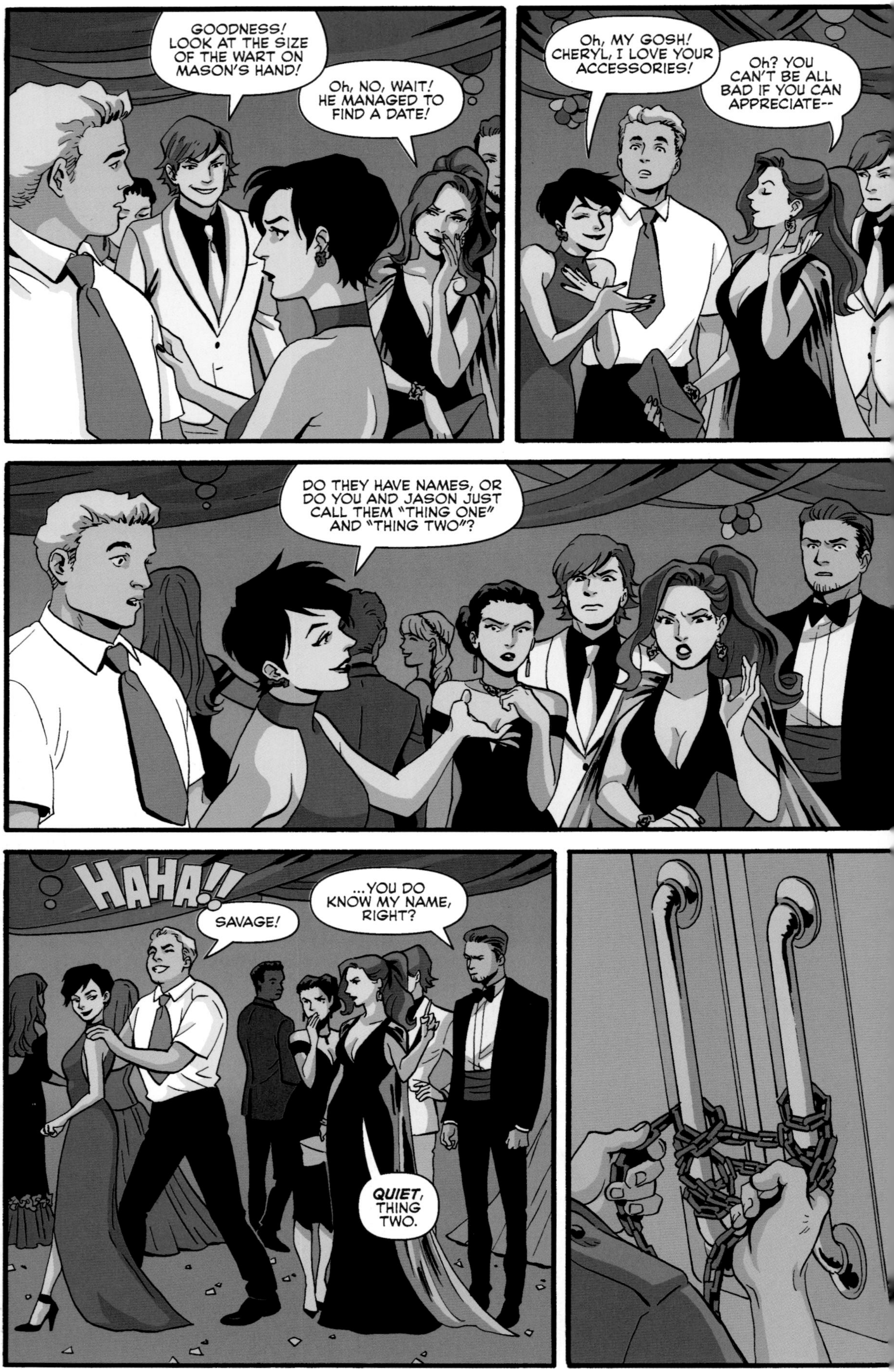
GOODNESS! LOOK AT THE SIZE OF THE WART ON MASON'S HAND!
Oh, NO, WAIT! HE MANAGED TO FIND A DATE!
Oh, MY GOSH! CHERYL, I LOVE YOUR ACCESSORIES!
Oh? YOU CAN'T BE ALL BAD IF YOU CAN APPRECIATE--
DO THEY HAVE NAMES, OR DO YOU AND JASON JUST CALL THEM "THING ONE" AND "THING TWO"?
HAHA!!
SAVAGE!
...YOU DO KNOW MY NAME, RIGHT?
QUIET, THING TWO.

CHAPTER THREE: POWDERKEG

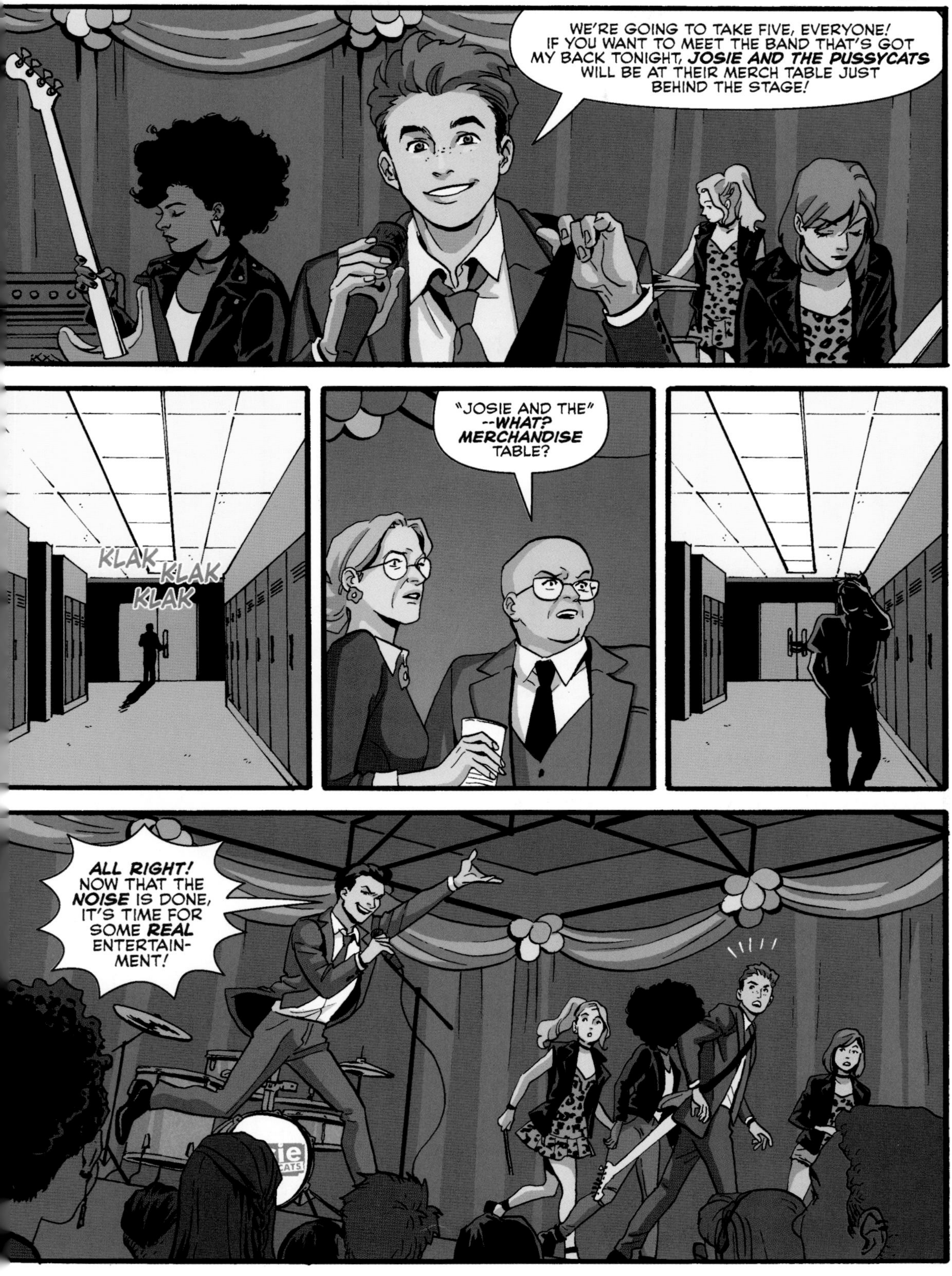
WE'RE GOING TO TAKE FIVE, EVERYONE! IF YOU WANT TO MEET THE BAND THAT'S GOT MY BACK TONIGHT, ***JOSIE AND THE PUSSYCATS*** WILL BE AT THEIR MERCH TABLE JUST BEHIND THE STAGE!
KLAK KLAK KLAK
"JOSIE AND THE" ***--WHAT? MERCHANDISE*** TABLE?
ALL RIGHT! NOW THAT THE ***NOISE*** IS DONE, IT'S TIME FOR SOME ***REAL*** ENTERTAIN-MENT!

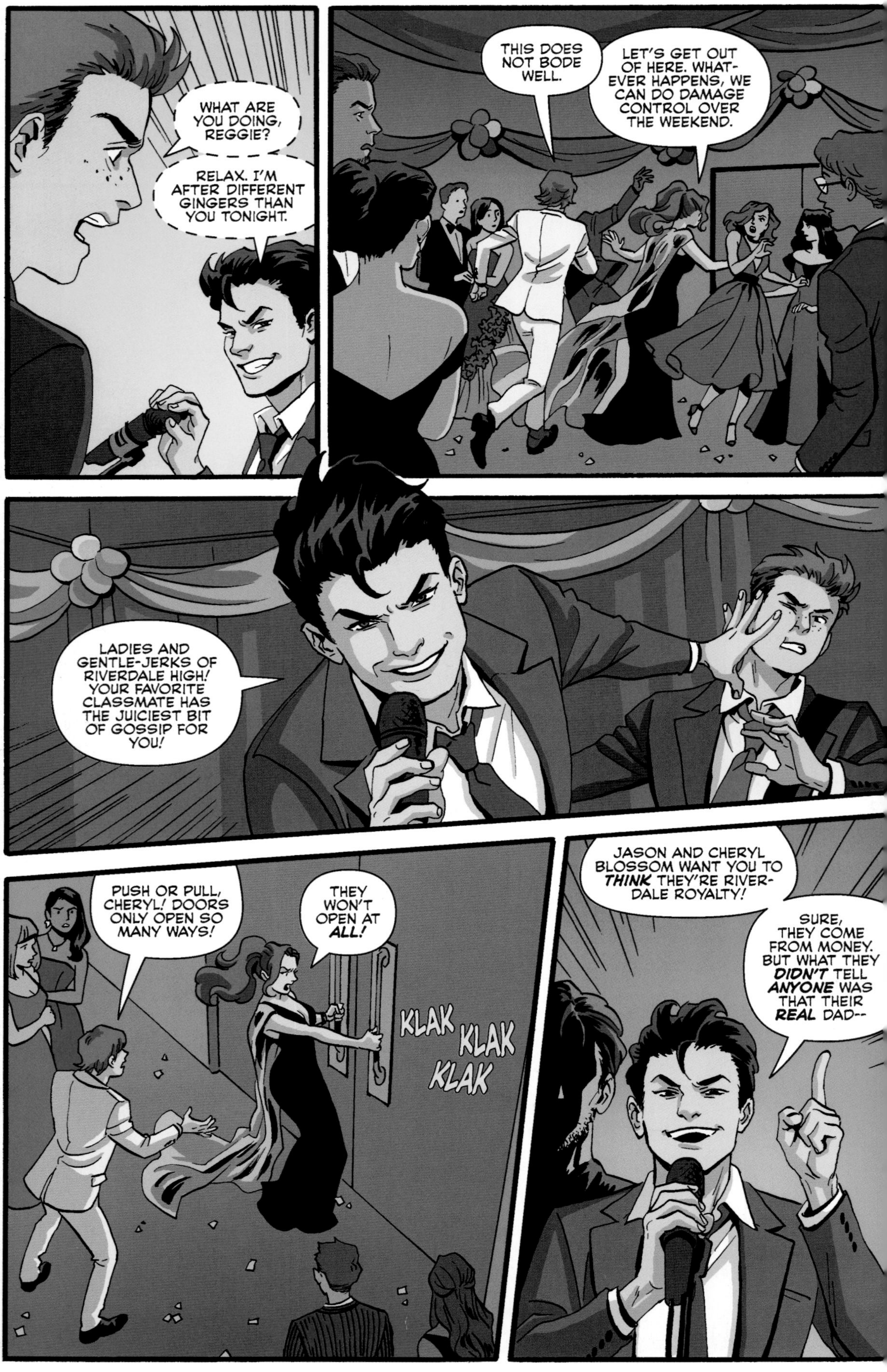
WHAT ARE YOU DOING, REGGIE?
RELAX. I'M AFTER DIFFERENT GINGERS THAN YOU TONIGHT.
THIS DOES NOT BODE WELL.
LET'S GET OUT OF HERE. WHAT-EVER HAPPENS, WE CAN DO DAMAGE CONTROL OVER THE WEEKEND.
LADIES AND GENTLE-JERKS OF RIVERDALE HIGH! YOUR FAVORITE CLASSMATE HAS THE JUICIEST BIT OF GOSSIP FOR YOU!
PUSH OR PULL, CHERYL! DOORS ONLY OPEN SO MANY WAYS!
THEY WON'T OPEN AT ALL!
KLAK KLAK KLAK
JASON AND CHERYL BLOSSOM WANT YOU TO THINK THEY'RE RIVER-DALE ROYALTY!
SURE, THEY COME FROM MONEY. BUT WHAT THEY DIDN'T TELL ANYONE WAS THAT THEIR REAL DAD--

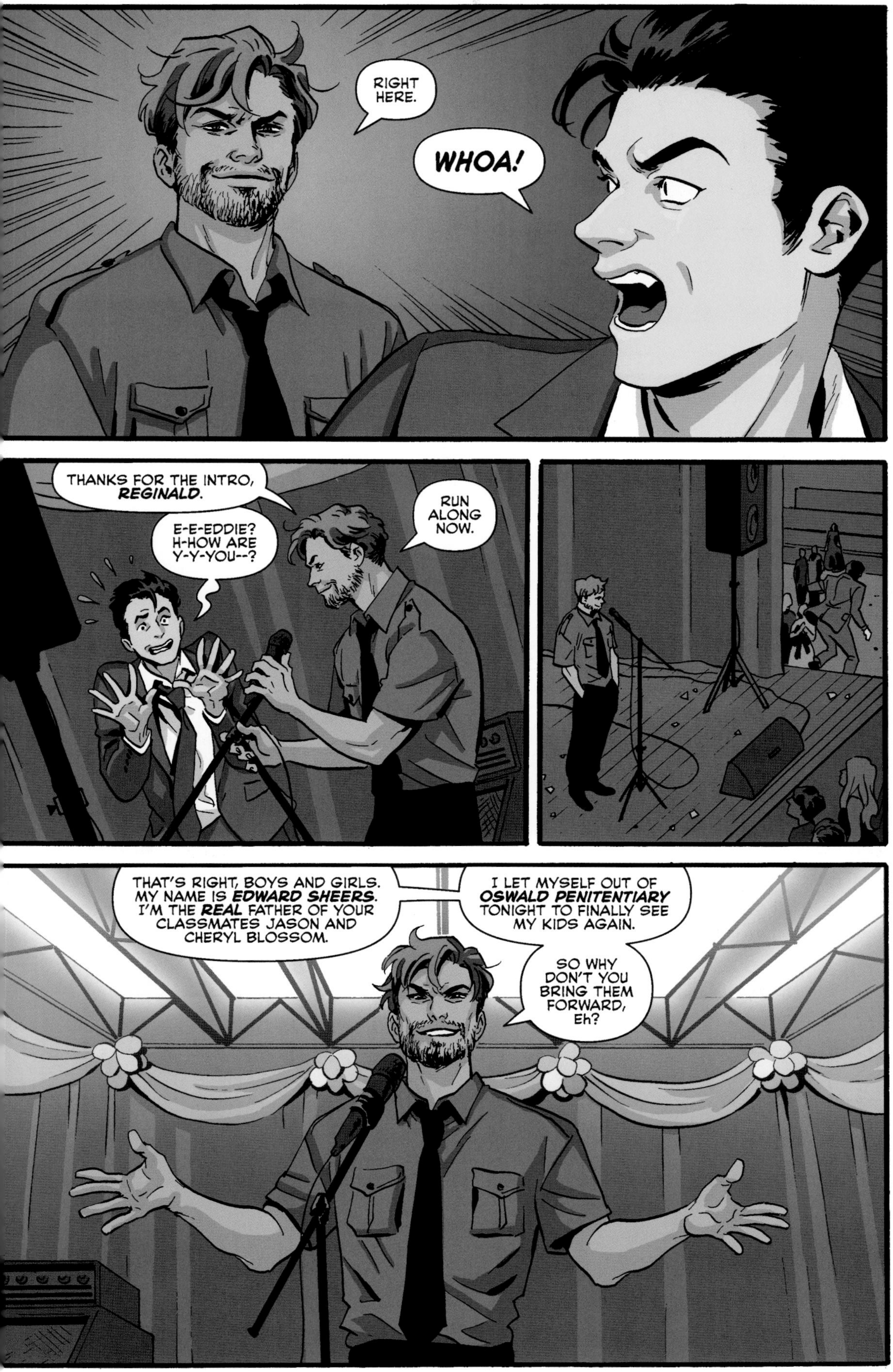
RIGHT HERE.
WHOA!
THANKS FOR THE INTRO, **REGINALD**.
E-E-EDDIE? H-HOW ARE Y-Y-YOU--?
RUN ALONG NOW.
THAT'S RIGHT, BOYS AND GIRLS. MY NAME IS **EDWARD SHEERS**. I'M THE **REAL** FATHER OF YOUR CLASSMATES JASON AND CHERYL BLOSSOM.
I LET MYSELF OUT OF **OSWALD PENITENTIARY** TONIGHT TO FINALLY SEE MY KIDS AGAIN.
SO WHY DON'T YOU BRING THEM FORWARD, Eh?

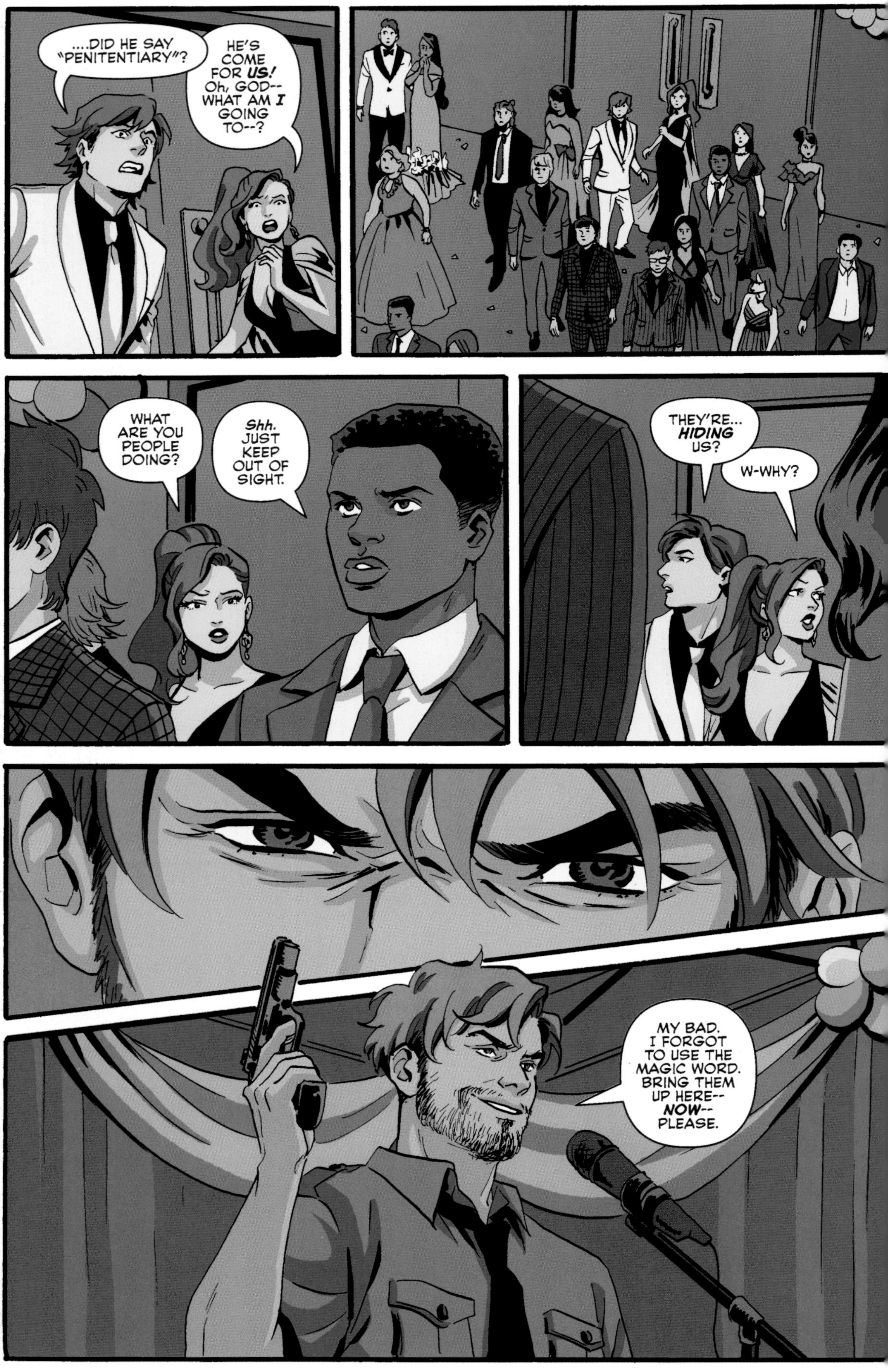
....DID HE SAY "PENITENTIARY"?
HE'S COME FOR US! Oh, GOD-- WHAT AM I GOING TO--?
WHAT ARE YOU PEOPLE DOING?
Shh. JUST KEEP OUT OF SIGHT.
THEY'RE... HIDING US?
W-WHY?
MY BAD. I FORGOT TO USE THE MAGIC WORD. BRING THEM UP HERE-- NOW-- PLEASE.

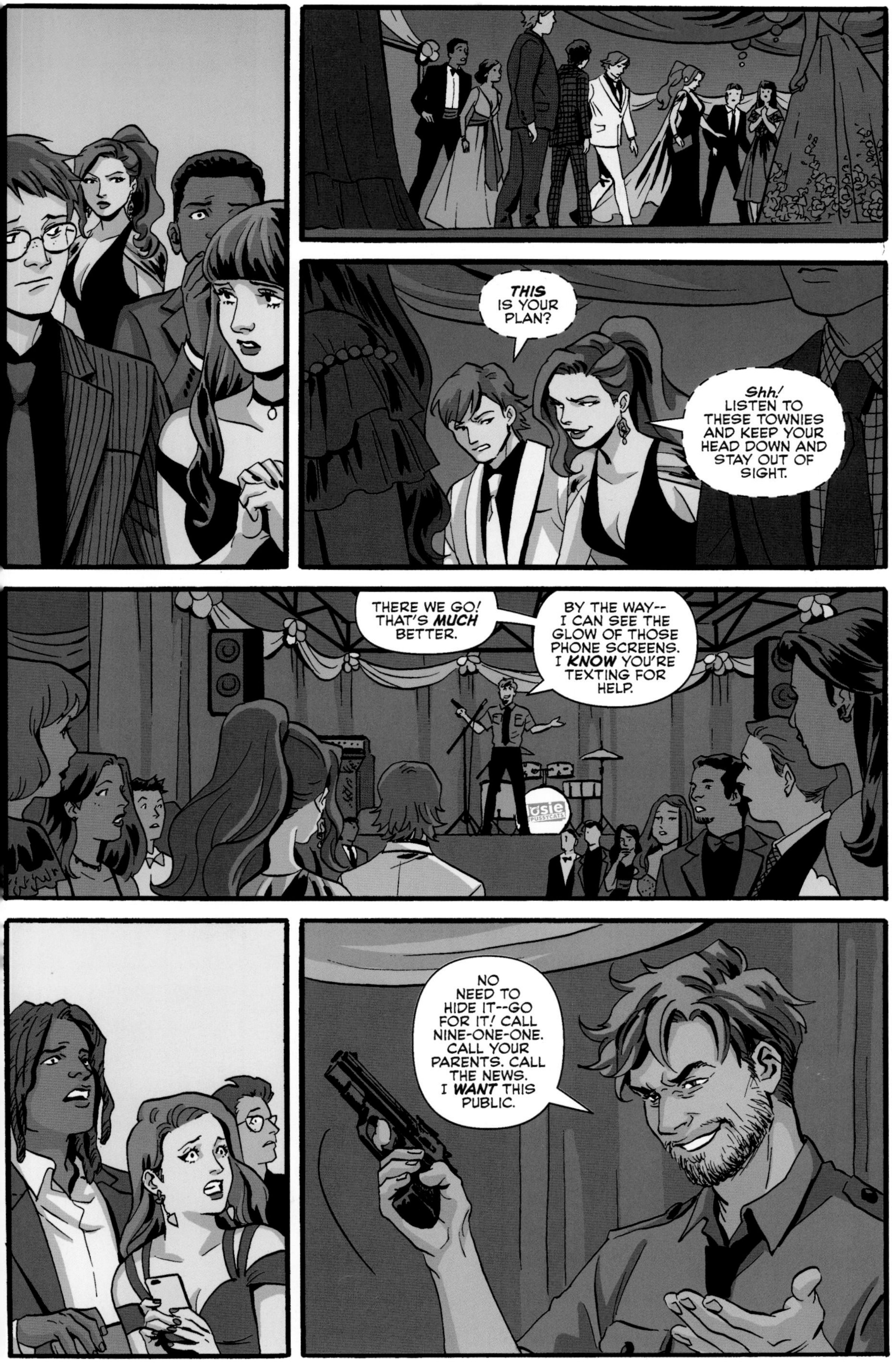
THIS IS YOUR PLAN?
Shh! LISTEN TO THESE TOWNIES AND KEEP YOUR HEAD DOWN AND STAY OUT OF SIGHT.
THERE WE GO! THAT'S MUCH BETTER.
BY THE WAY-- I CAN SEE THE GLOW OF THOSE PHONE SCREENS. I KNOW YOU'RE TEXTING FOR HELP.
NO NEED TO HIDE IT--GO FOR IT! CALL NINE-ONE-ONE. CALL YOUR PARENTS. CALL THE NEWS. I WANT THIS PUBLIC.

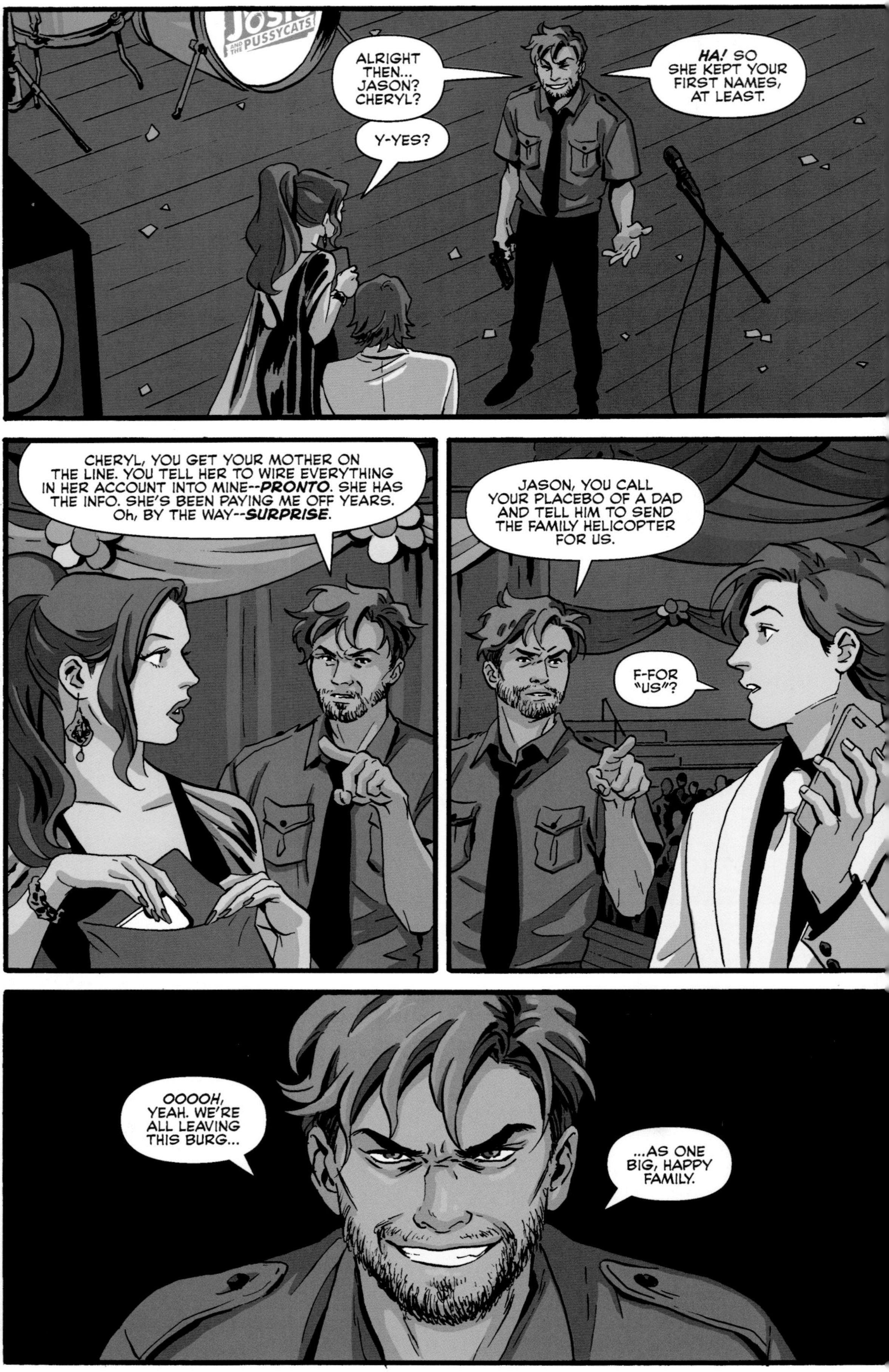
JOSIE AND THE PUSSYCATS
ALRIGHT THEN... JASON? CHERYL?
HA! SO SHE KEPT YOUR FIRST NAMES, AT LEAST.
Y-YES?
CHERYL, YOU GET YOUR MOTHER ON THE LINE. YOU TELL HER TO WIRE EVERYTHING IN HER ACCOUNT INTO MINE--PRONTO. SHE HAS THE INFO. SHE'S BEEN PAYING ME OFF YEARS. Oh, BY THE WAY--SURPRISE.
JASON, YOU CALL YOUR PLACEBO OF A DAD AND TELL HIM TO SEND THE FAMILY HELICOPTER FOR US.
F-FOR "US"?
OOOOH, YEAH. WE'RE ALL LEAVING THIS BURG...
...AS ONE BIG, HAPPY FAMILY.

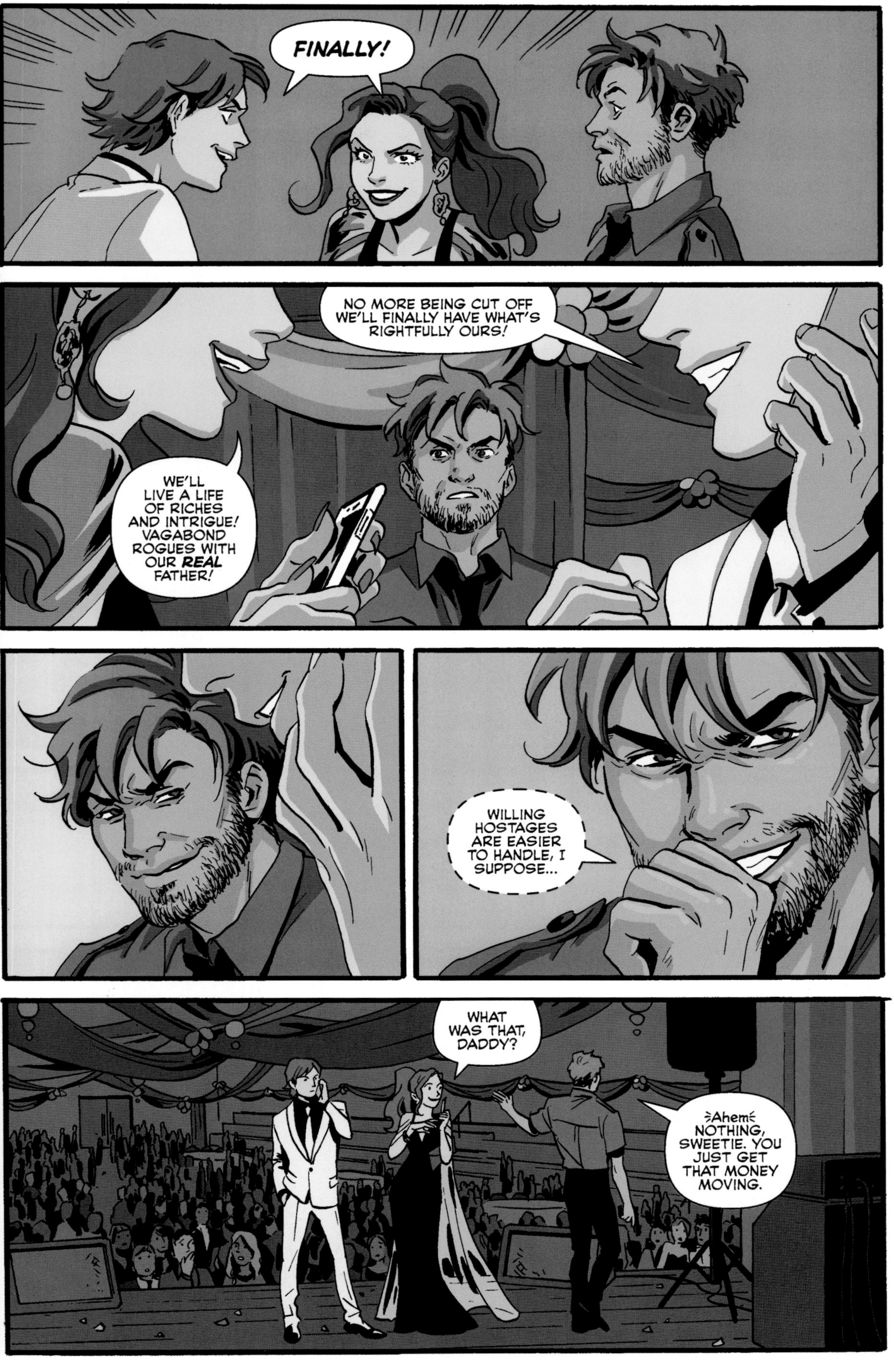
FINALLY!
NO MORE BEING CUT OFF WE'LL FINALLY HAVE WHAT'S RIGHTFULLY OURS!
WE'LL LIVE A LIFE OF RICHES AND INTRIGUE! VAGABOND ROGUES WITH OUR *REAL* FATHER!
WILLING HOSTAGES ARE EASIER TO HANDLE, I SUPPOSE...
WHAT WAS THAT, DADDY?
Ahem NOTHING, SWEETIE. YOU JUST GET THAT MONEY MOVING.

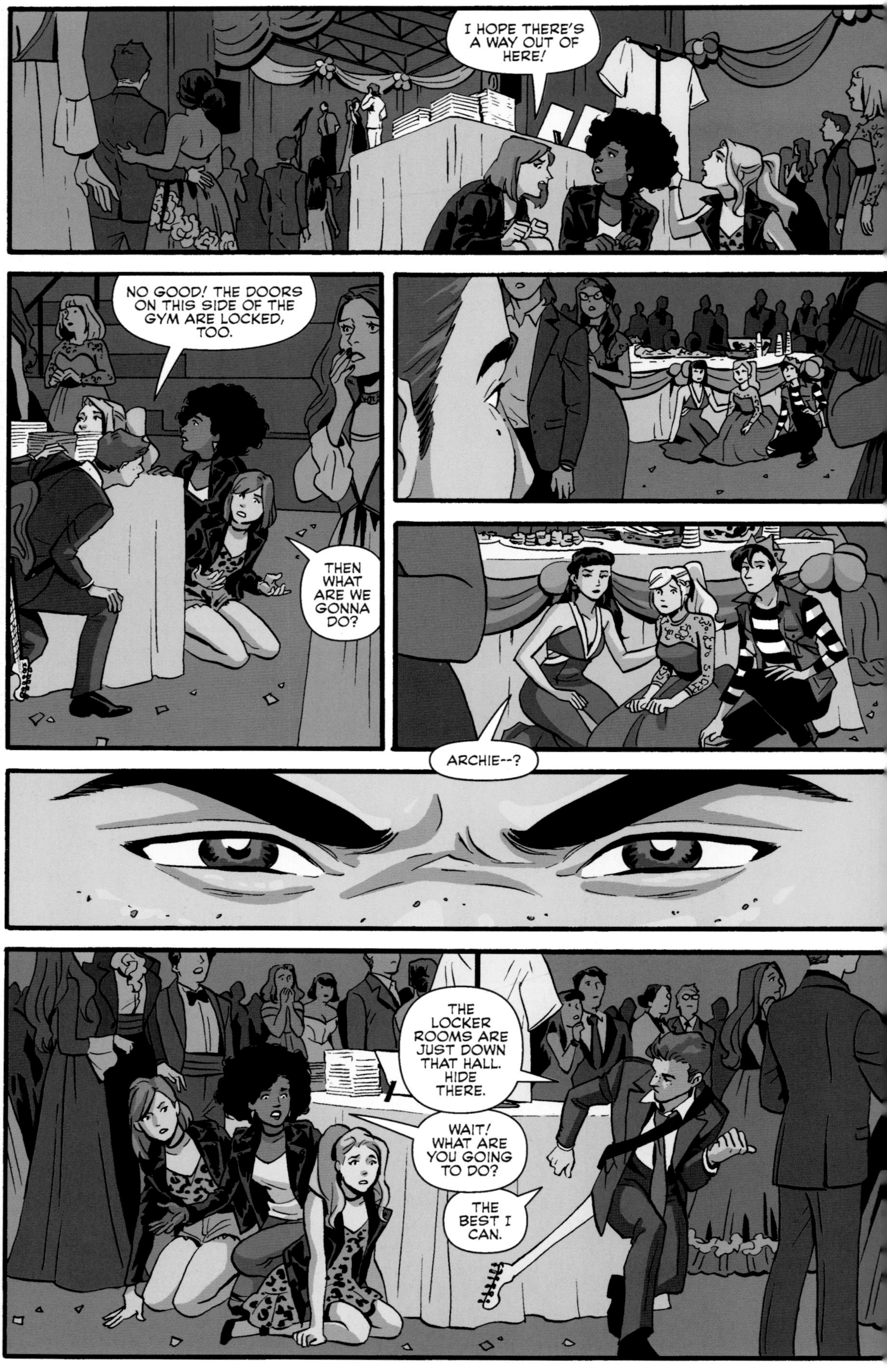
I HOPE THERE'S A WAY OUT OF HERE!
NO GOOD! THE DOORS ON THIS SIDE OF THE GYM ARE LOCKED, TOO.
THEN WHAT ARE WE GONNA DO?
ARCHIE--?
THE LOCKER ROOMS ARE JUST DOWN THAT HALL. HIDE THERE.
WAIT! WHAT ARE YOU GOING TO DO?
THE BEST I CAN.

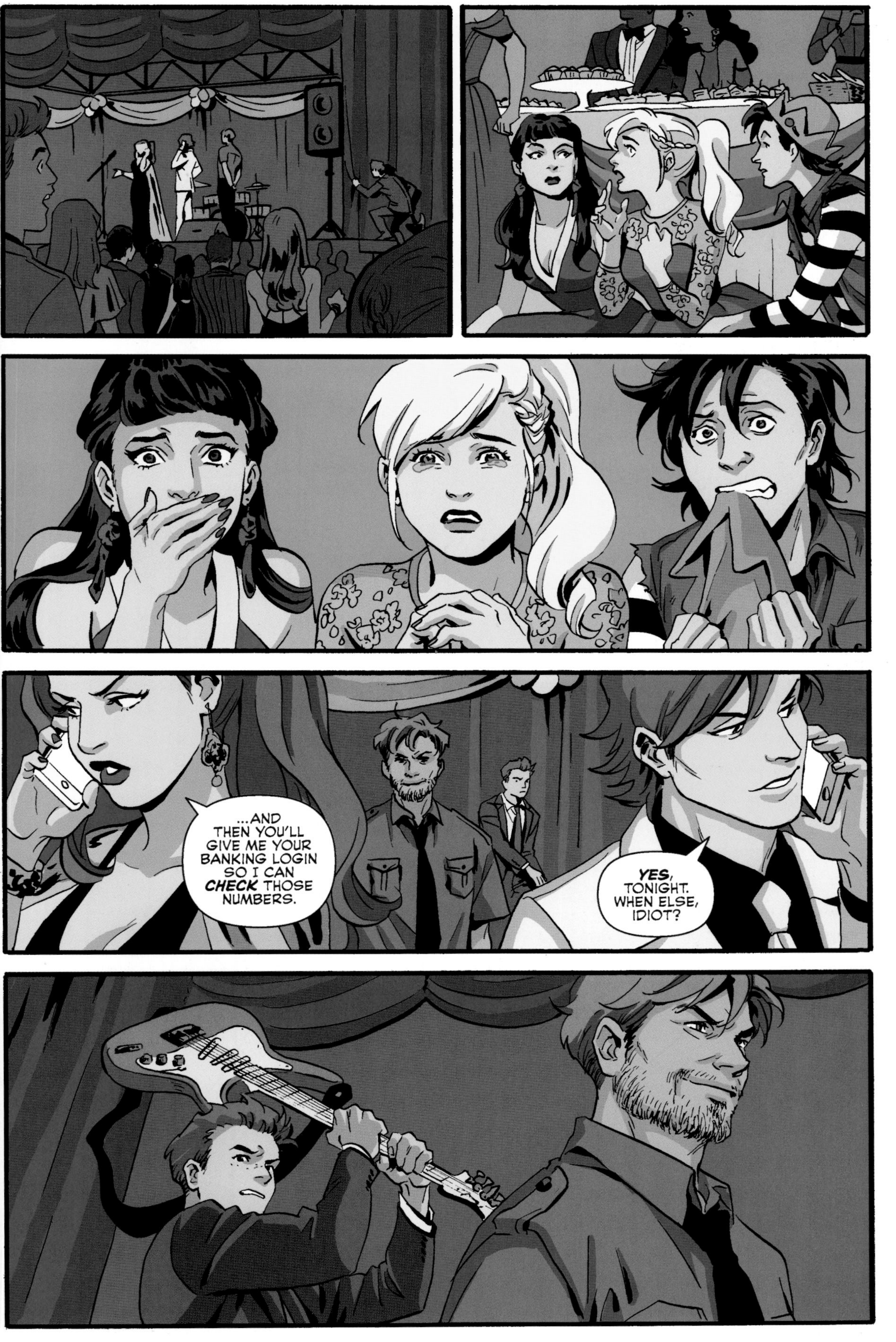
...AND THEN YOU'LL GIVE ME YOUR BANKING LOGIN SO I CAN CHECK THOSE NUMBERS.
YES, TONIGHT. WHEN ELSE, IDIOT?

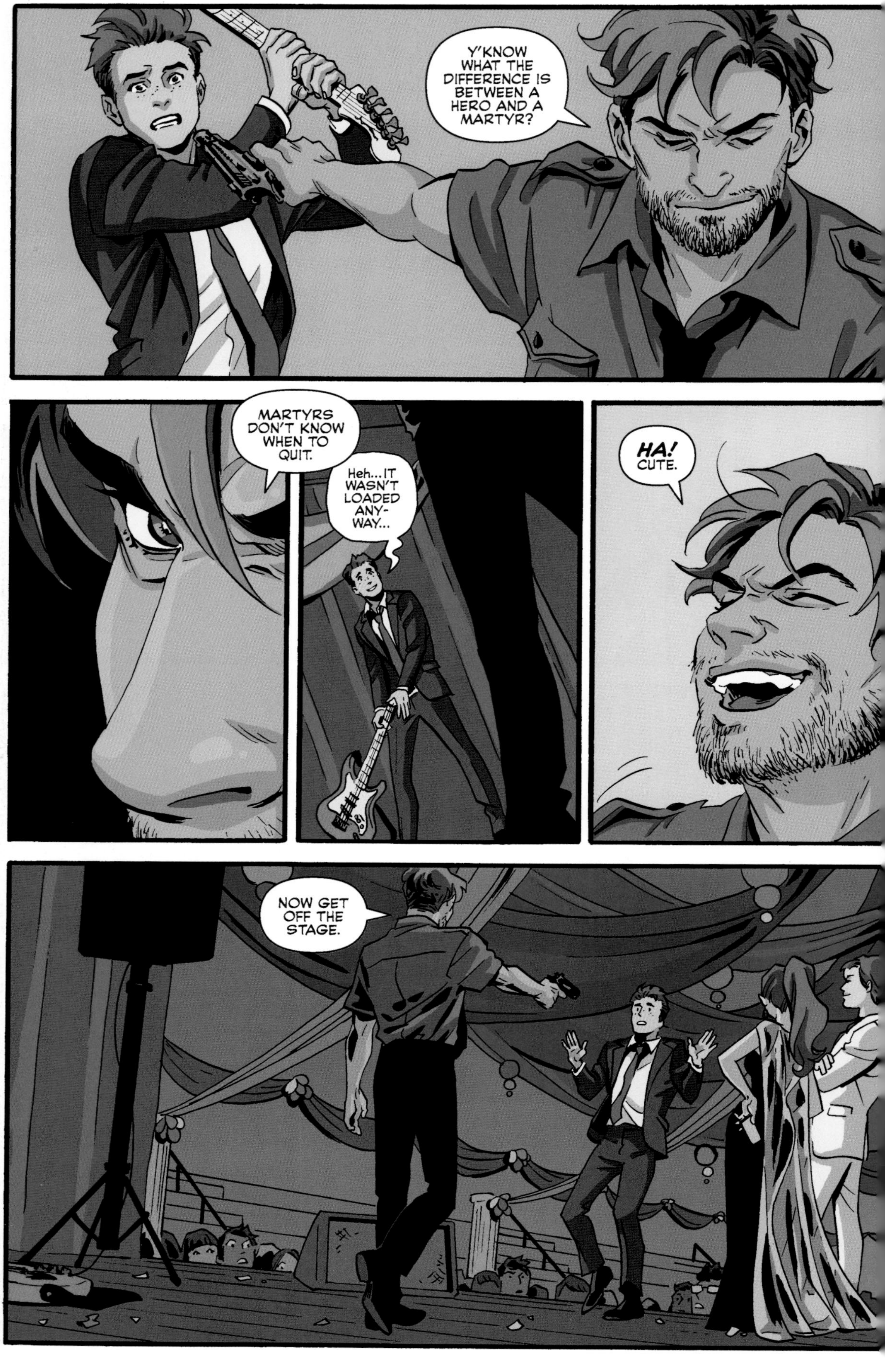
Y'KNOW WHAT THE DIFFERENCE IS BETWEEN A HERO AND A MARTYR?
MARTYRS DON'T KNOW WHEN TO QUIT.
Heh...IT WASN'T LOADED ANY-WAY...
HA! CUTE.
NOW GET OFF THE STAGE.

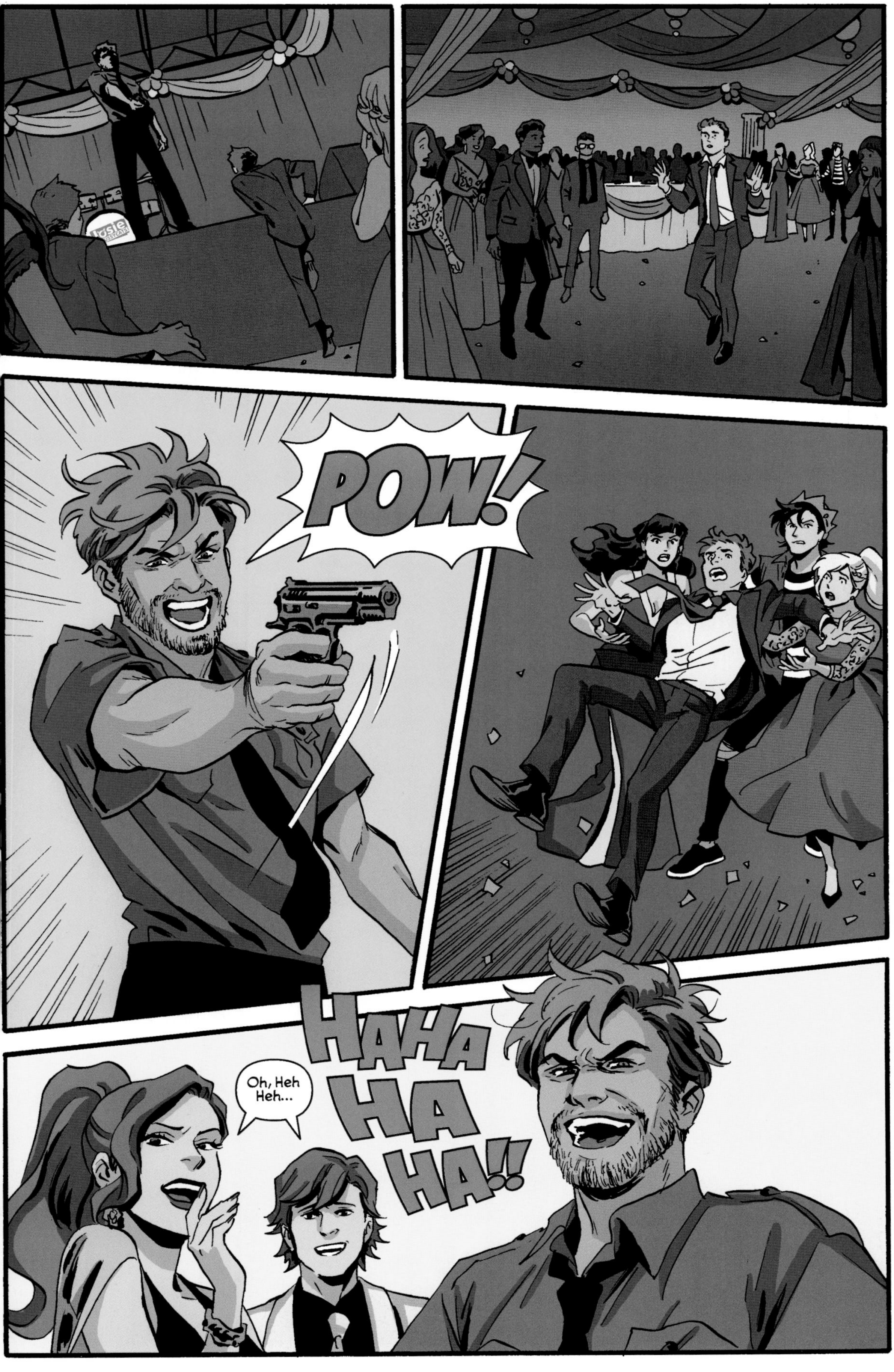
POW!
HAHA HA HA HA!!
Oh, Heh Heh...

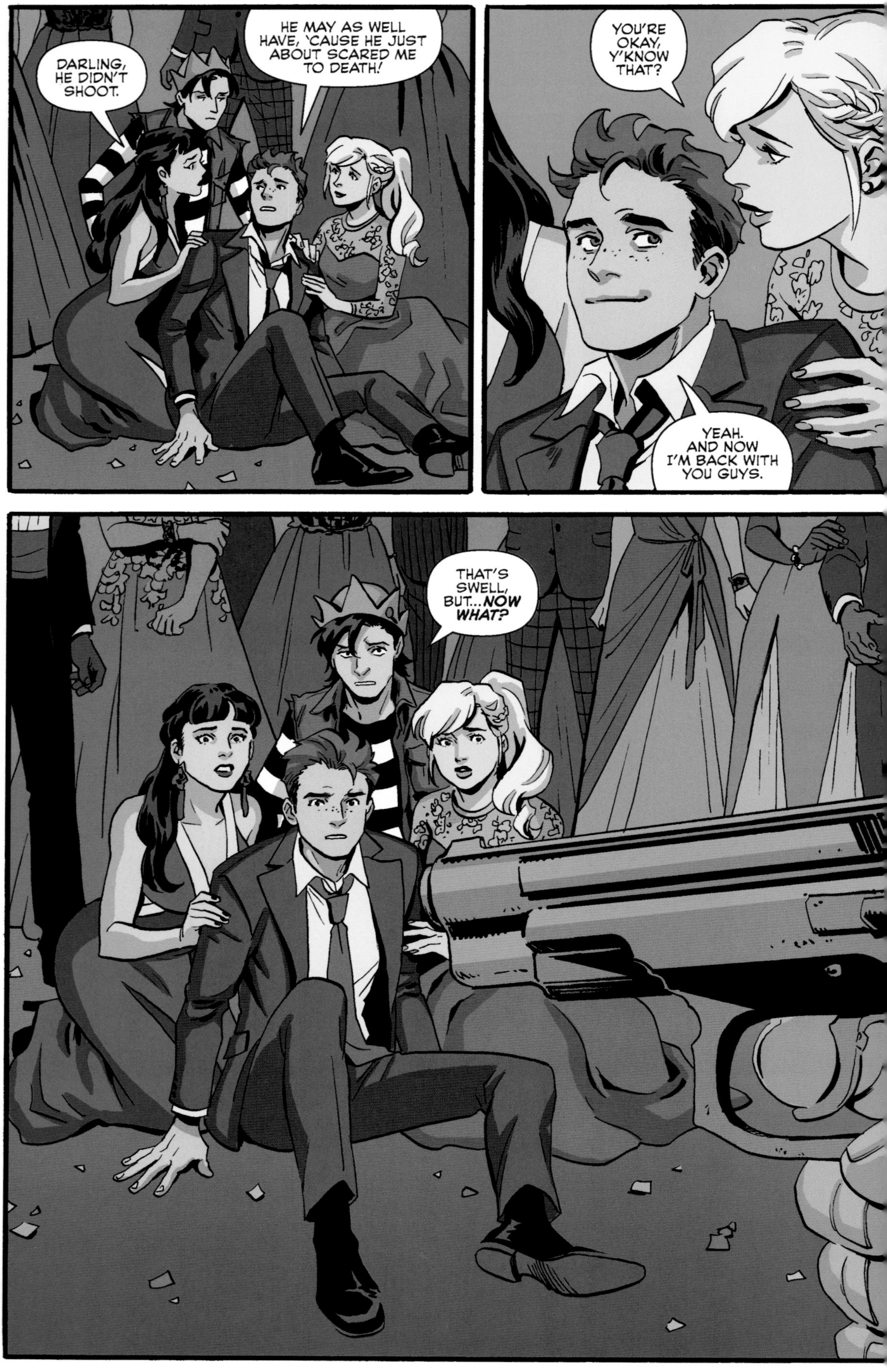
DARLING, HE DIDN'T SHOOT.
HE MAY AS WELL HAVE, 'CAUSE HE JUST ABOUT SCARED ME TO DEATH!
YOU'RE OKAY, Y'KNOW THAT?
YEAH. AND NOW I'M BACK WITH YOU GUYS.
THAT'S SWELL, BUT... ***NOW WHAT?***

TO BE CONTINUED...

ISSUE THIRTY-TWO

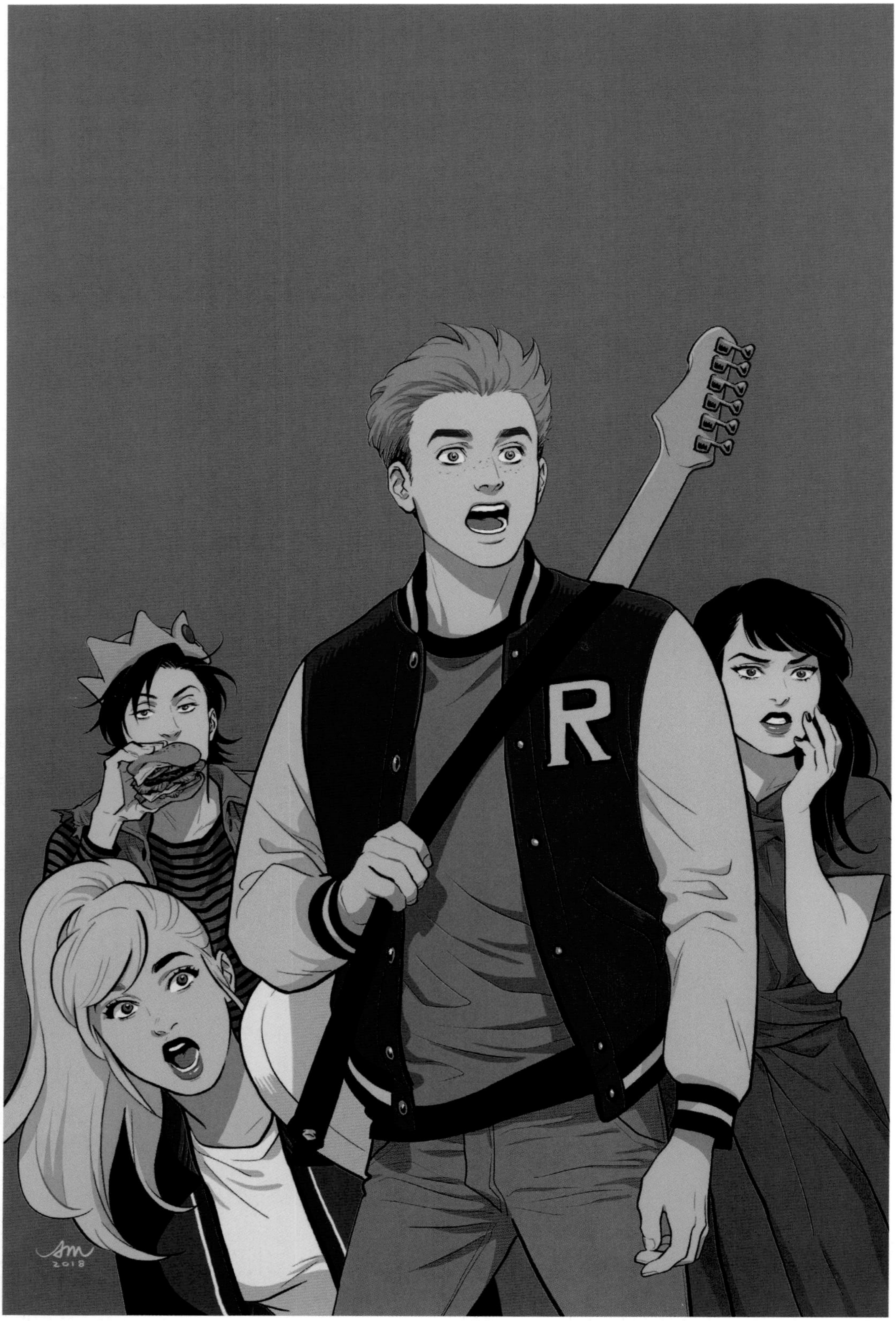

R

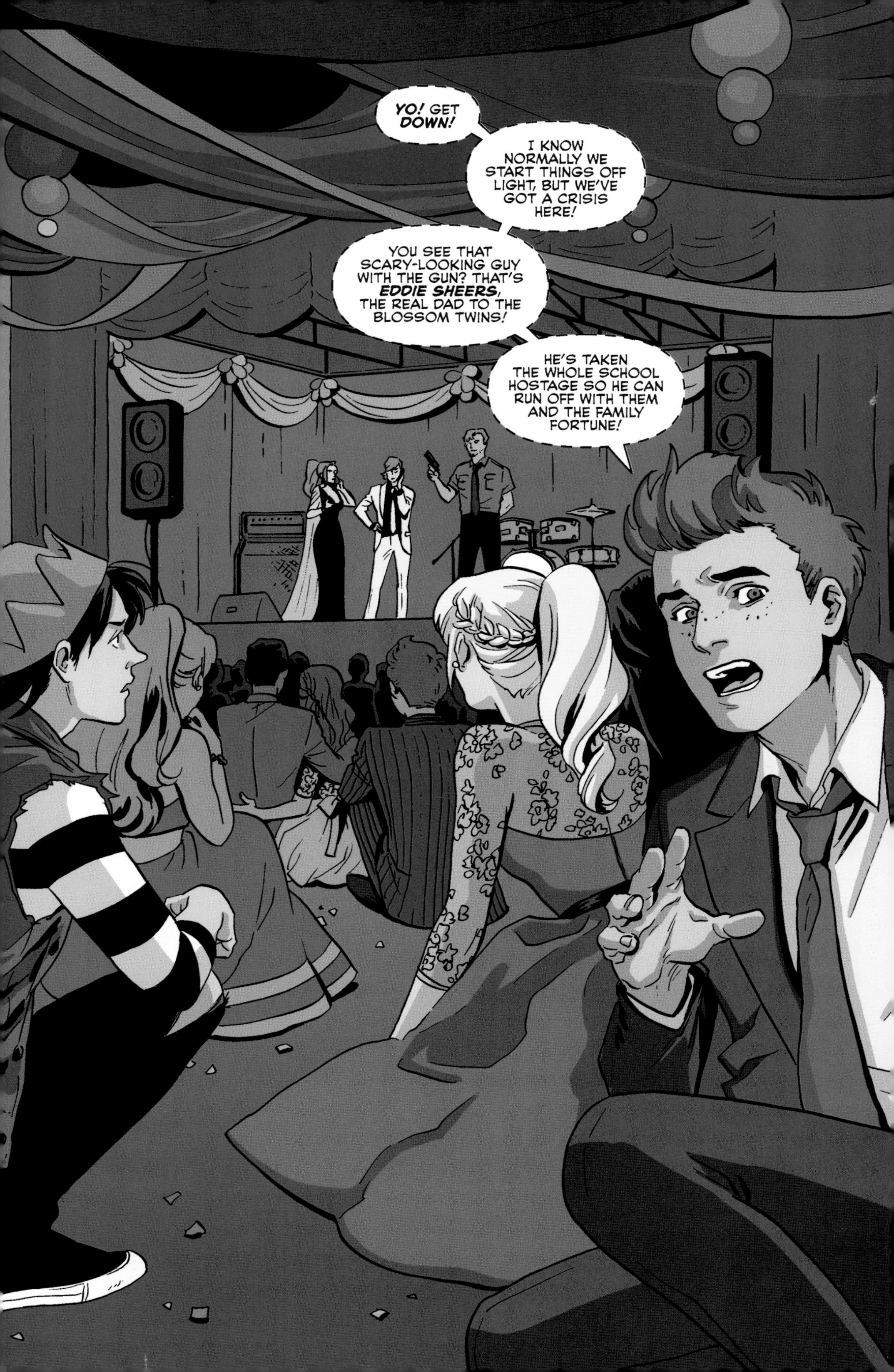
YO! GET DOWN!
I KNOW NORMALLY WE START THINGS OFF LIGHT, BUT WE'VE GOT A CRISIS HERE!
YOU SEE THAT SCARY-LOOKING GUY WITH THE GUN? THAT'S EDDIE SHEERS, THE REAL DAD TO THE BLOSSOM TWINS!
HE'S TAKEN THE WHOLE SCHOOL HOSTAGE SO HE CAN RUN OFF WITH THEM AND THE FAMILY FORTUNE!

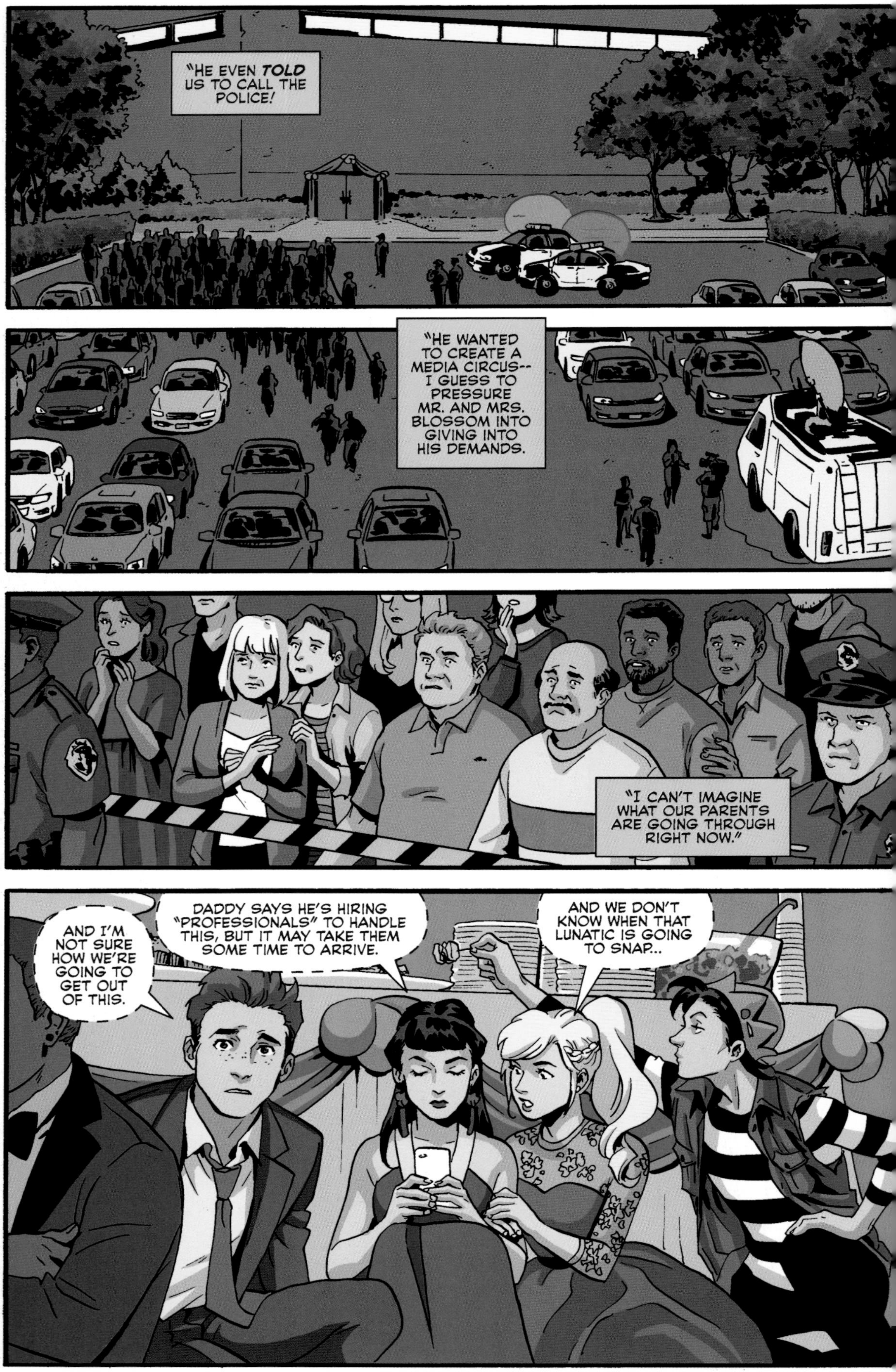
"HE EVEN TOLD US TO CALL THE POLICE!
"HE WANTED TO CREATE A MEDIA CIRCUS-- I GUESS TO PRESSURE MR. AND MRS. BLOSSOM INTO GIVING INTO HIS DEMANDS.
"I CAN'T IMAGINE WHAT OUR PARENTS ARE GOING THROUGH RIGHT NOW."
AND I'M NOT SURE HOW WE'RE GOING TO GET OUT OF THIS.
DADDY SAYS HE'S HIRING "PROFESSIONALS" TO HANDLE THIS, BUT IT MAY TAKE THEM SOME TIME TO ARRIVE.
AND WE DON'T KNOW WHEN THAT LUNATIC IS GOING TO SNAP...

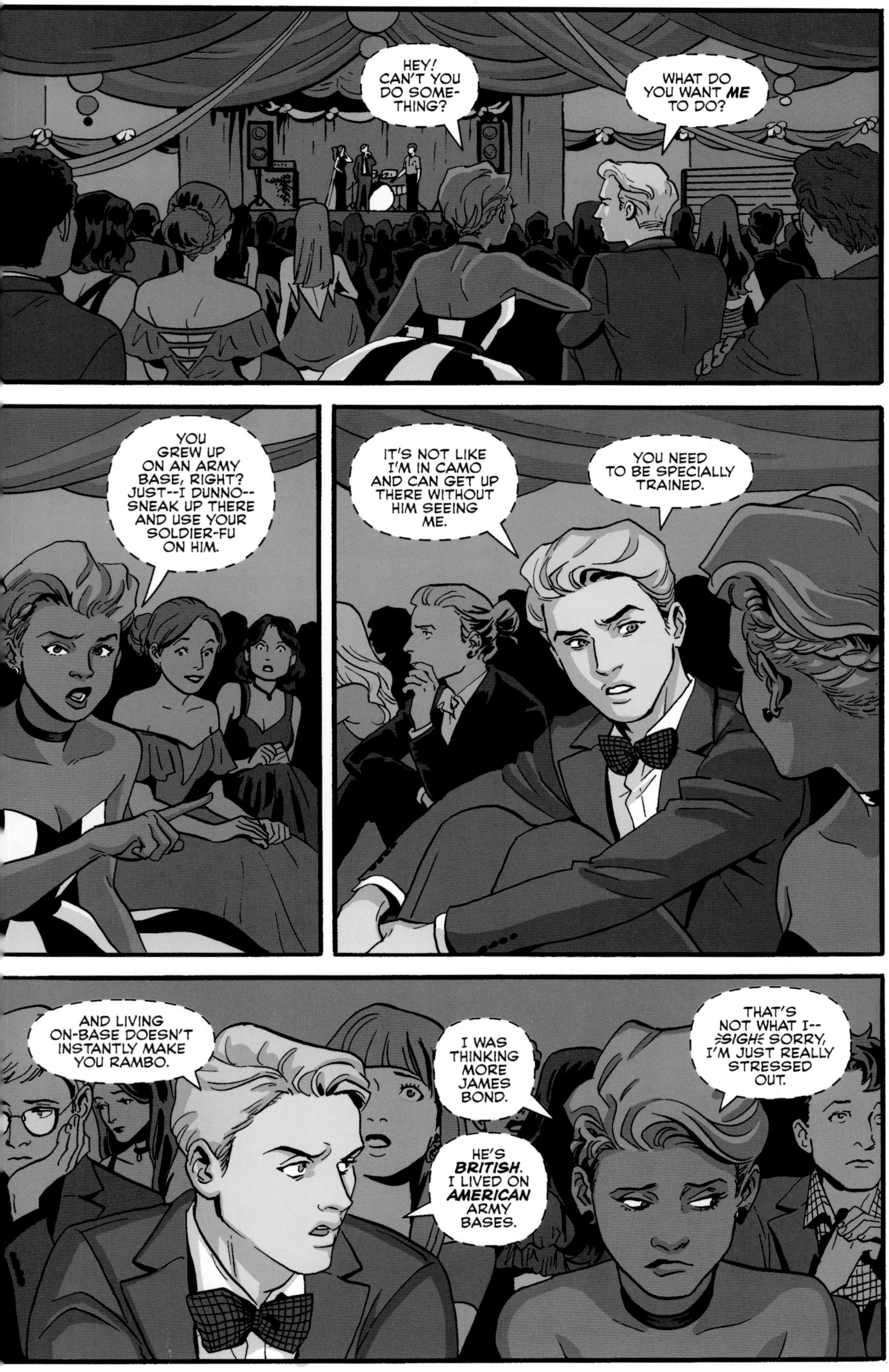
HEY! CAN'T YOU DO SOME-THING?
WHAT DO YOU WANT ME TO DO?
YOU GREW UP ON AN ARMY BASE, RIGHT? JUST--I DUNNO--SNEAK UP THERE AND USE YOUR SOLDIER-FU ON HIM.
IT'S NOT LIKE I'M IN CAMO AND CAN GET UP THERE WITHOUT HIM SEEING ME.
YOU NEED TO BE SPECIALLY TRAINED.
AND LIVING ON-BASE DOESN'T INSTANTLY MAKE YOU RAMBO.
I WAS THINKING MORE JAMES BOND.
HE'S BRITISH. I LIVED ON AMERICAN ARMY BASES.
THAT'S NOT WHAT I-- SIGH SORRY, I'M JUST REALLY STRESSED OUT.

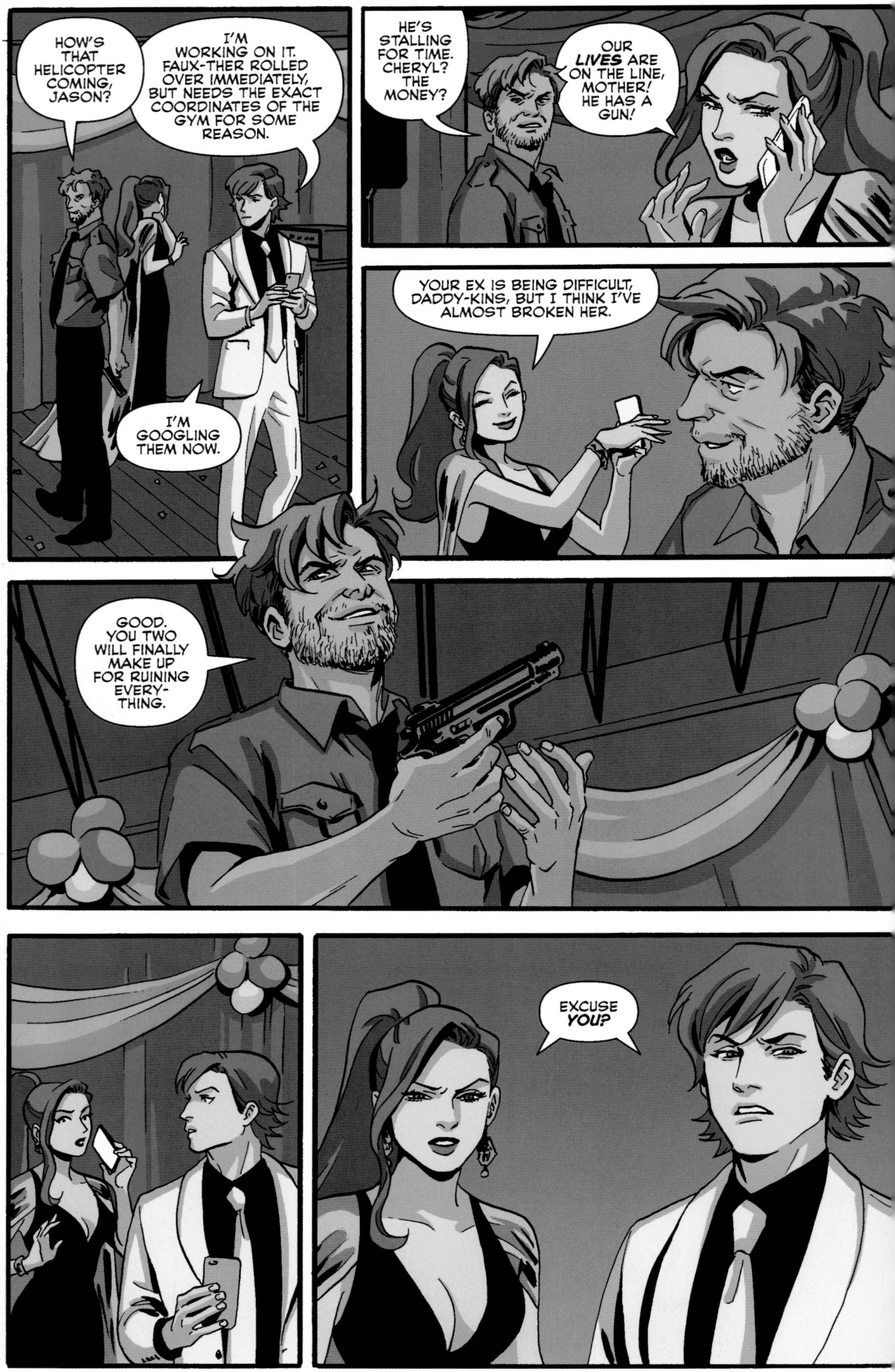
HOW'S THAT HELICOPTER COMING, JASON?
I'M WORKING ON IT. FAUX-THER ROLLED OVER IMMEDIATELY, BUT NEEDS THE EXACT COORDINATES OF THE GYM FOR SOME REASON.
I'M GOOGLING THEM NOW.
HE'S STALLING FOR TIME. CHERYL? THE MONEY?
OUR LIVES ARE ON THE LINE, MOTHER! HE HAS A GUN!
YOUR EX IS BEING DIFFICULT, DADDY-KINS, BUT I THINK I'VE ALMOST BROKEN HER.
GOOD. YOU TWO WILL FINALLY MAKE UP FOR RUINING EVERY-THING.
EXCUSE YOU?

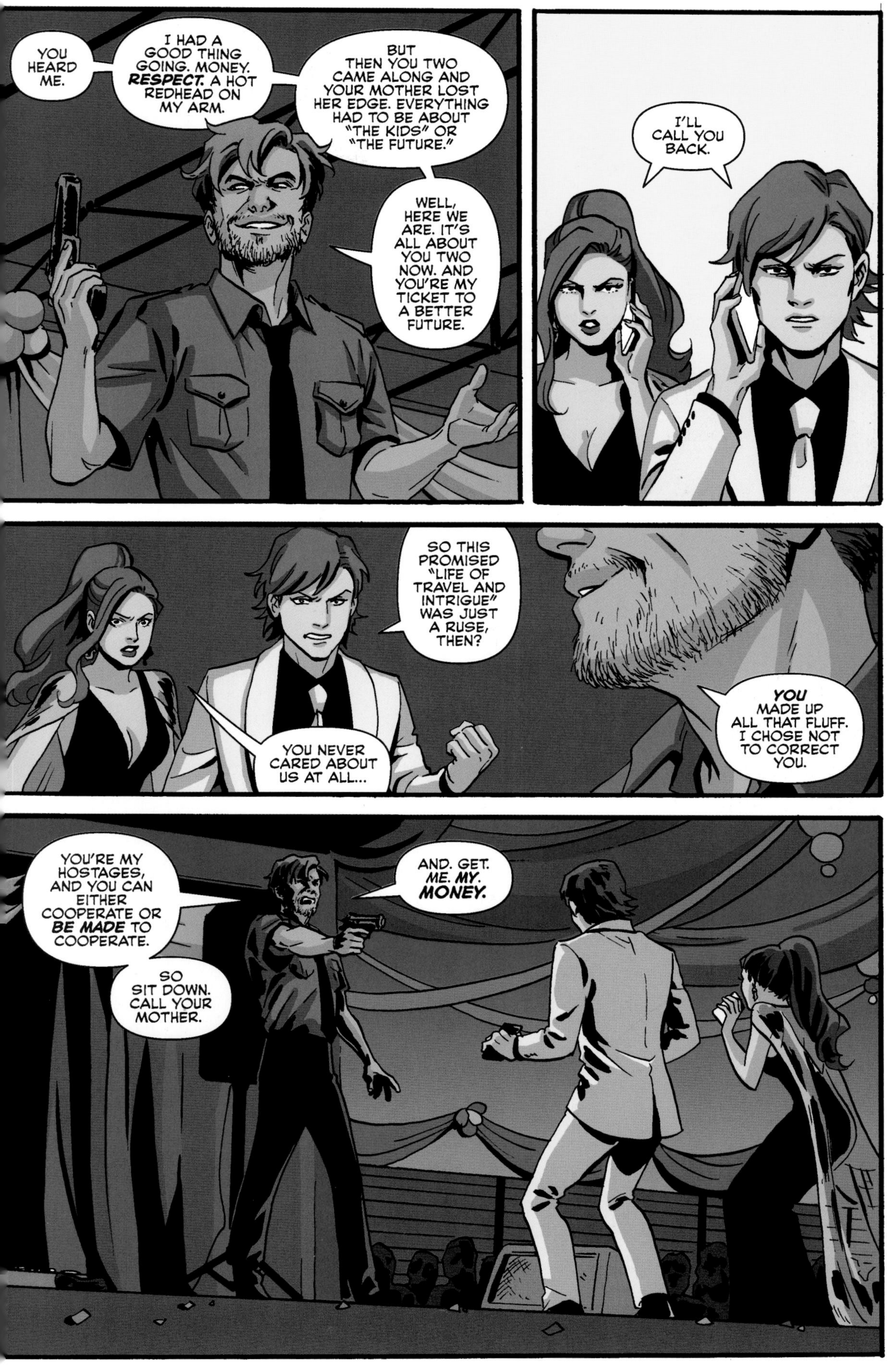
YOU HEARD ME.
I HAD A GOOD THING GOING. MONEY. **RESPECT.** A HOT REDHEAD ON MY ARM.
BUT THEN YOU TWO CAME ALONG AND YOUR MOTHER LOST HER EDGE. EVERYTHING HAD TO BE ABOUT "THE KIDS" OR "THE FUTURE."
WELL, HERE WE ARE. IT'S ALL ABOUT YOU TWO NOW. AND YOU'RE MY TICKET TO A BETTER FUTURE.
I'LL CALL YOU BACK.
YOU NEVER CARED ABOUT US AT ALL...
SO THIS PROMISED "LIFE OF TRAVEL AND INTRIGUE" WAS JUST A RUSE, THEN?
YOU MADE UP ALL THAT FLUFF. I CHOSE NOT TO CORRECT YOU.
YOU'RE MY HOSTAGES, AND YOU CAN EITHER COOPERATE OR **BE MADE** TO COOPERATE.
SO SIT DOWN. CALL YOUR MOTHER.
AND. GET. **ME. MY. MONEY.**

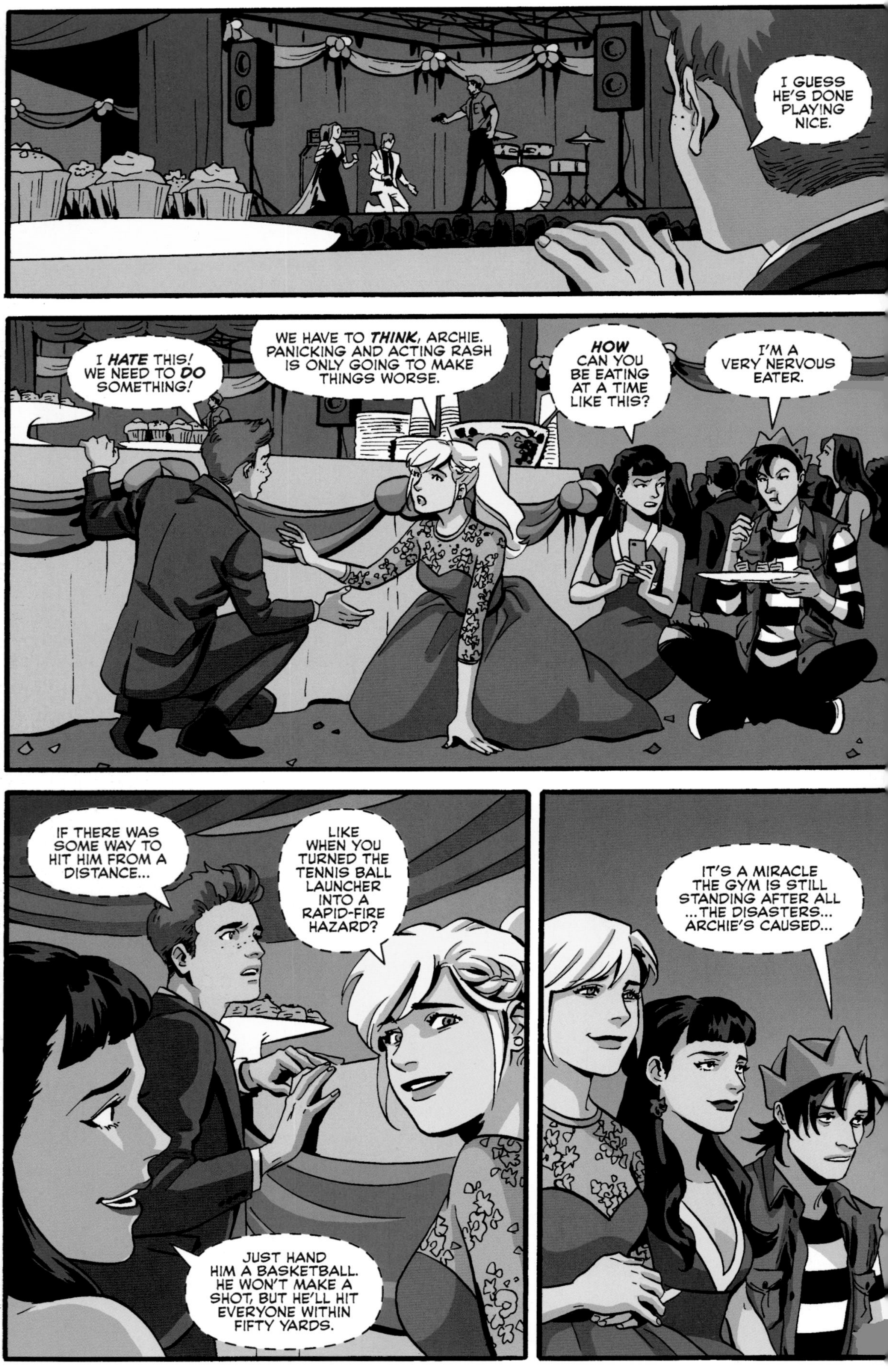
I GUESS HE'S DONE PLAYING NICE.
I HATE THIS! WE NEED TO DO SOMETHING!
WE HAVE TO THINK, ARCHIE. PANICKING AND ACTING RASH IS ONLY GOING TO MAKE THINGS WORSE.
HOW CAN YOU BE EATING AT A TIME LIKE THIS?
I'M A VERY NERVOUS EATER.
IF THERE WAS SOME WAY TO HIT HIM FROM A DISTANCE...
LIKE WHEN YOU TURNED THE TENNIS BALL LAUNCHER INTO A RAPID-FIRE HAZARD?
JUST HAND HIM A BASKETBALL. HE WON'T MAKE A SHOT, BUT HE'LL HIT EVERYONE WITHIN FIFTY YARDS.
IT'S A MIRACLE THE GYM IS STILL STANDING AFTER ALL ...THE DISASTERS... ARCHIE'S CAUSED...

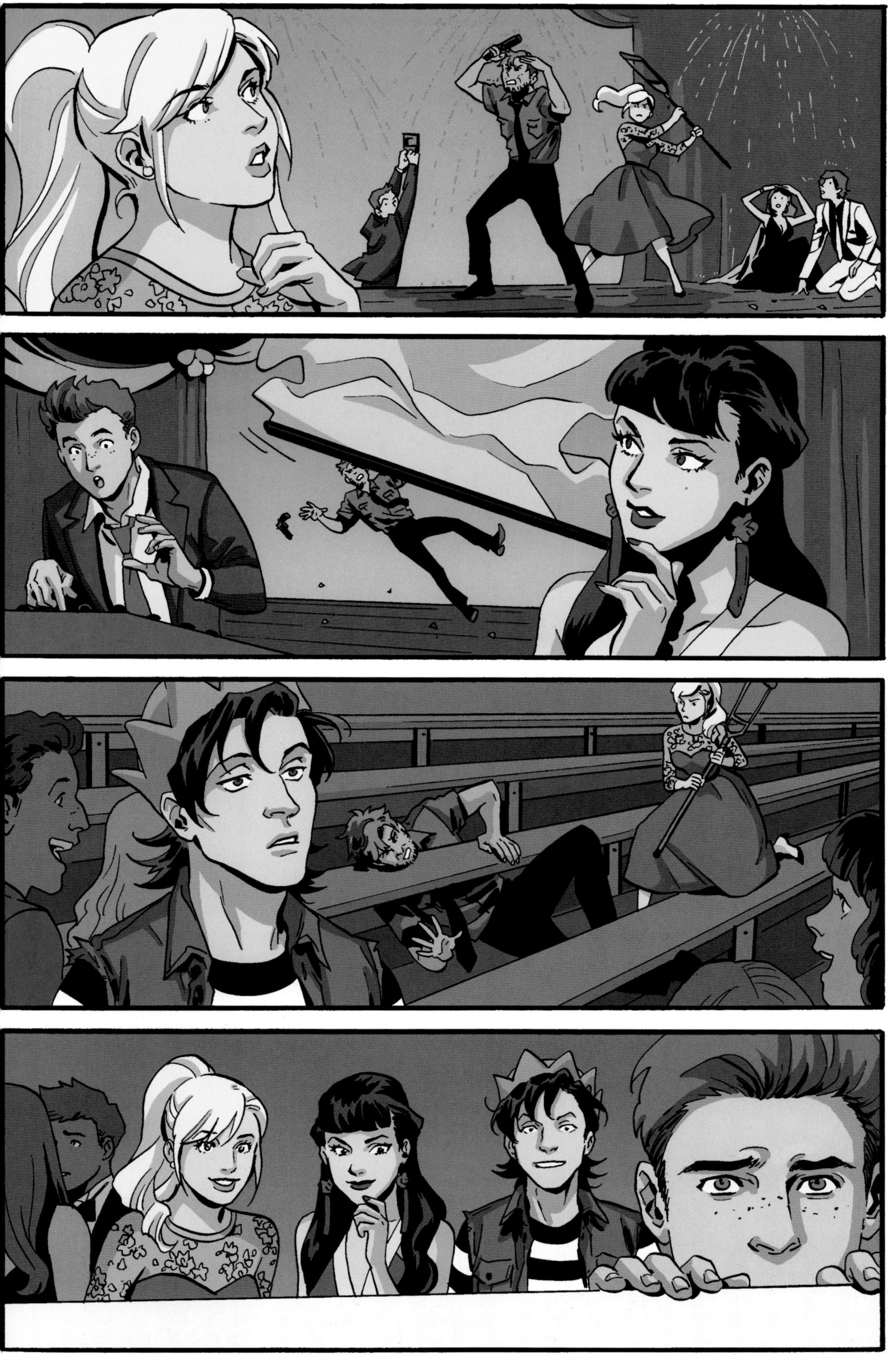

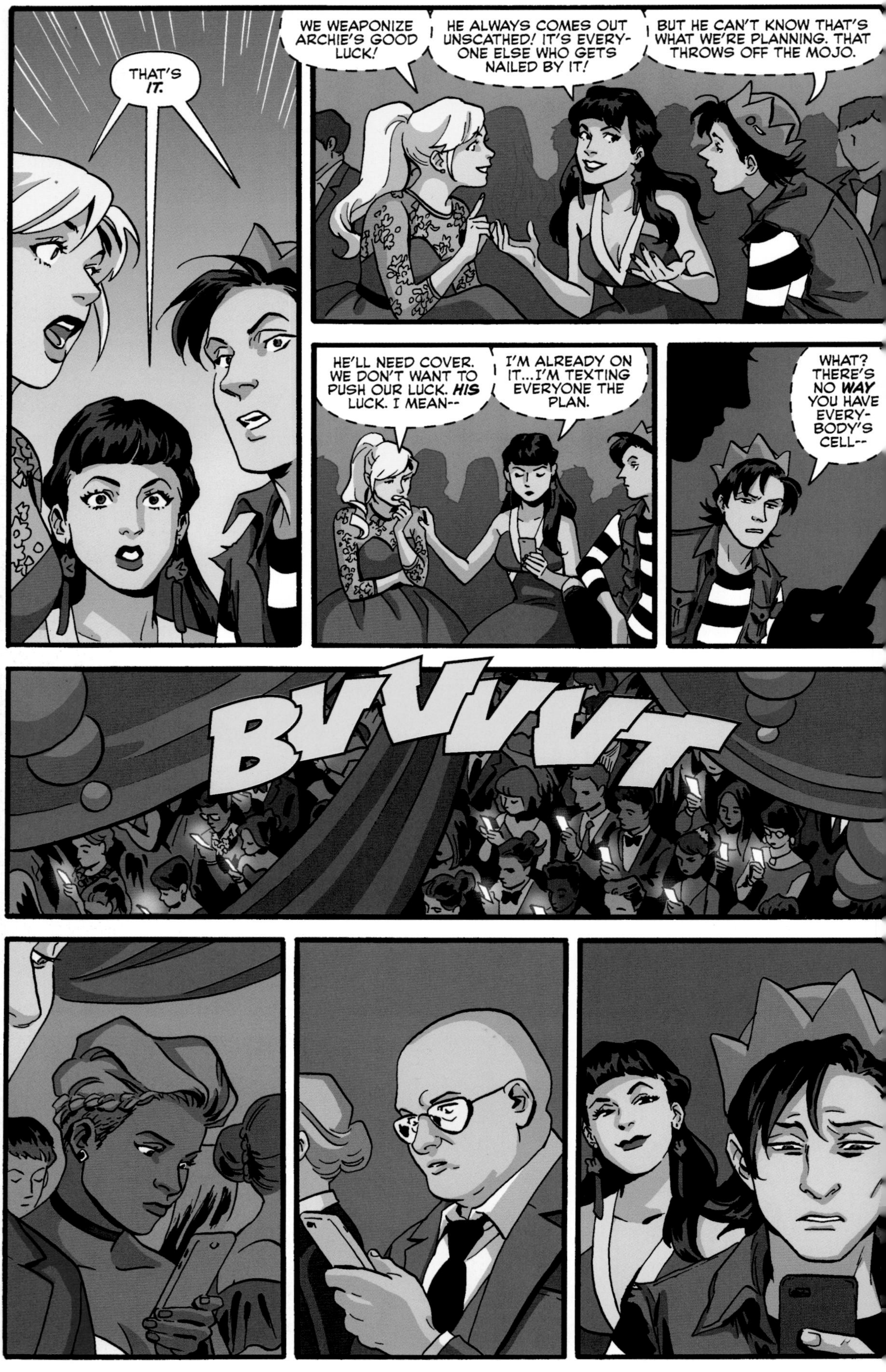
THAT'S IT.
WE WEAPONIZE ARCHIE'S GOOD LUCK!
HE ALWAYS COMES OUT UNSCATHED! IT'S EVERY-ONE ELSE WHO GETS NAILED BY IT!
BUT HE CAN'T KNOW THAT'S WHAT WE'RE PLANNING. THAT THROWS OFF THE MOJO.
HE'LL NEED COVER. WE DON'T WANT TO PUSH OUR LUCK. HIS LUCK. I MEAN--
I'M ALREADY ON IT...I'M TEXTING EVERYONE THE PLAN.
WHAT? THERE'S NO WAY YOU HAVE EVERY-BODY'S CELL--
BVVVVT

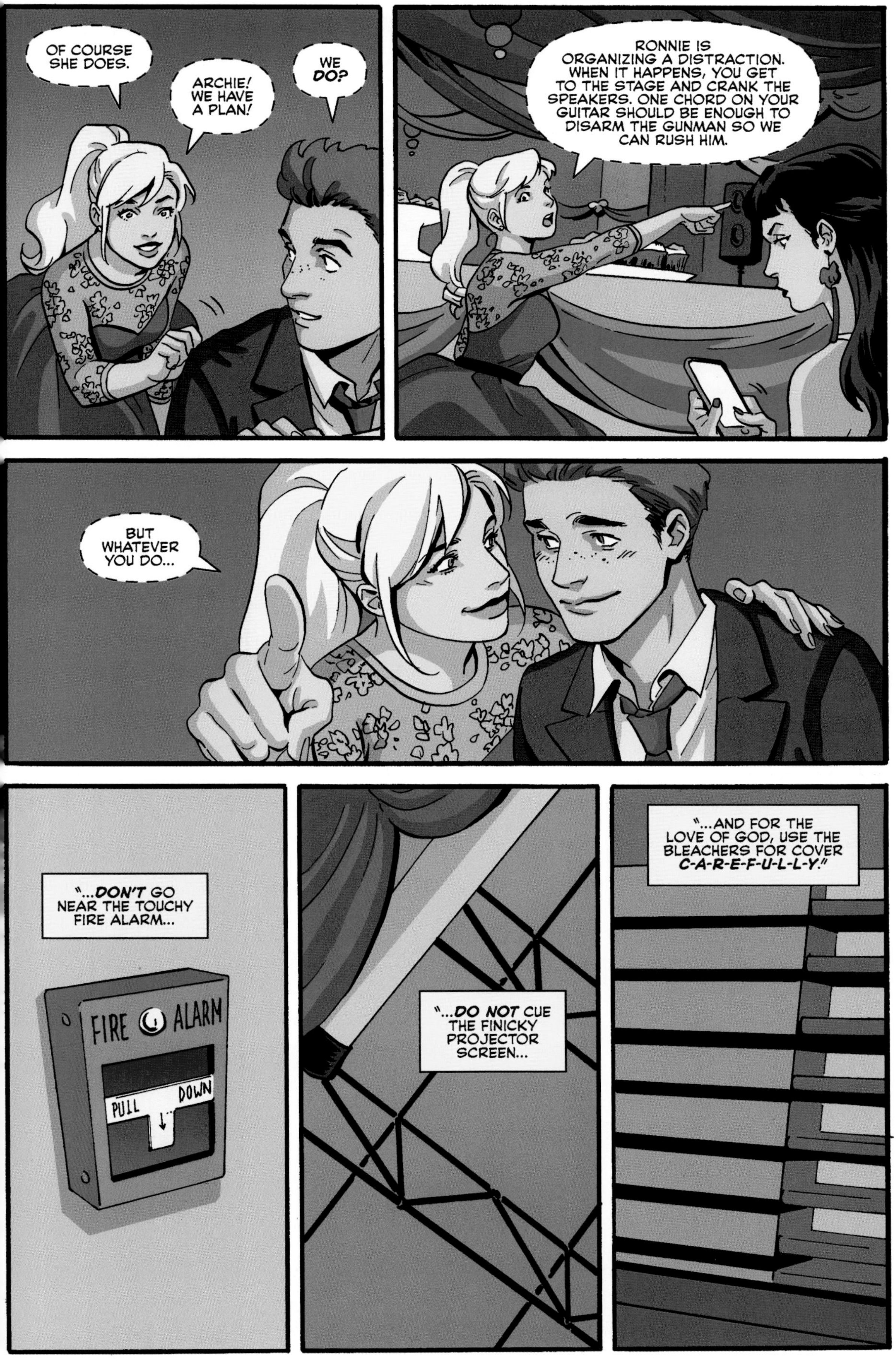
OF COURSE SHE DOES.
ARCHIE! WE HAVE A PLAN!
WE ***DO?***
RONNIE IS ORGANIZING A DISTRACTION. WHEN IT HAPPENS, YOU GET TO THE STAGE AND CRANK THE SPEAKERS. ONE CHORD ON YOUR GUITAR SHOULD BE ENOUGH TO DISARM THE GUNMAN SO WE CAN RUSH HIM.
BUT WHATEVER YOU DO...
"...***DON'T*** GO NEAR THE TOUCHY FIRE ALARM...
FIRE ALARM
PULL DOWN
"...***DO NOT*** CUE THE FINICKY PROJECTOR SCREEN...
"...AND FOR THE LOVE OF GOD, USE THE BLEACHERS FOR COVER ***C-A-R-E-F-U-L-L-Y.***"

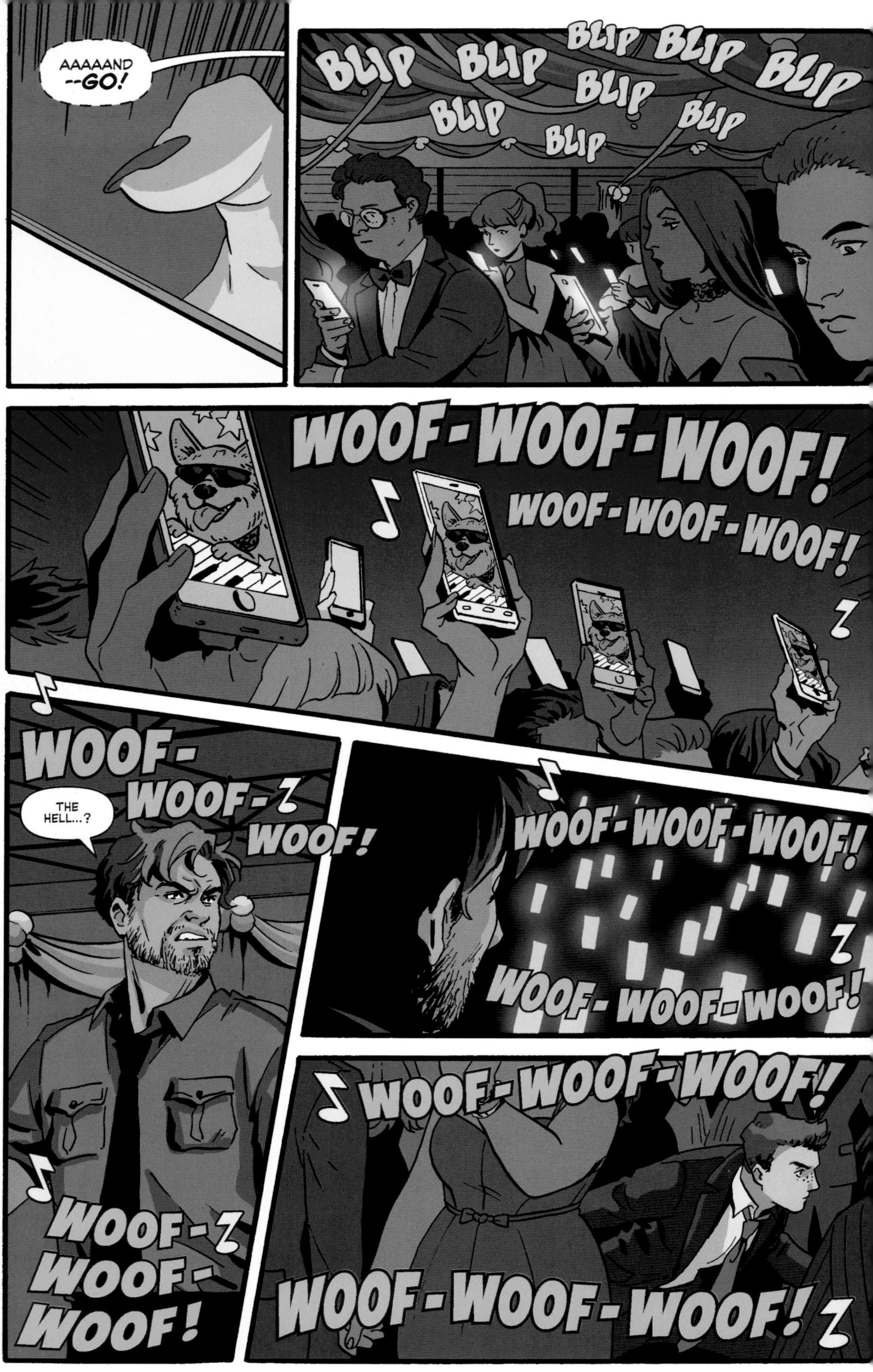
AAAAAND --GO!
BLIP BLIP BLIP BLIP BLIP BLIP BLIP BLIP BLIP
WOOF-WOOF-WOOF!
WOOF-WOOF-WOOF!
WOOF-WOOF-WOOF!
THE HELL...?
WOOF-WOOF-WOOF!
WOOF-WOOF-WOOF!
WOOF-WOOF-WOOF!
WOOF-WOOF-WOOF!
WOOF-WOOF-WOOF!

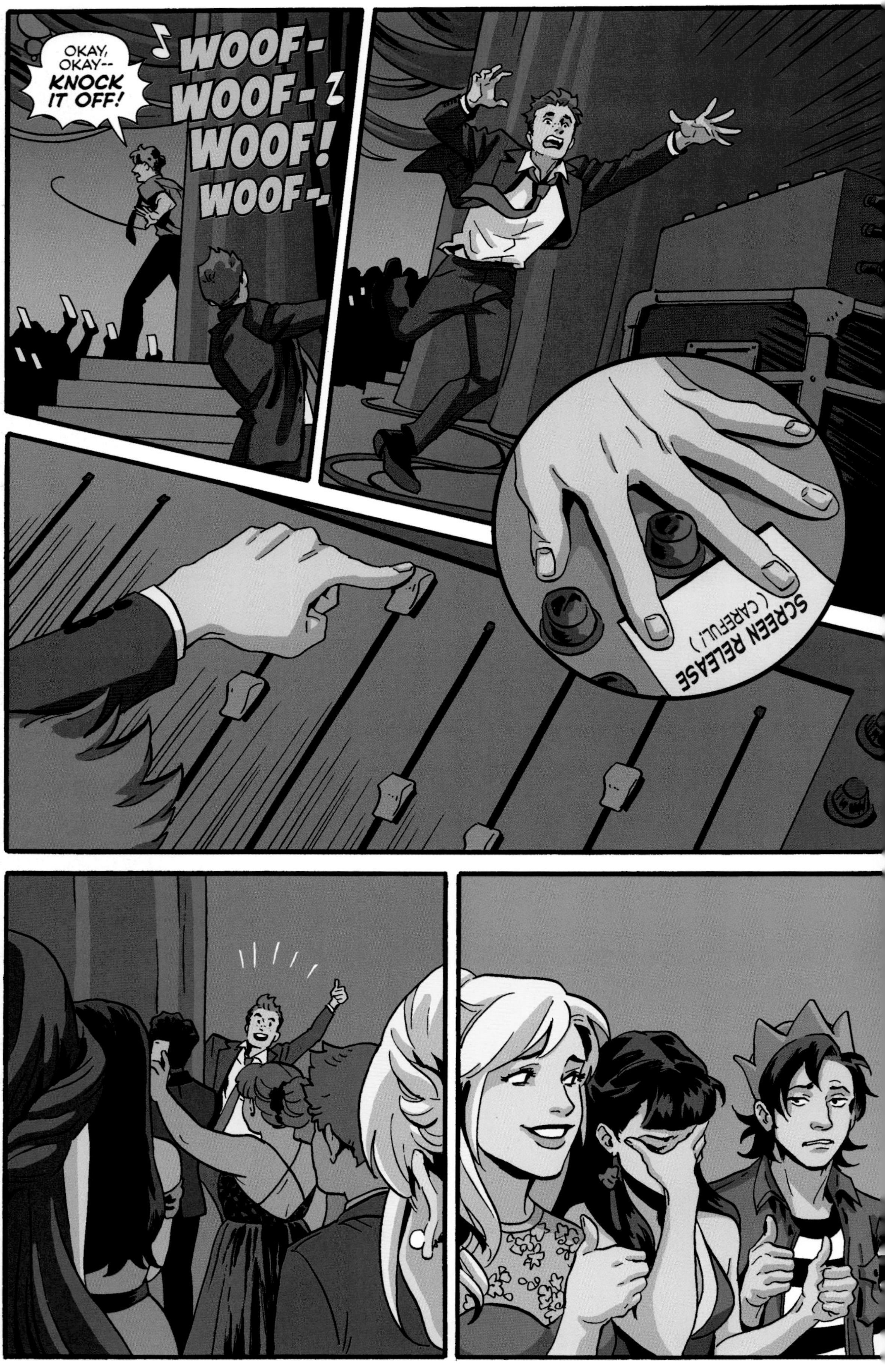
OKAY, OKAY-- KNOCK IT OFF!
WOOF- WOOF- WOOF! WOOF-
SCREEN RELEASE
(CAREFUL!)

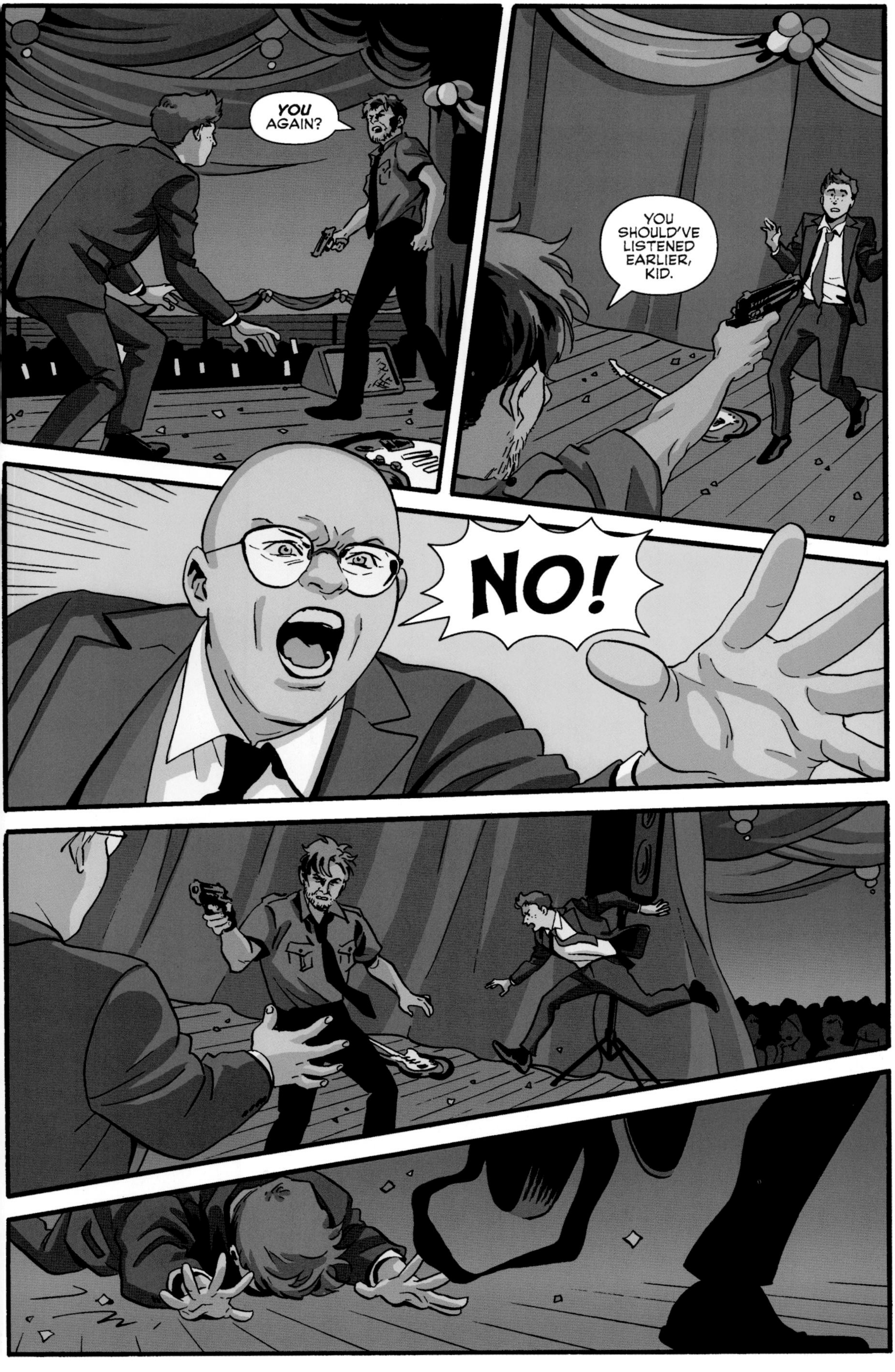
YOU AGAIN?
YOU SHOULD'VE LISTENED EARLIER, KID.
NO!

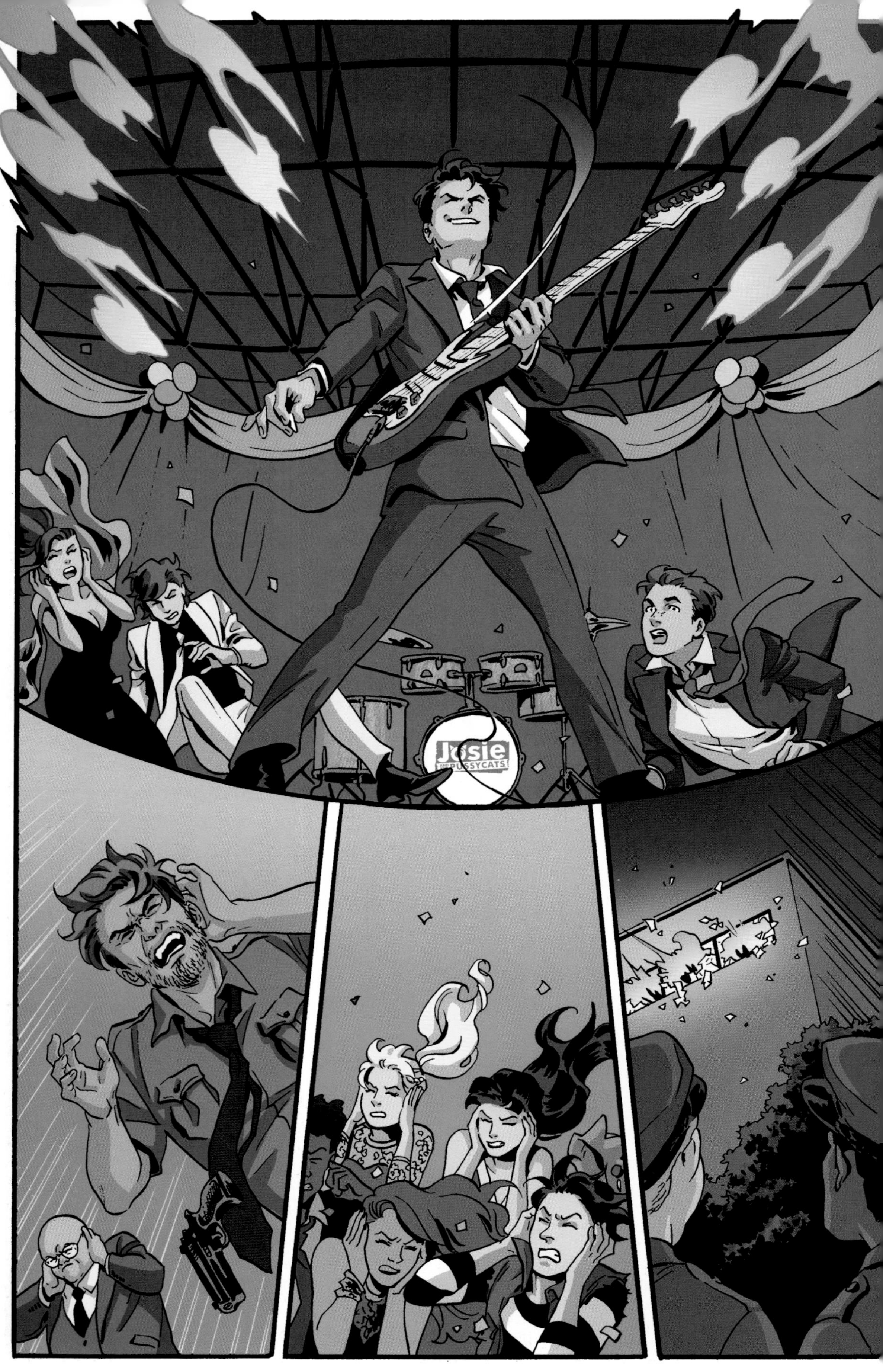
Josie
AND THE PUSSYCATS

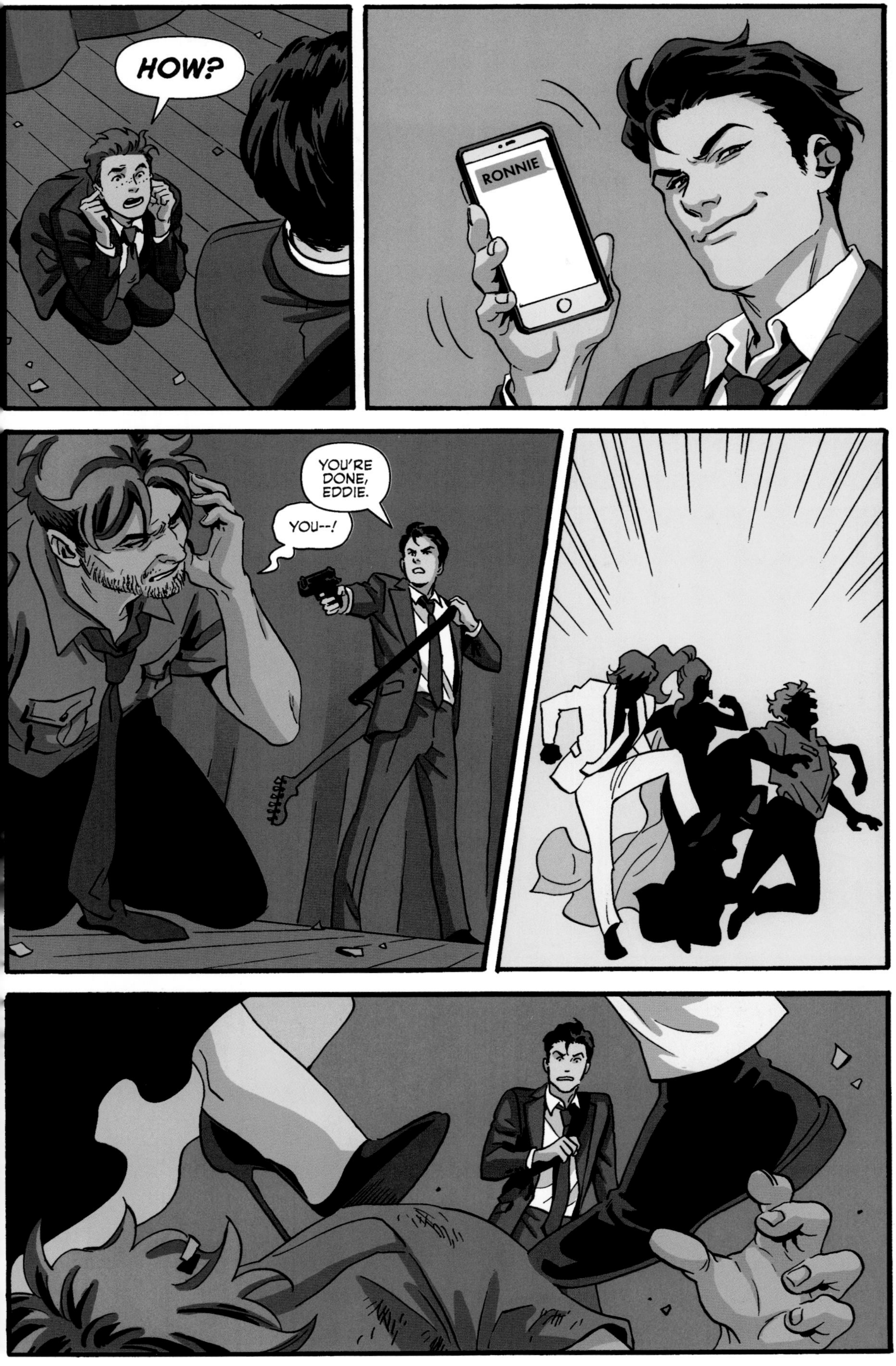
HOW?
RONNIE
YOU'RE DONE, EDDIE.
YOU--!

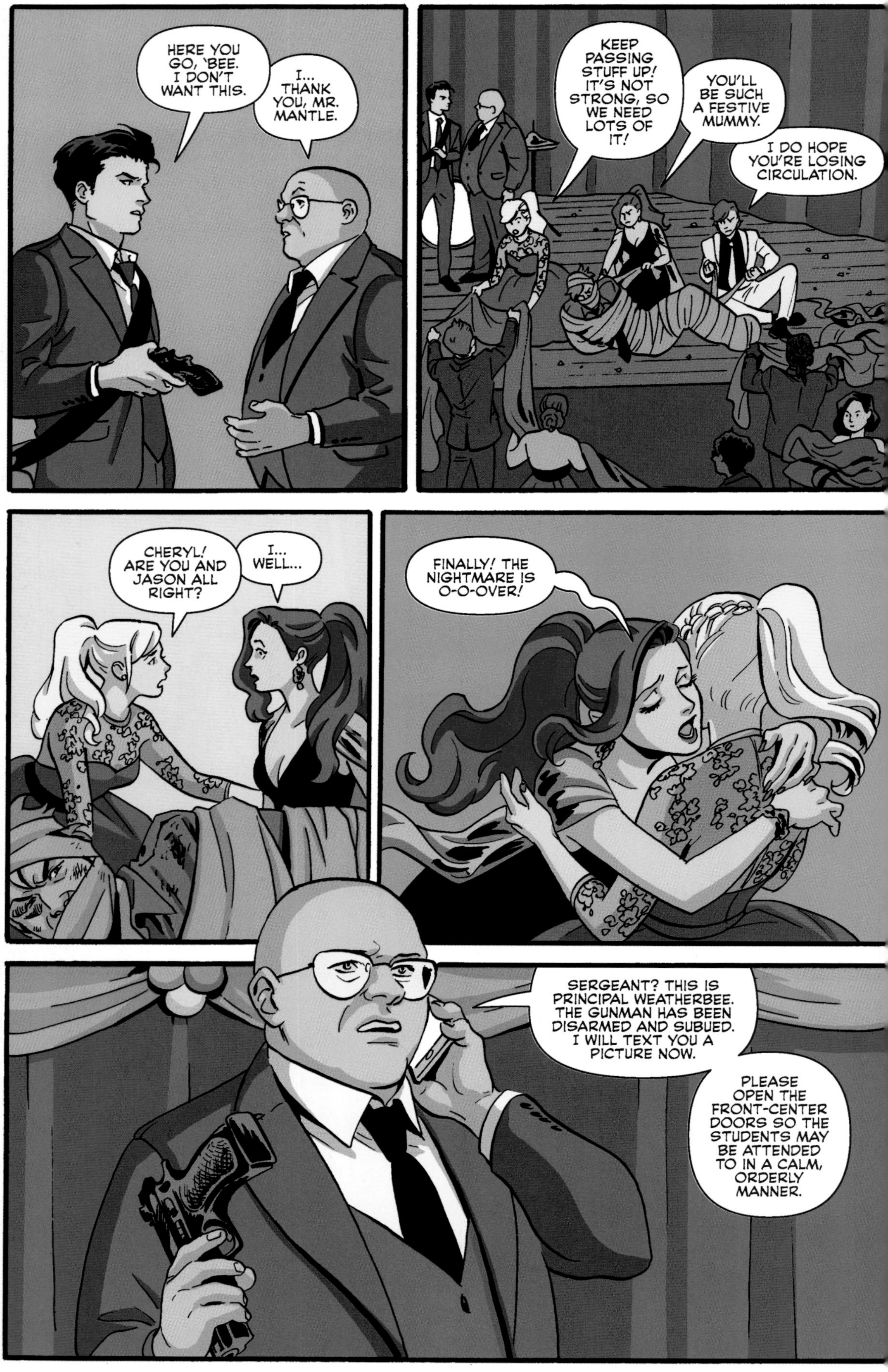
HERE YOU GO, 'BEE. I DON'T WANT THIS.
I... THANK YOU, MR. MANTLE.
KEEP PASSING STUFF UP! IT'S NOT STRONG, SO WE NEED LOTS OF IT!
YOU'LL BE SUCH A FESTIVE MUMMY.
I DO HOPE YOU'RE LOSING CIRCULATION.
CHERYL! ARE YOU AND JASON ALL RIGHT?
I... WELL...
FINALLY! THE NIGHTMARE IS O-O-OVER!
SERGEANT? THIS IS PRINCIPAL WEATHERBEE. THE GUNMAN HAS BEEN DISARMED AND SUBUED. I WILL TEXT YOU A PICTURE NOW.
PLEASE OPEN THE FRONT-CENTER DOORS SO THE STUDENTS MAY BE ATTENDED TO IN A CALM, ORDERLY MANNER.

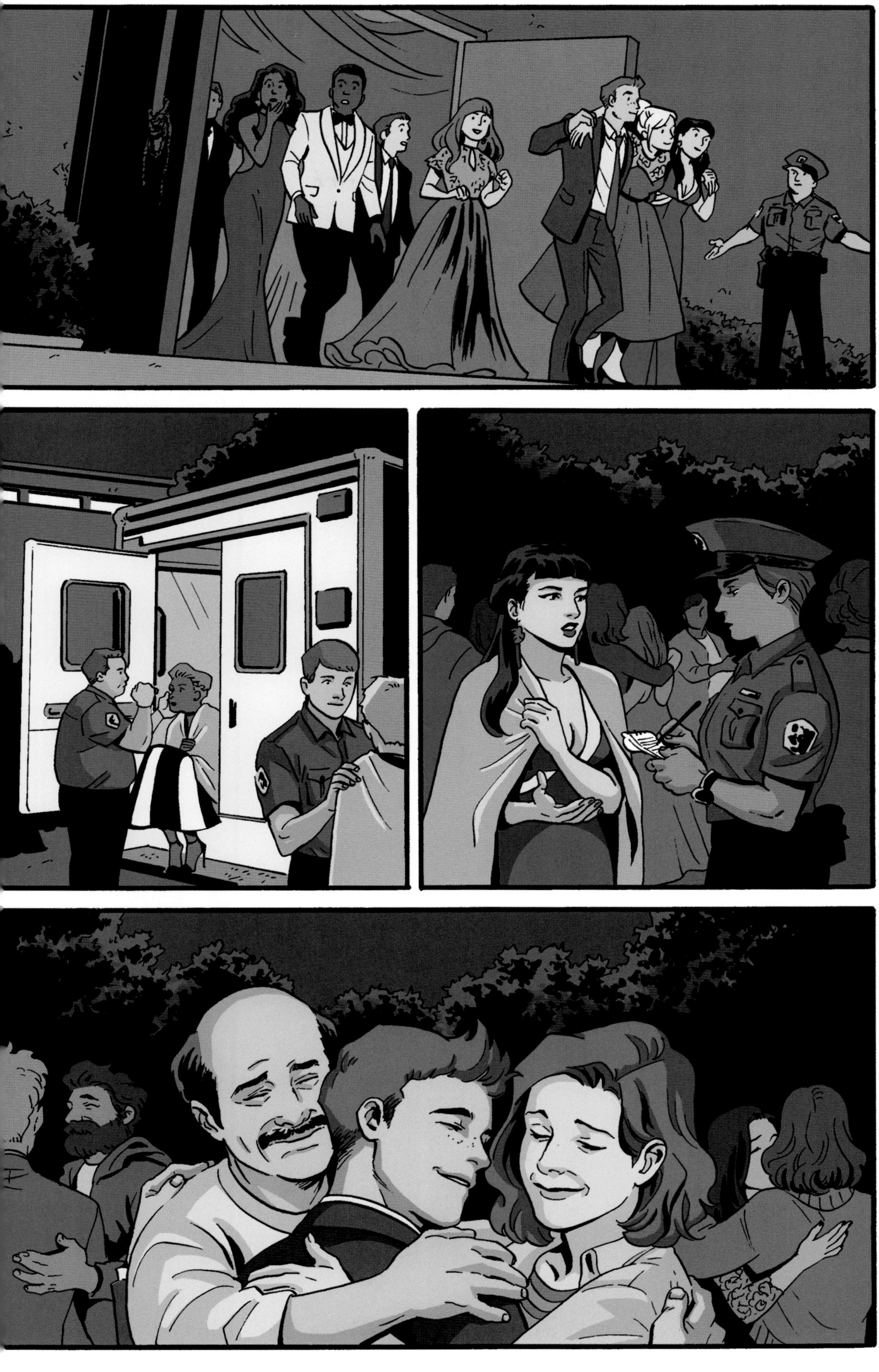

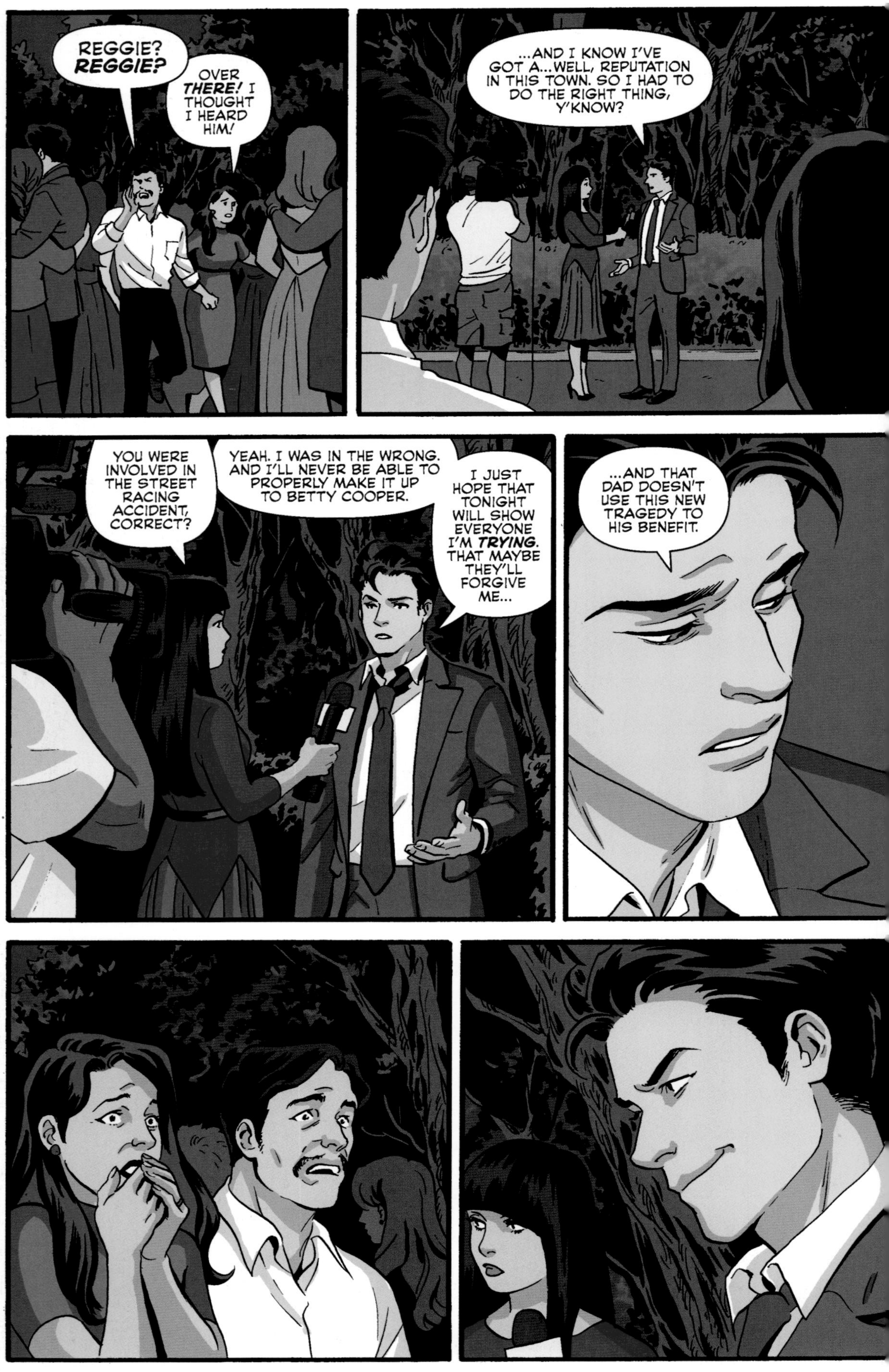
REGGIE? REGGIE?
OVER THERE! I THOUGHT I HEARD HIM!
...AND I KNOW I'VE GOT A...WELL, REPUTATION IN THIS TOWN. SO I HAD TO DO THE RIGHT THING, Y'KNOW?
YOU WERE INVOLVED IN THE STREET RACING ACCIDENT, CORRECT?
YEAH. I WAS IN THE WRONG. AND I'LL NEVER BE ABLE TO PROPERLY MAKE IT UP TO BETTY COOPER.
I JUST HOPE THAT TONIGHT WILL SHOW EVERYONE I'M TRYING. THAT MAYBE THEY'LL FORGIVE ME...
...AND THAT DAD DOESN'T USE THIS NEW TRAGEDY TO HIS BENEFIT.

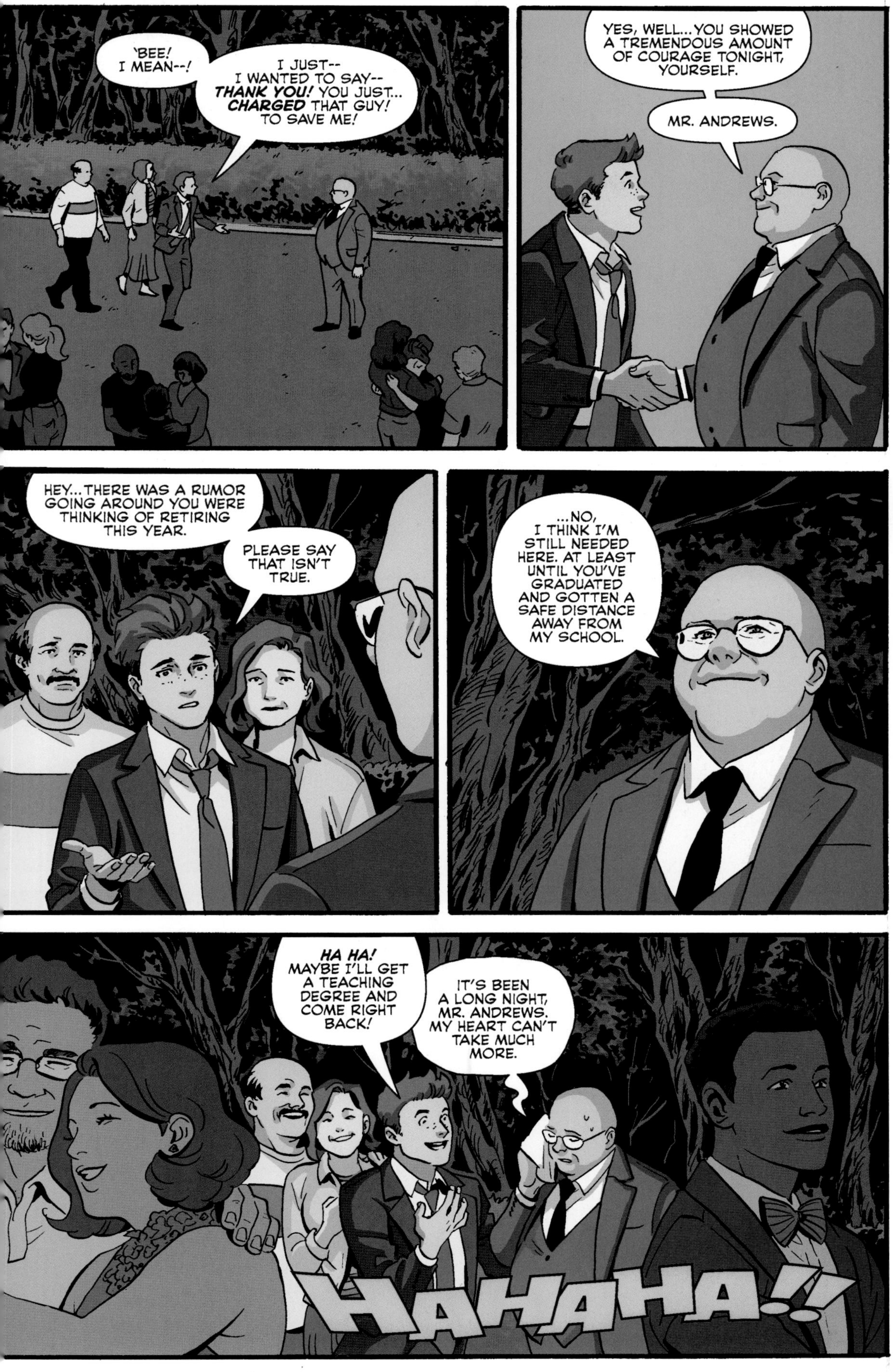

'BEE! I MEAN--!
I JUST-- I WANTED TO SAY-- *THANK YOU!* YOU JUST... *CHARGED* THAT GUY! TO SAVE ME!
YES, WELL...YOU SHOWED A TREMENDOUS AMOUNT OF COURAGE TONIGHT, YOURSELF.
MR. ANDREWS.
HEY...THERE WAS A RUMOR GOING AROUND YOU WERE THINKING OF RETIRING THIS YEAR.
PLEASE SAY THAT ISN'T TRUE.
...NO, I THINK I'M STILL NEEDED HERE. AT LEAST UNTIL YOU'VE GRADUATED AND GOTTEN A SAFE DISTANCE AWAY FROM MY SCHOOL.
HA HA! MAYBE I'LL GET A TEACHING DEGREE AND COME RIGHT BACK!
IT'S BEEN A LONG NIGHT, MR. ANDREWS. MY HEART CAN'T TAKE MUCH MORE.
HAHAHA!!

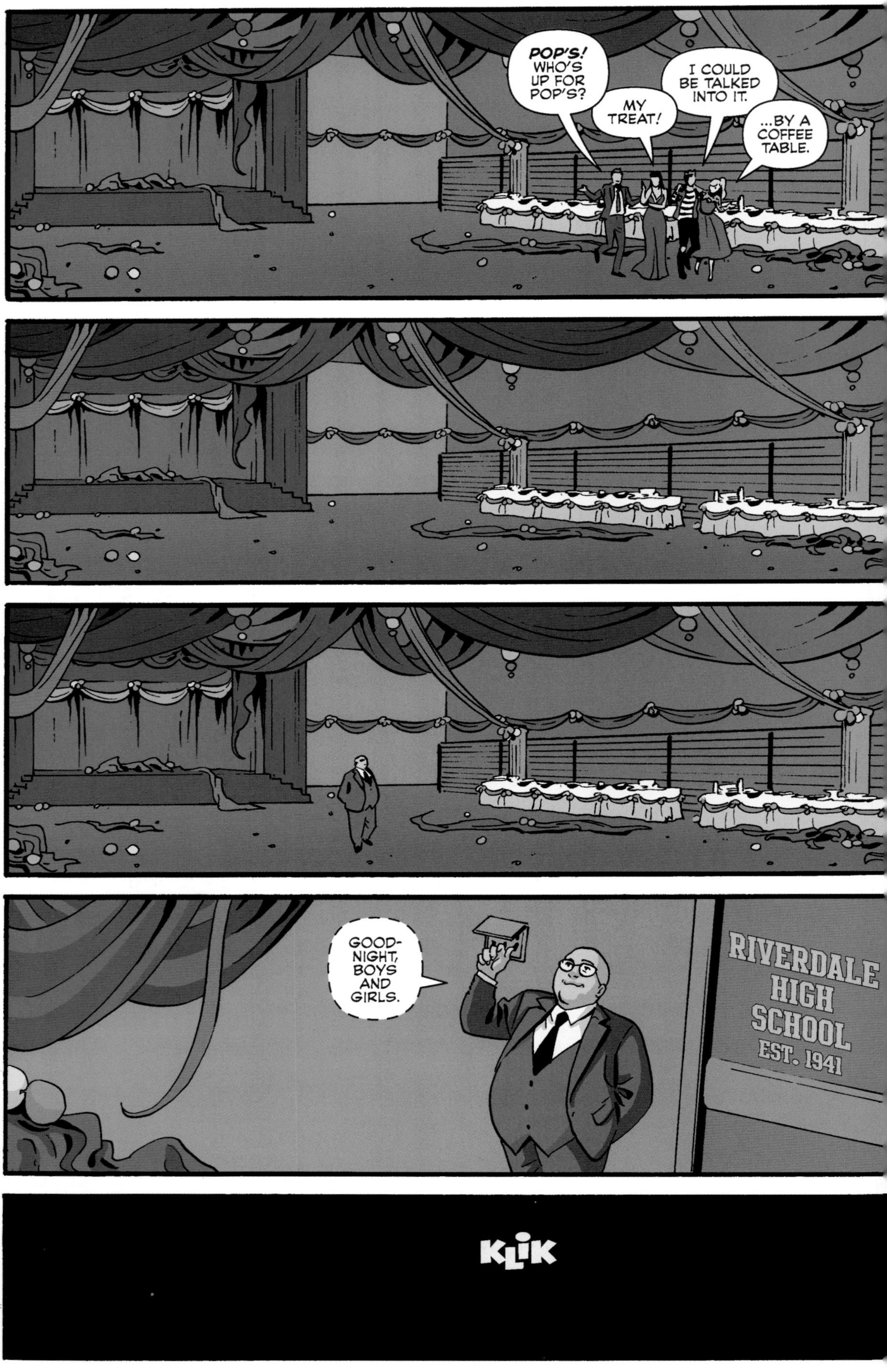
POP'S! WHO'S UP FOR POP'S?
MY TREAT!
I COULD BE TALKED INTO IT.
...BY A COFFEE TABLE.
GOOD-NIGHT, BOYS AND GIRLS.
RIVERDALE HIGH SCHOOL EST. 1941
KLIK

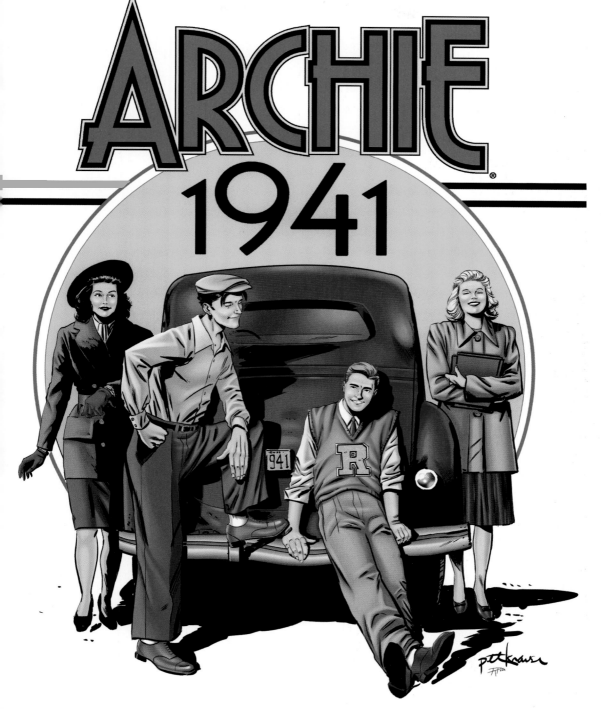

THE NEXT CHAPTER OF ARCHIE BEGINS...
MARK WAID CONTINUES HIS HISTORIC RUN
IN ARCHIE COMICS WITH

ARCHIE 1941

MARK WAID · BRIAN AUGUSTYN · PETER KRAUSE
KELLY FITZPATRICK · JACK MORELLI

ARCHIE®

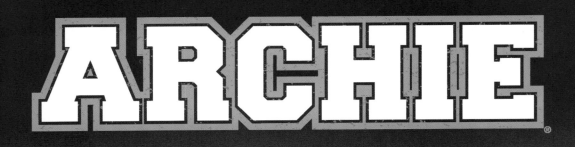

COVER GALLERY

In addition to the amazing main covers we have for each issue, we also receive gorgeous artwork from an array of talented artists for our direct market exclusive covers. Here are all of the main and variant covers for each of the five issues in *Archie Volume Six*.

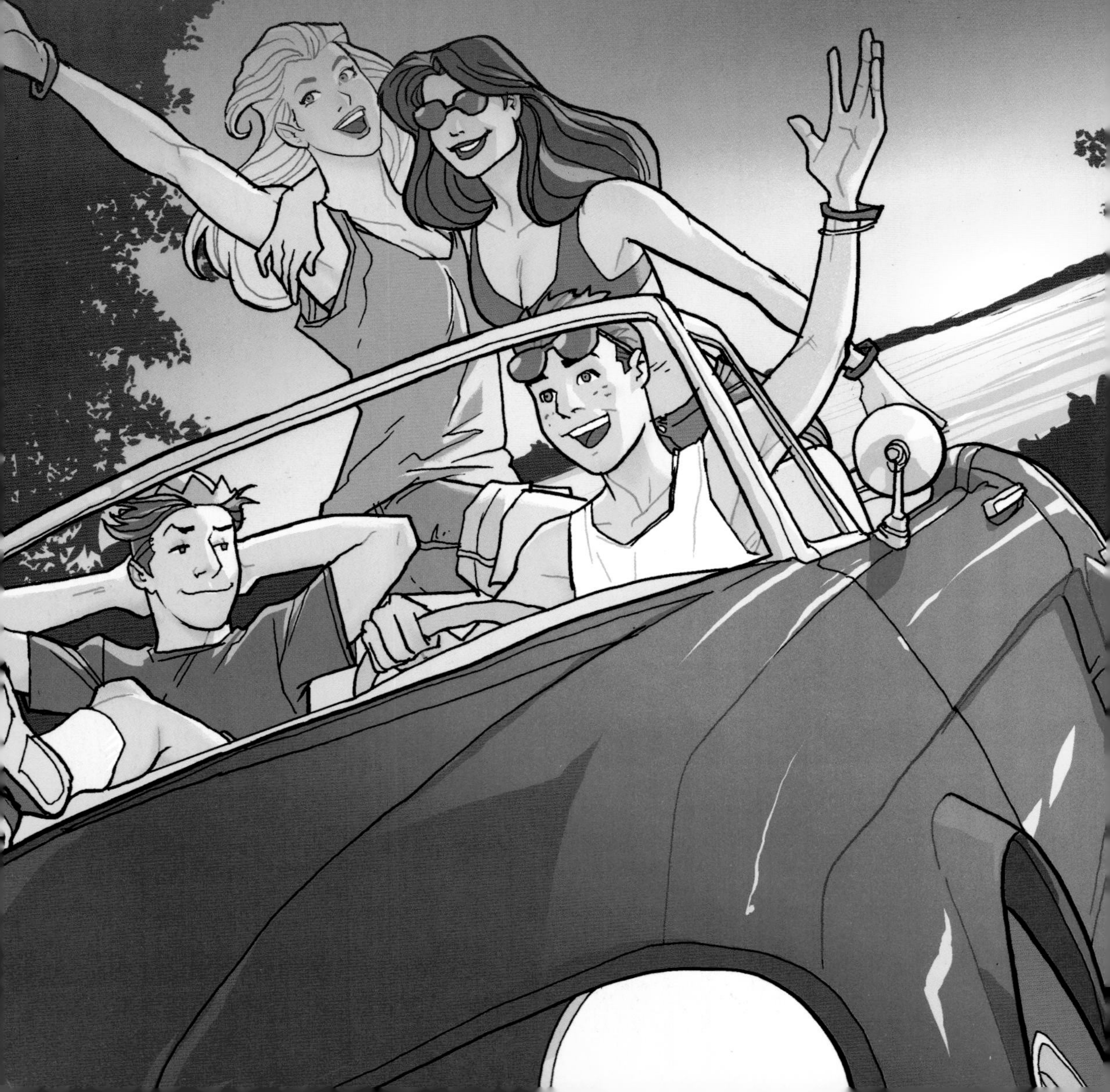

ISSUE
TWENTY
EIGHT

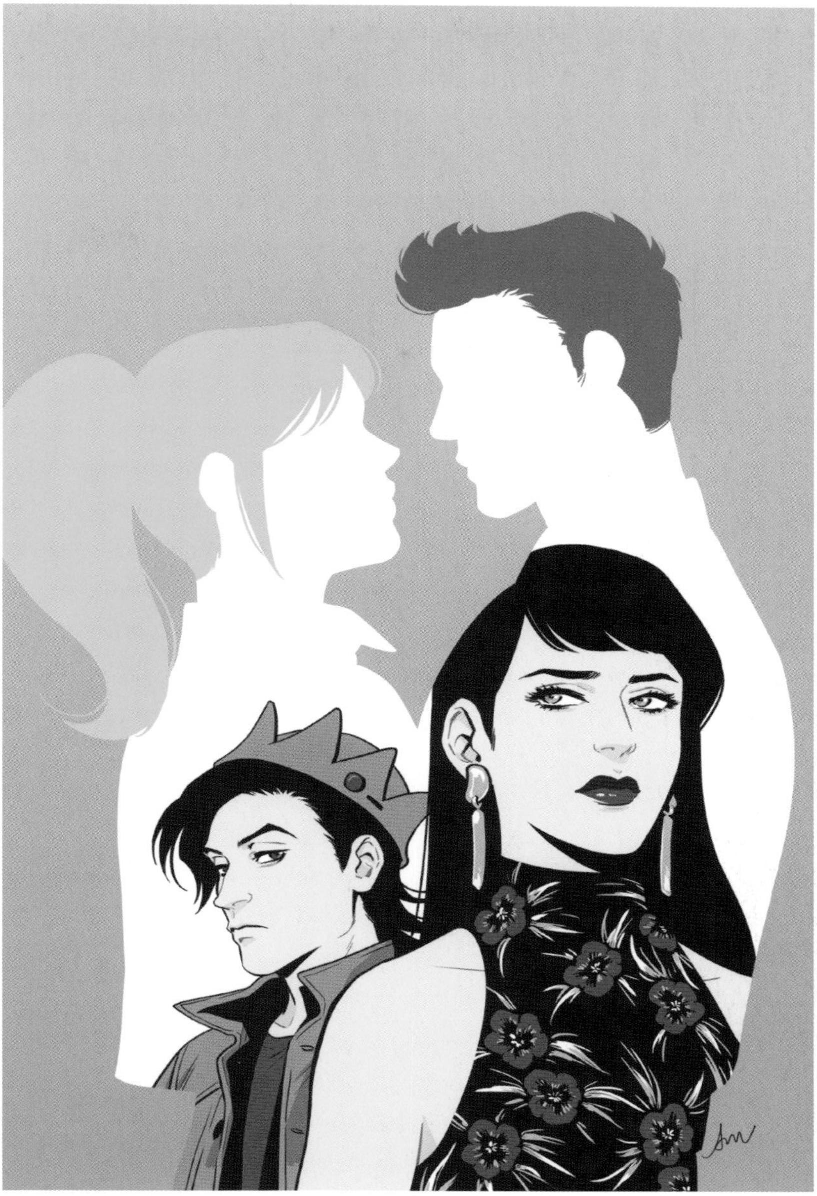

AUDREY
MOK

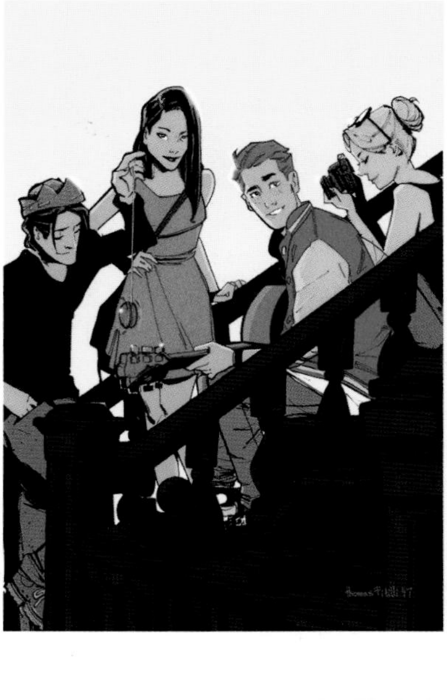

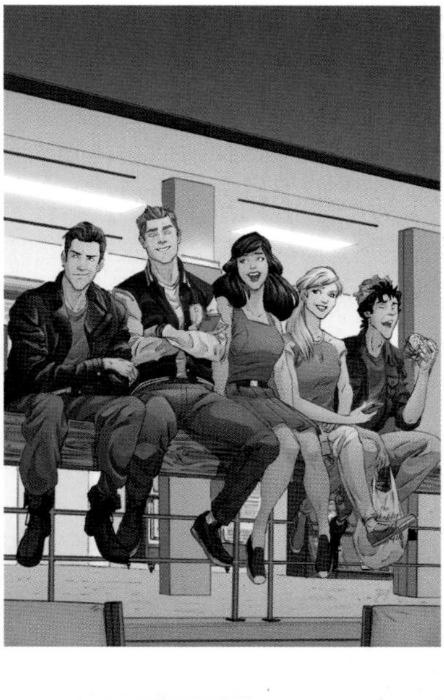

(L)
THOMAS
PITILLI

(R)
DAN
SCHOENING

ISSUE TWENTY NINE

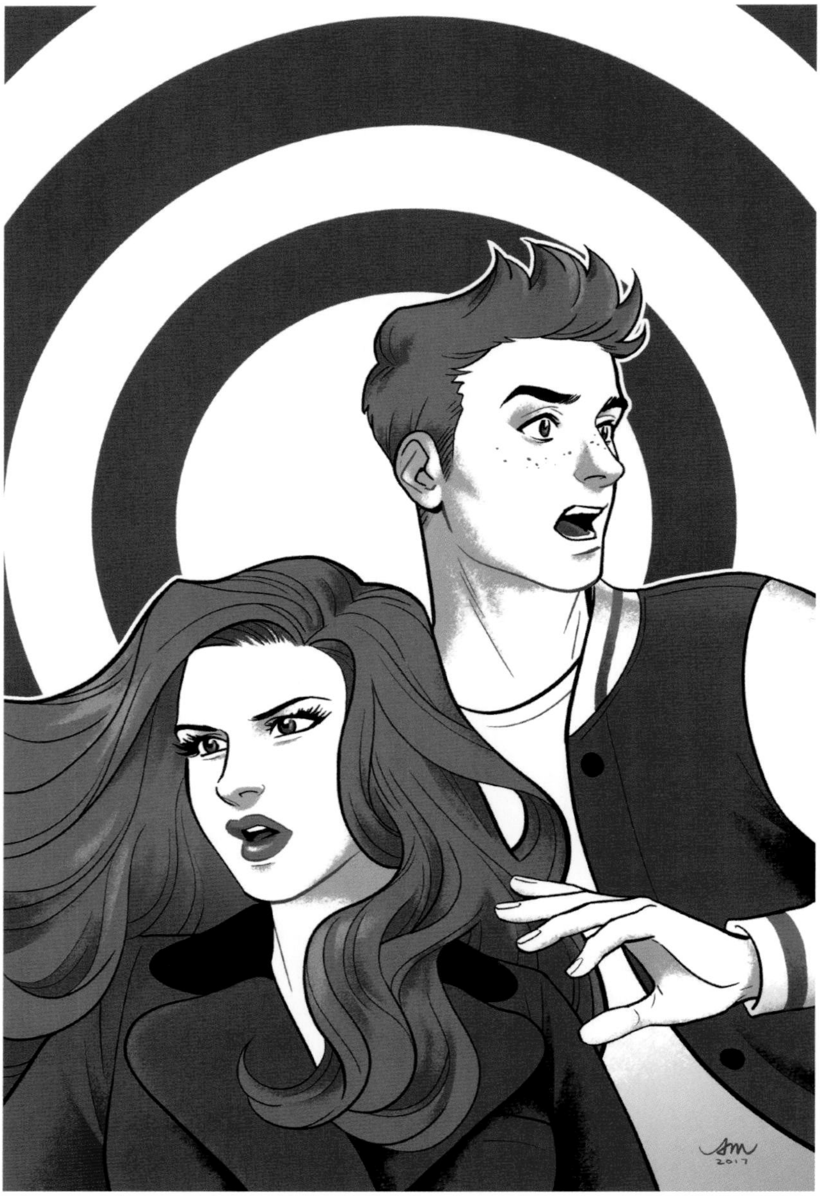

AUDREY MOK

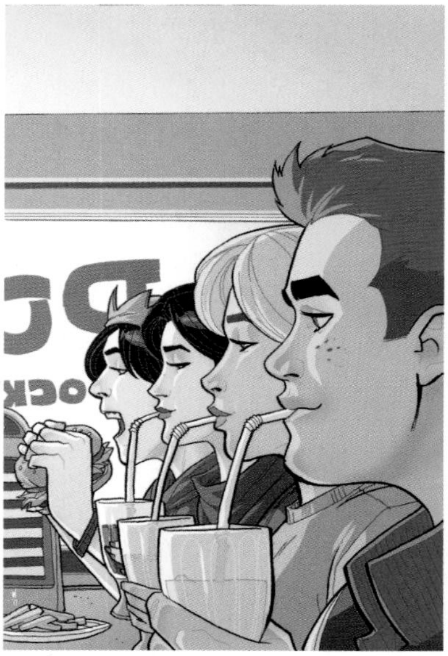

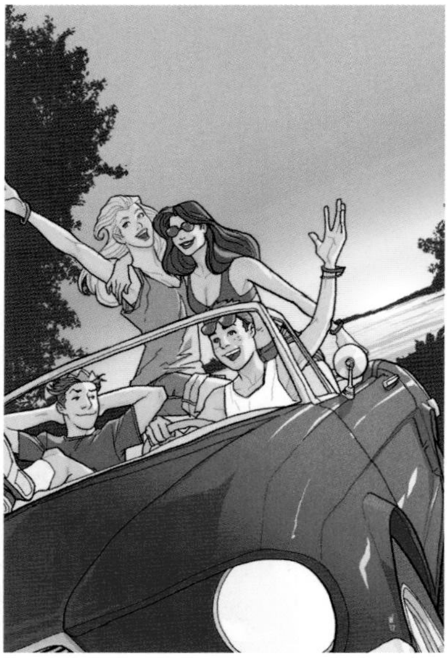

(L)
PETE WOODS

(R)
PETE WOODS

ISSUE THIRTY

AUDREY MOK

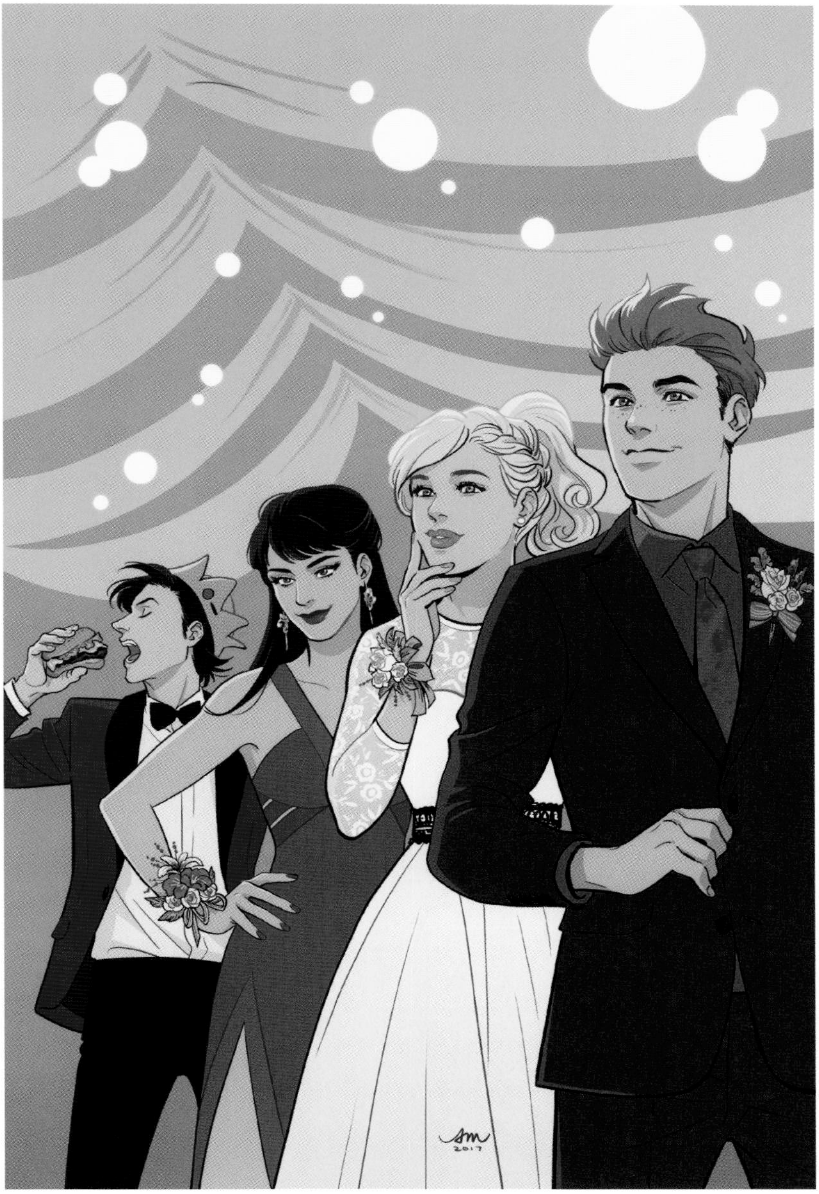

(L) ADAM GORHAM

(R) SANDY JARRELL

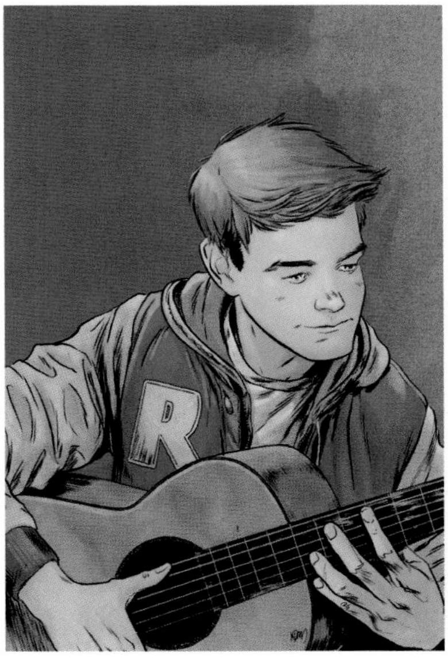

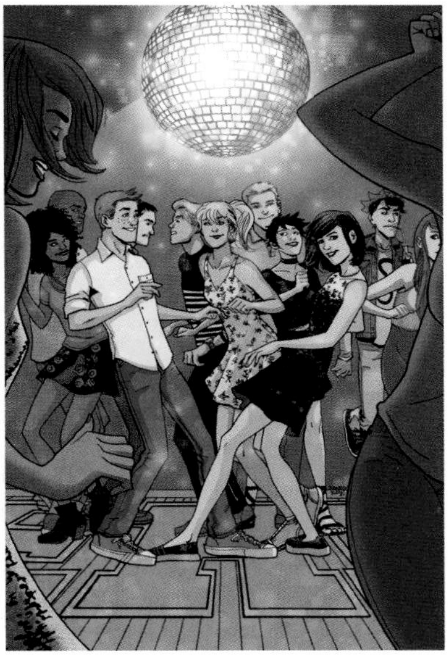

ISSUE THIRTY ONE

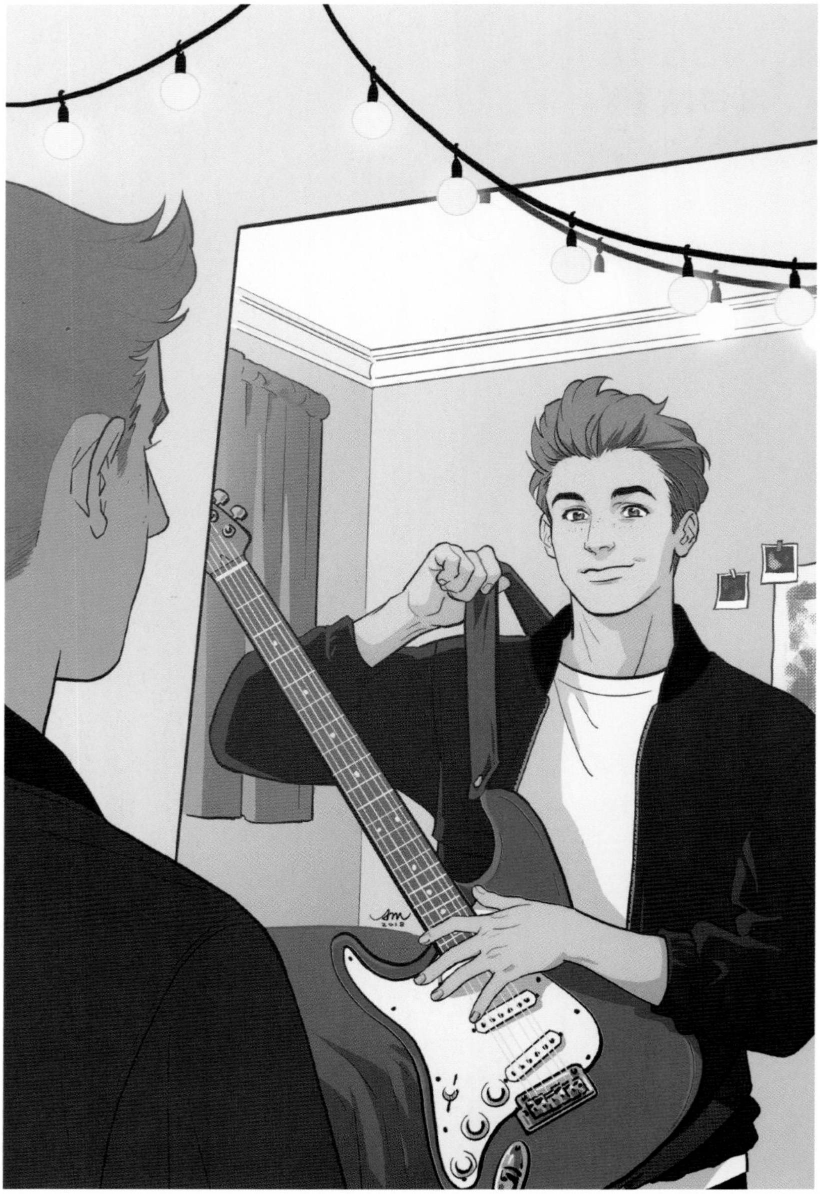

AUDREY MOK

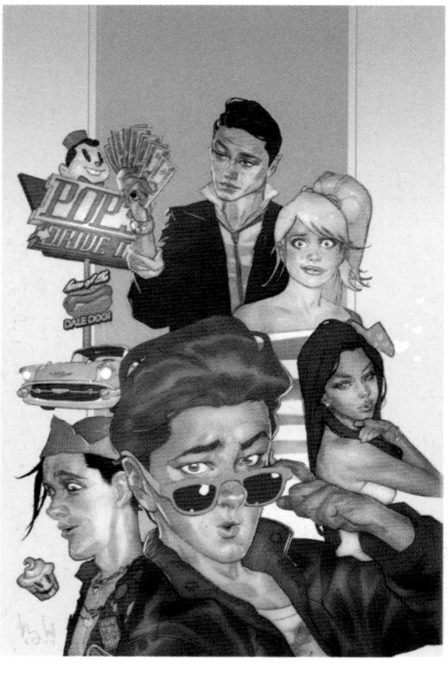

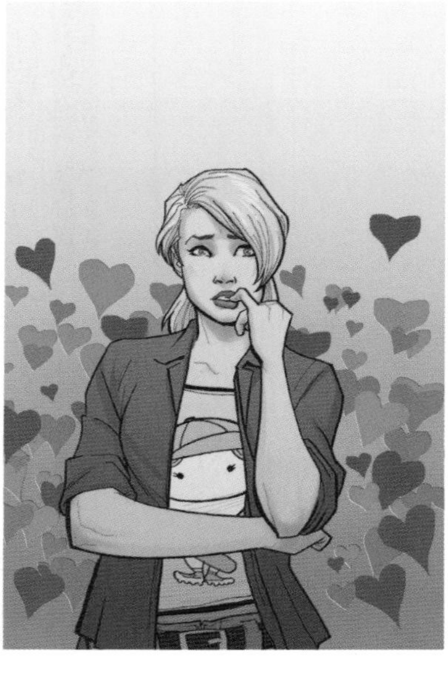

(L) BEN CALDWELL

(R) PETE WOODS

ISSUE
THIRTY
TWO

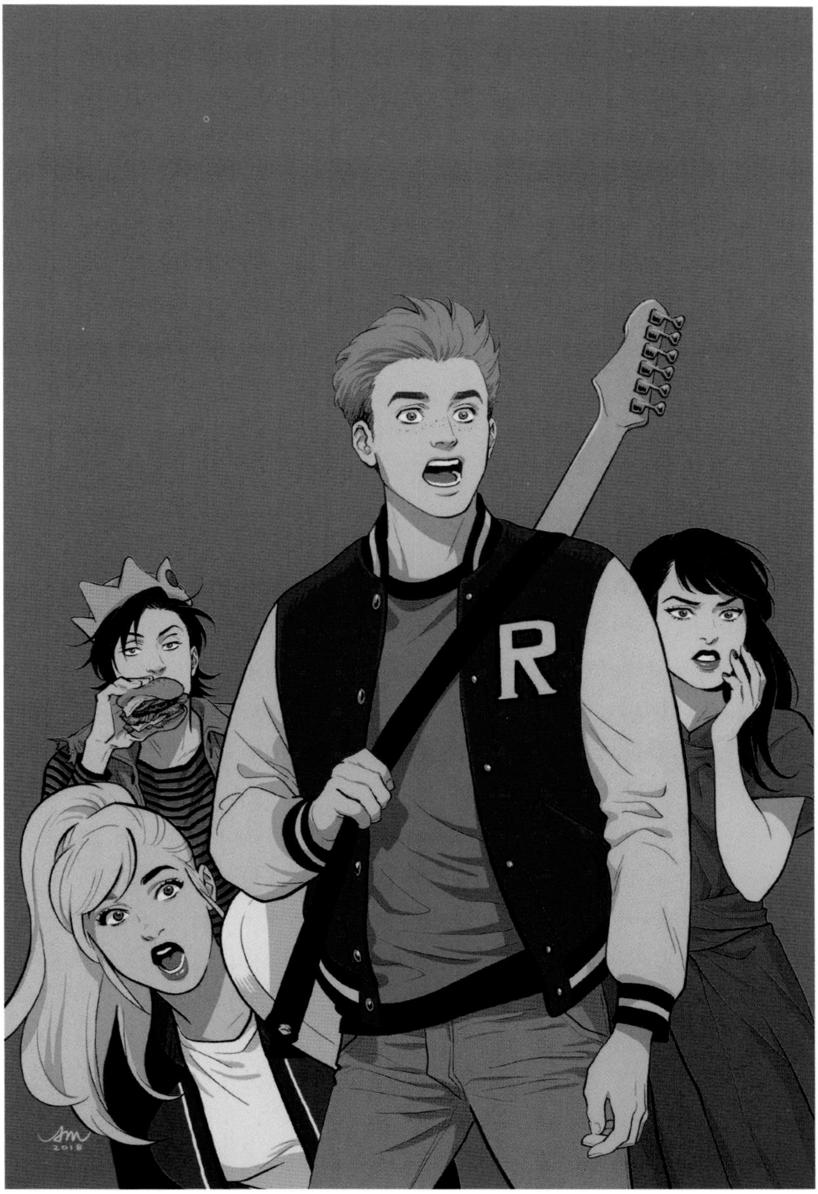

AUDREY
MOK

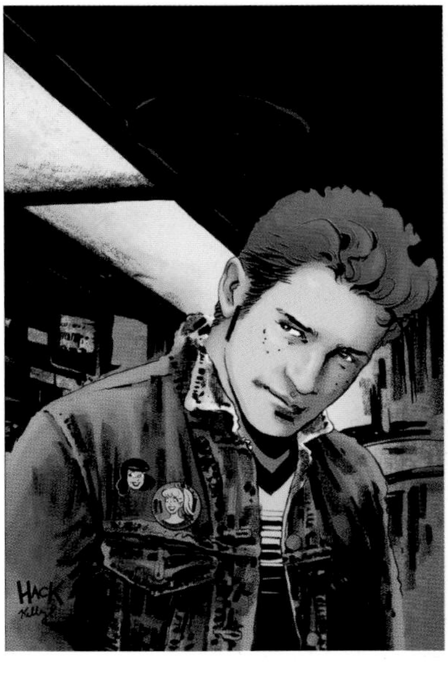

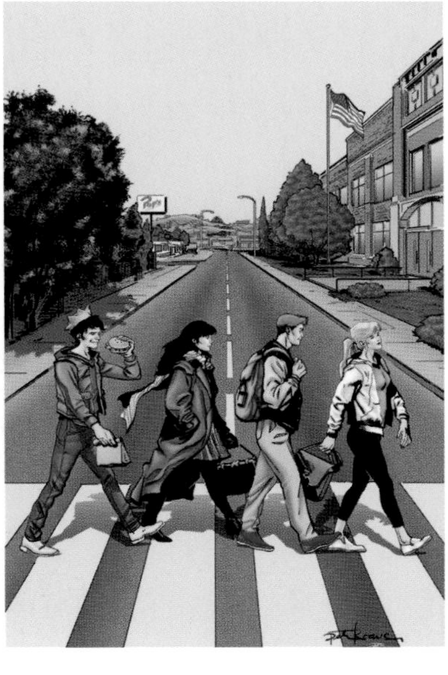

(L)
ROBERT
HACK

(R)
PETER
KRAUSE

ARCHIE®

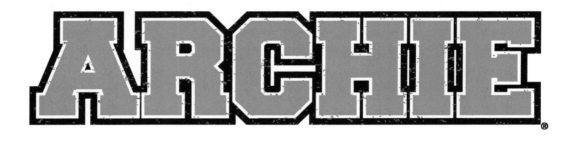

COVER SKETCHES

Before each issue goes through the solicitation process, our writers MARK WAID and IAN FLYNN give us a synopsis of what will occur in each upcoming issue, and from that our talented interior artist will come up with some main cover ideas and send in rough drafts of how they would like the cover to look. Here are a few of AUDREY MOK's brilliant cover sketches along with how they appeared in the final versions.

ISSUE TWENTY EIGHT

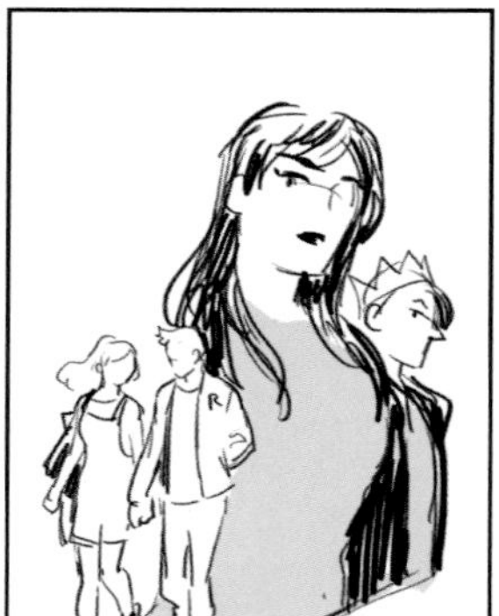

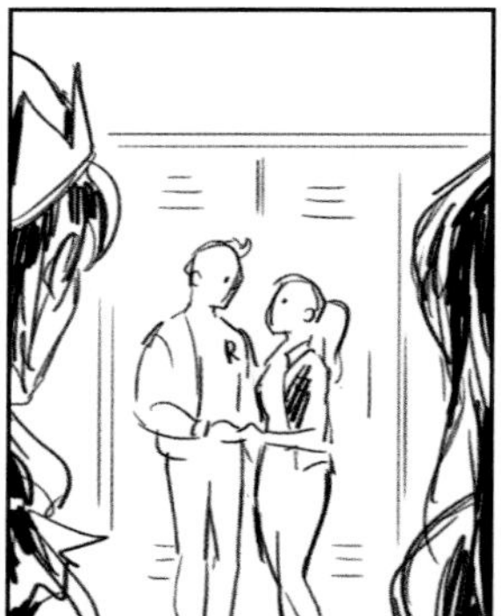

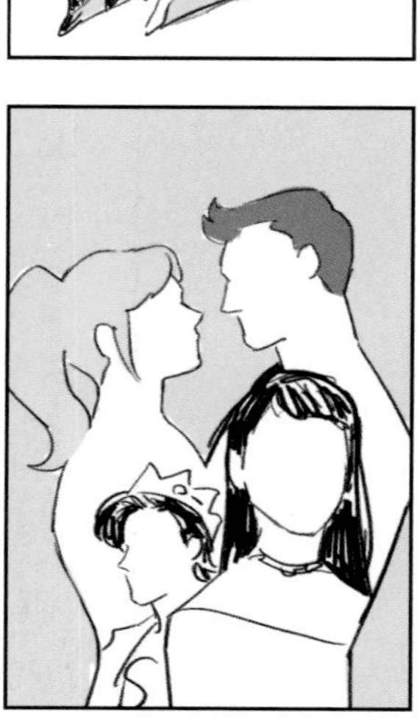

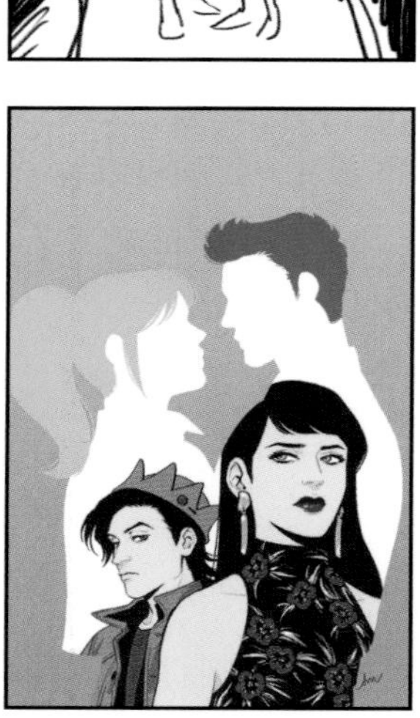

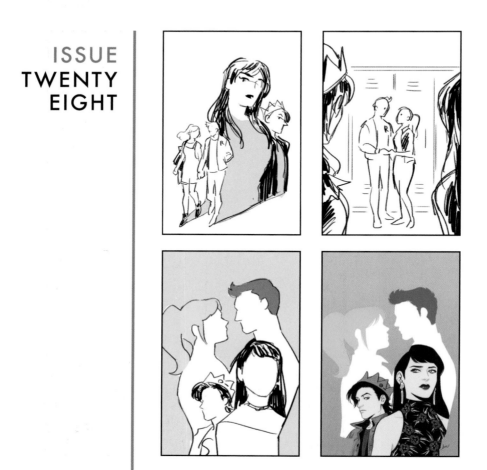

ISSUE TWENTY NINE

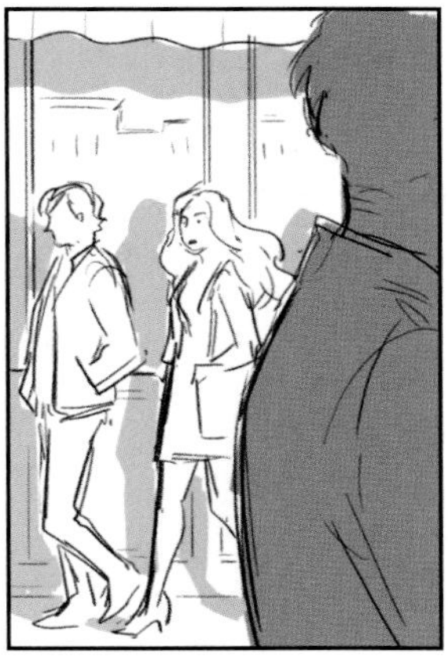

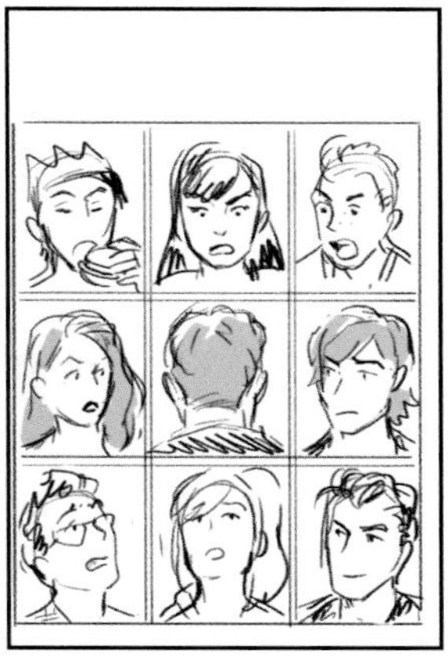

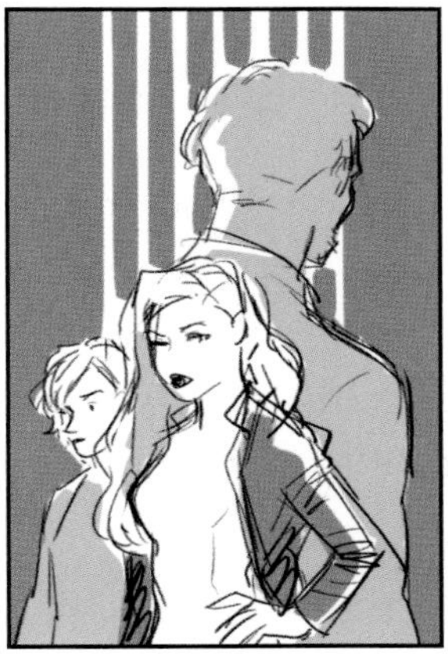

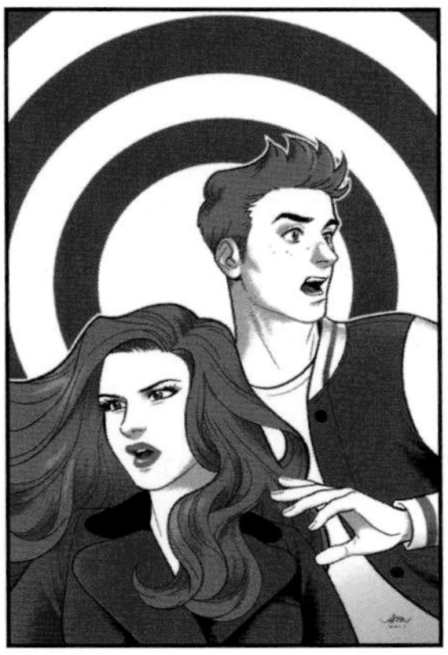

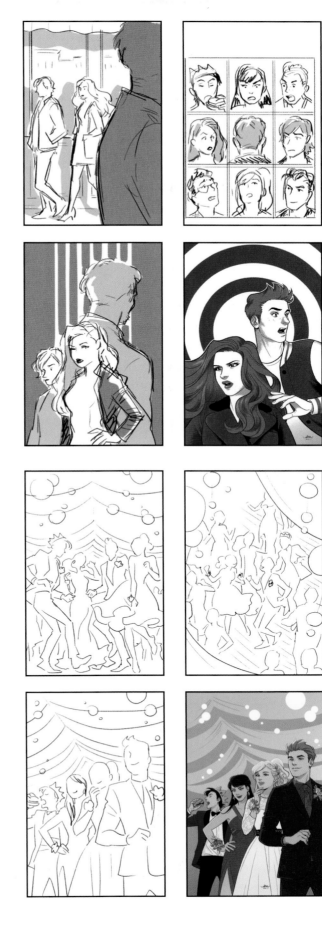

ISSUE THIRTY

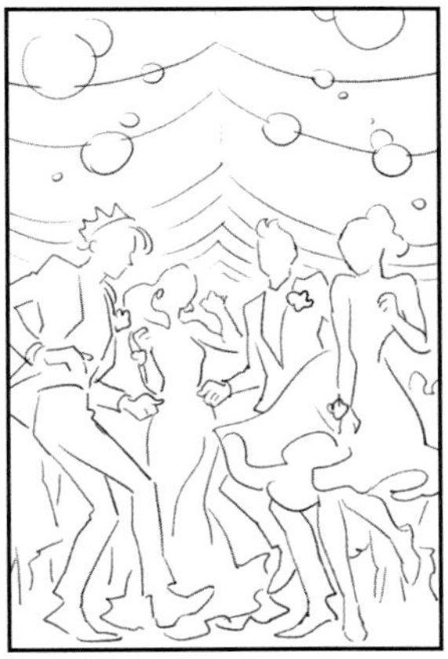

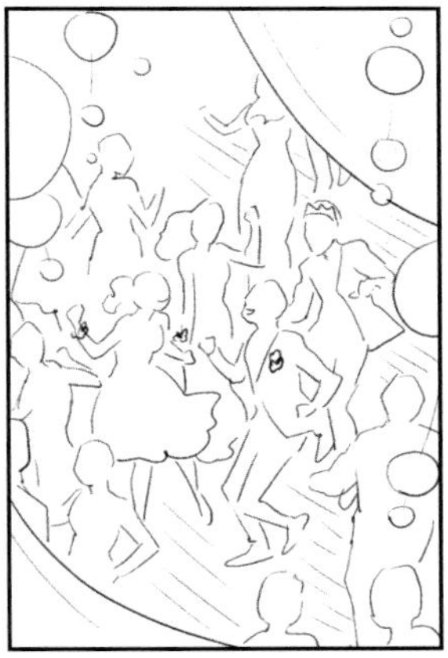

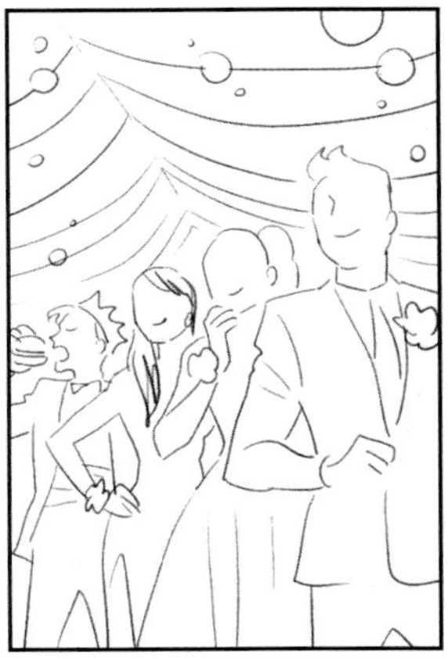

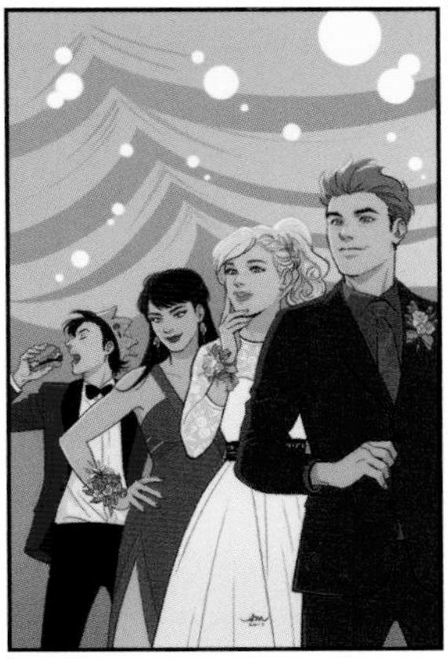

ISSUE THIRTY ONE

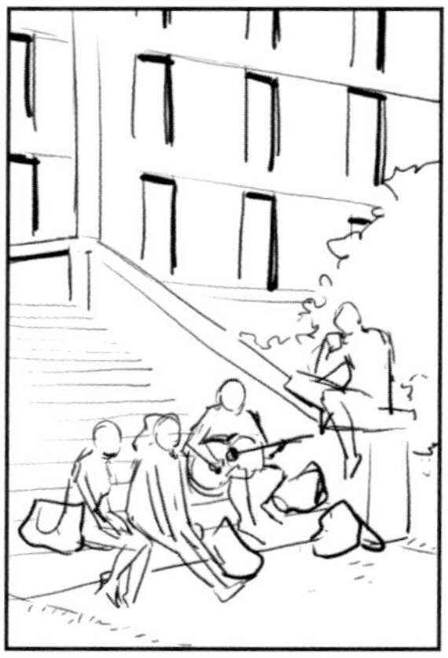

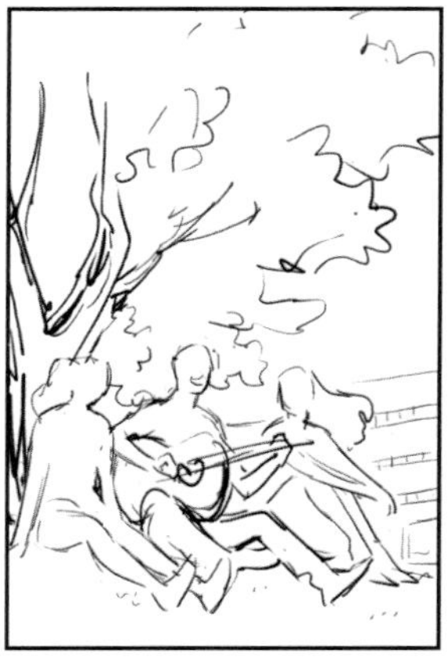

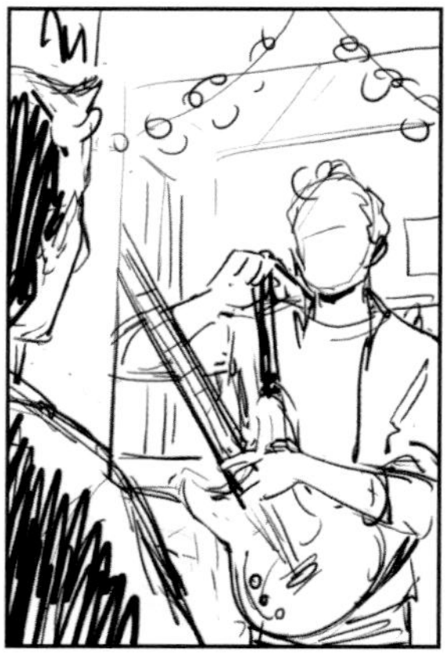

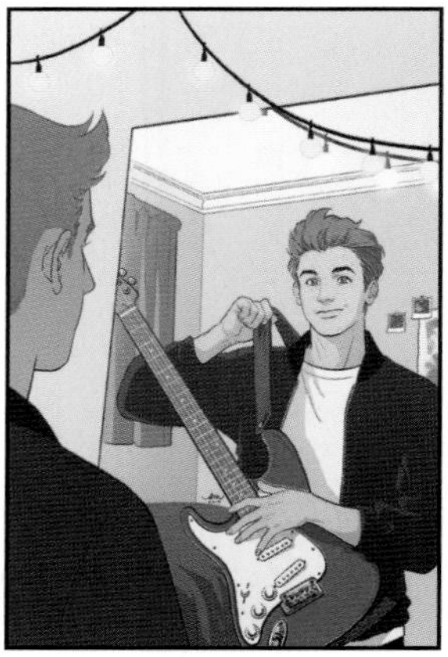

ISSUE THIRTY TWO

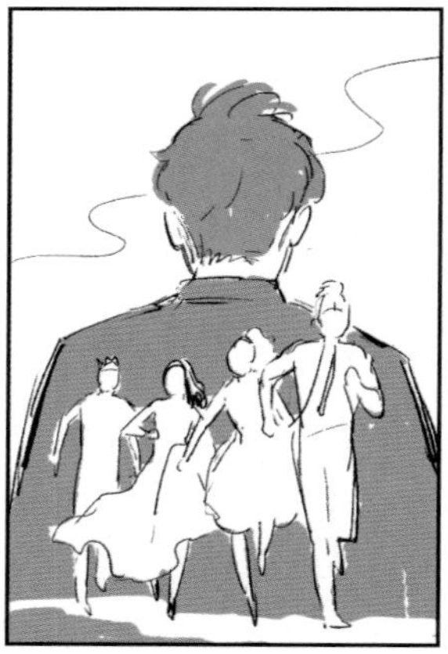

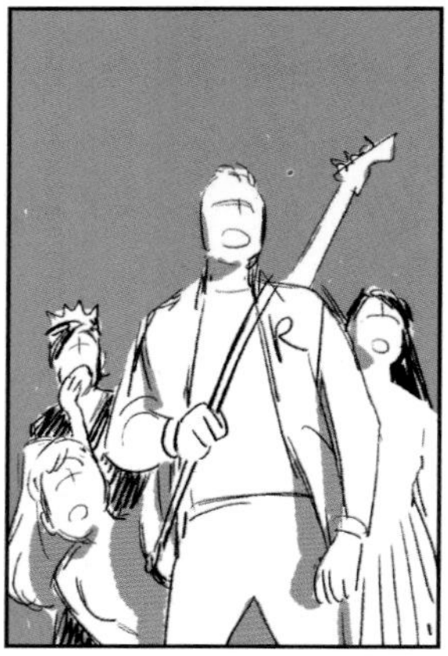

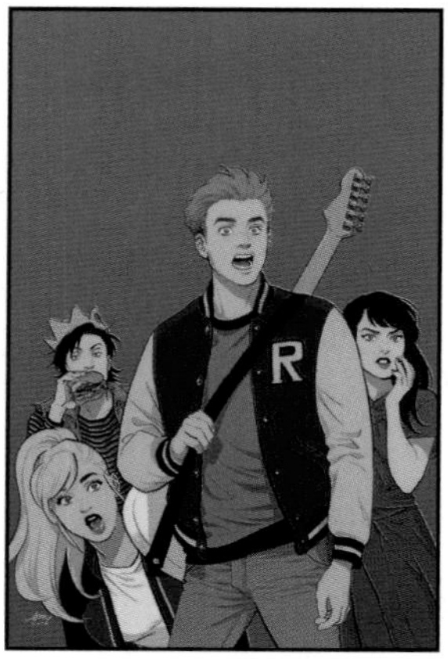

SPECIAL PREVIEW

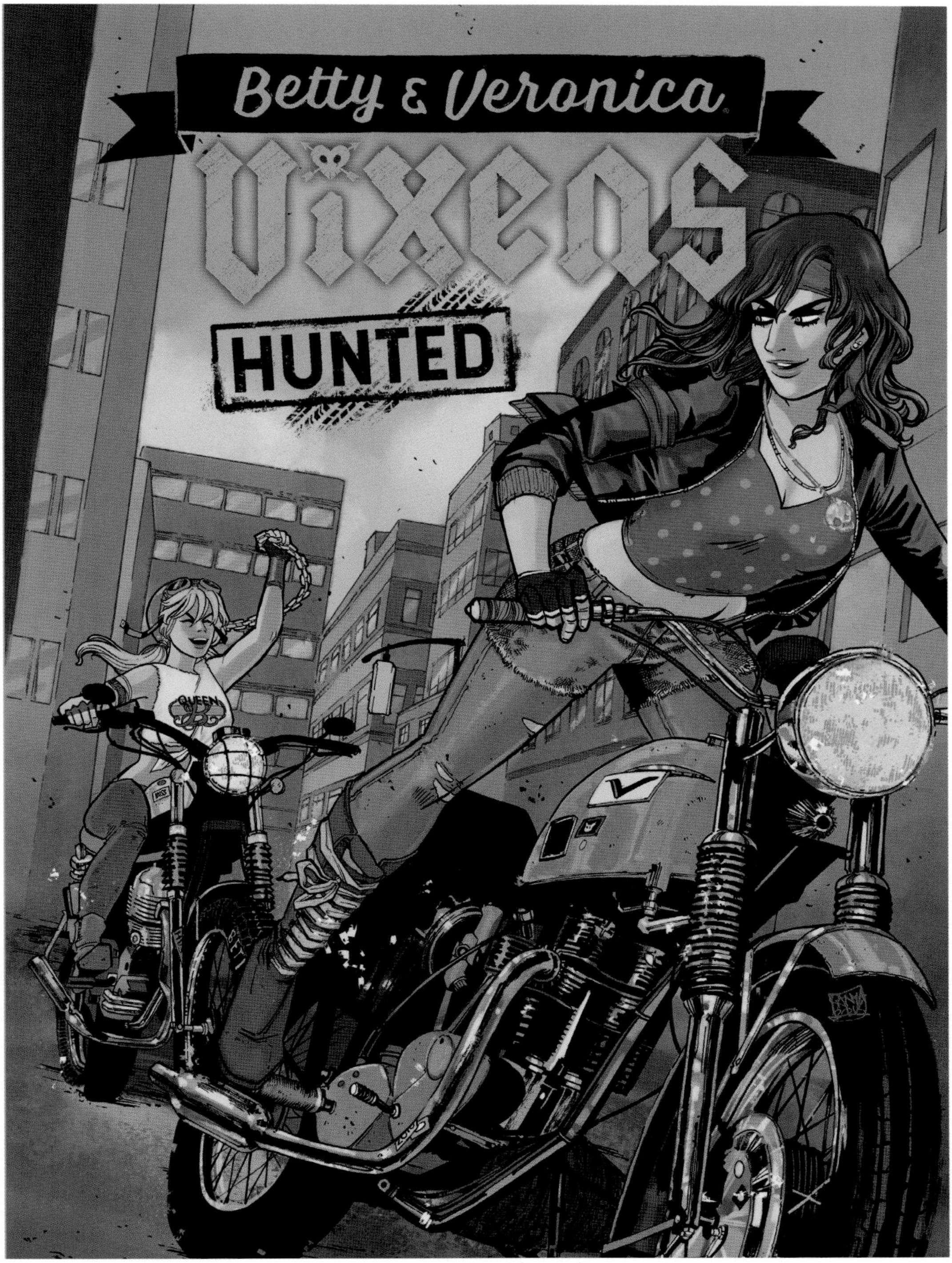
Betty & Veronica
Vixens
HUNTED

STORY BY
JAMIE LEE ROTANTE

PENCILS BY
JEN VAUGHN

COLORING BY
ELAINA UNGER

LETTERING BY
RACHEL DEERING

ISSUE SIX

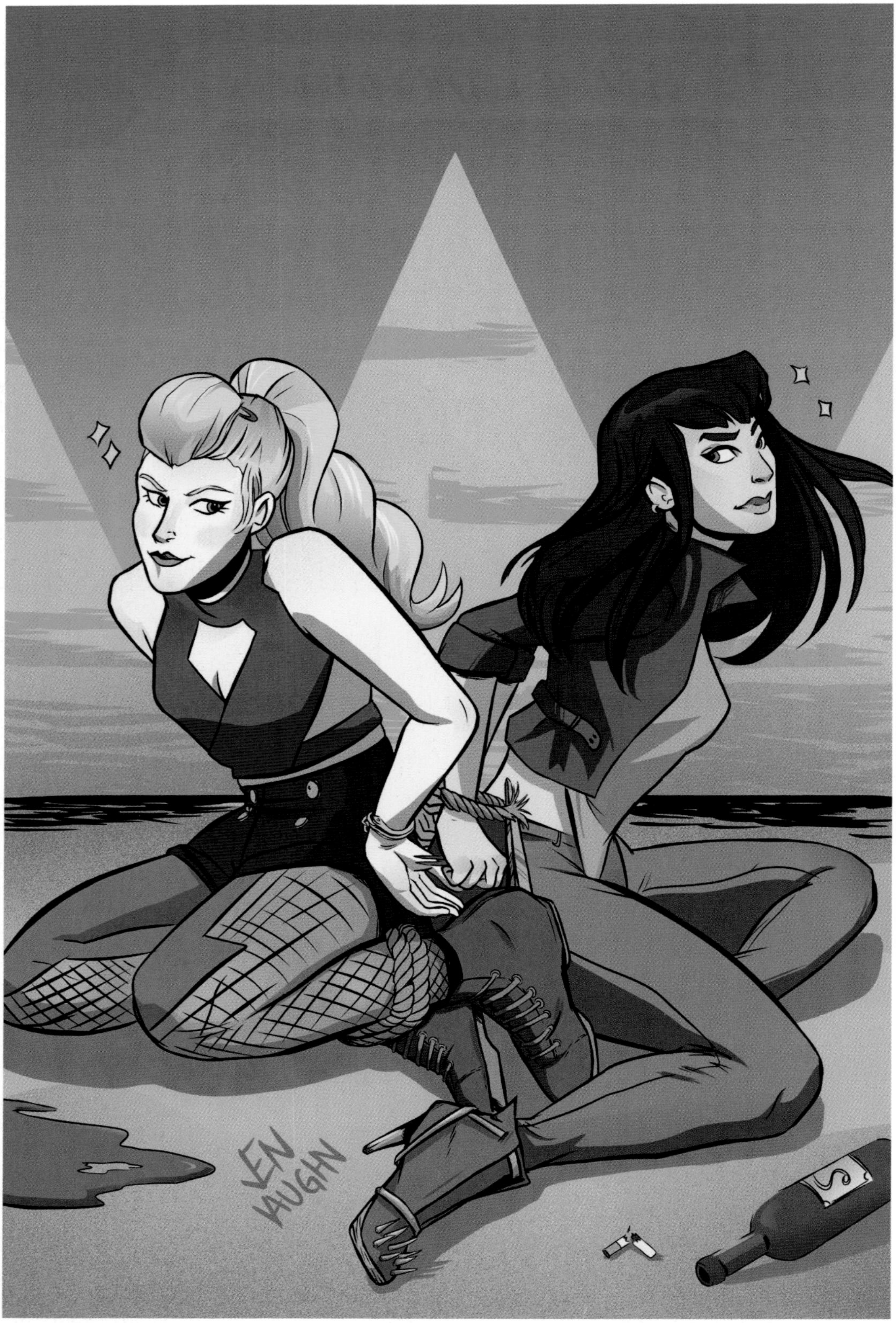
JEN VAUGHN

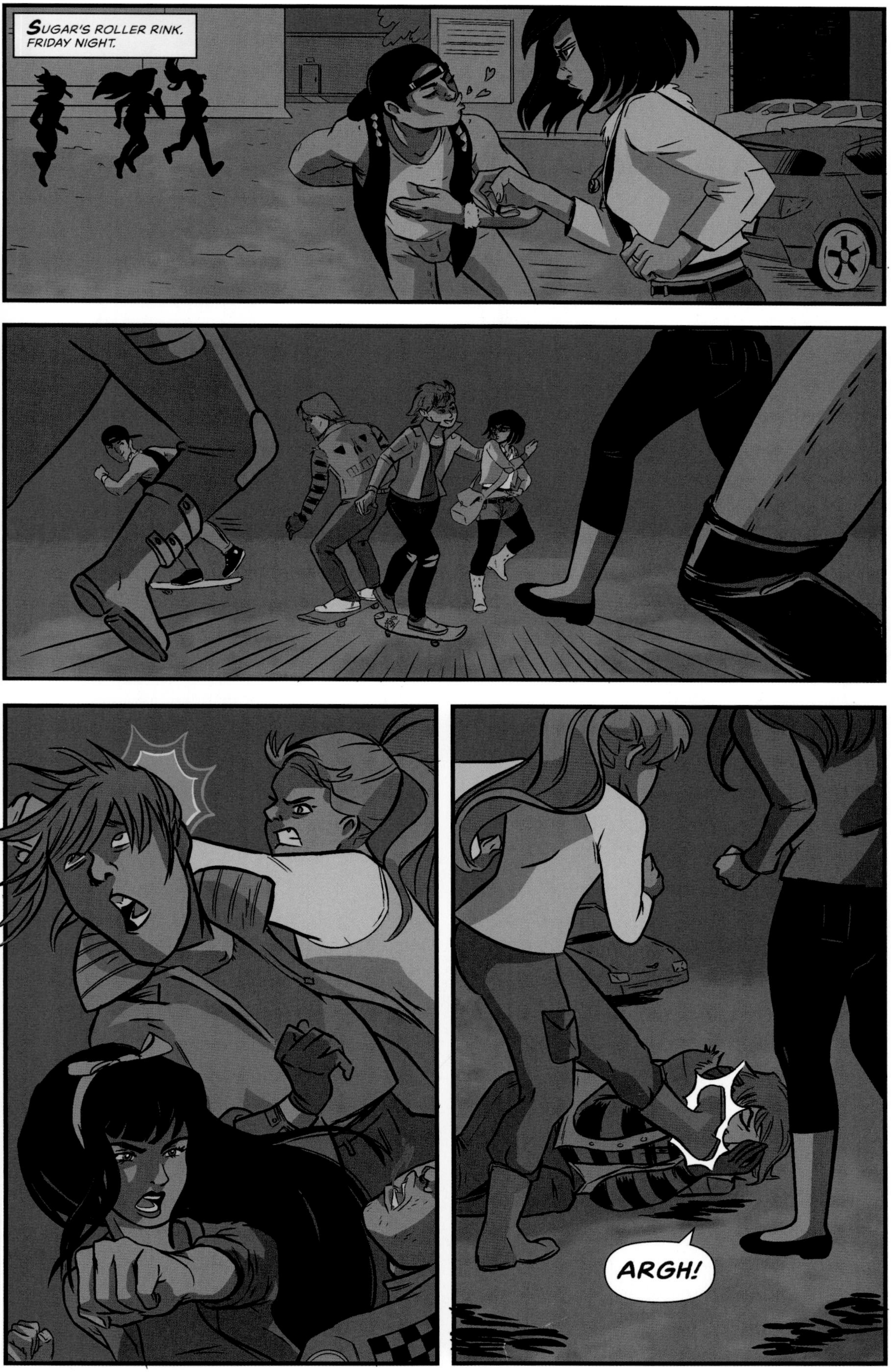
SUGAR'S ROLLER RINK, FRIDAY NIGHT.
ARGH!

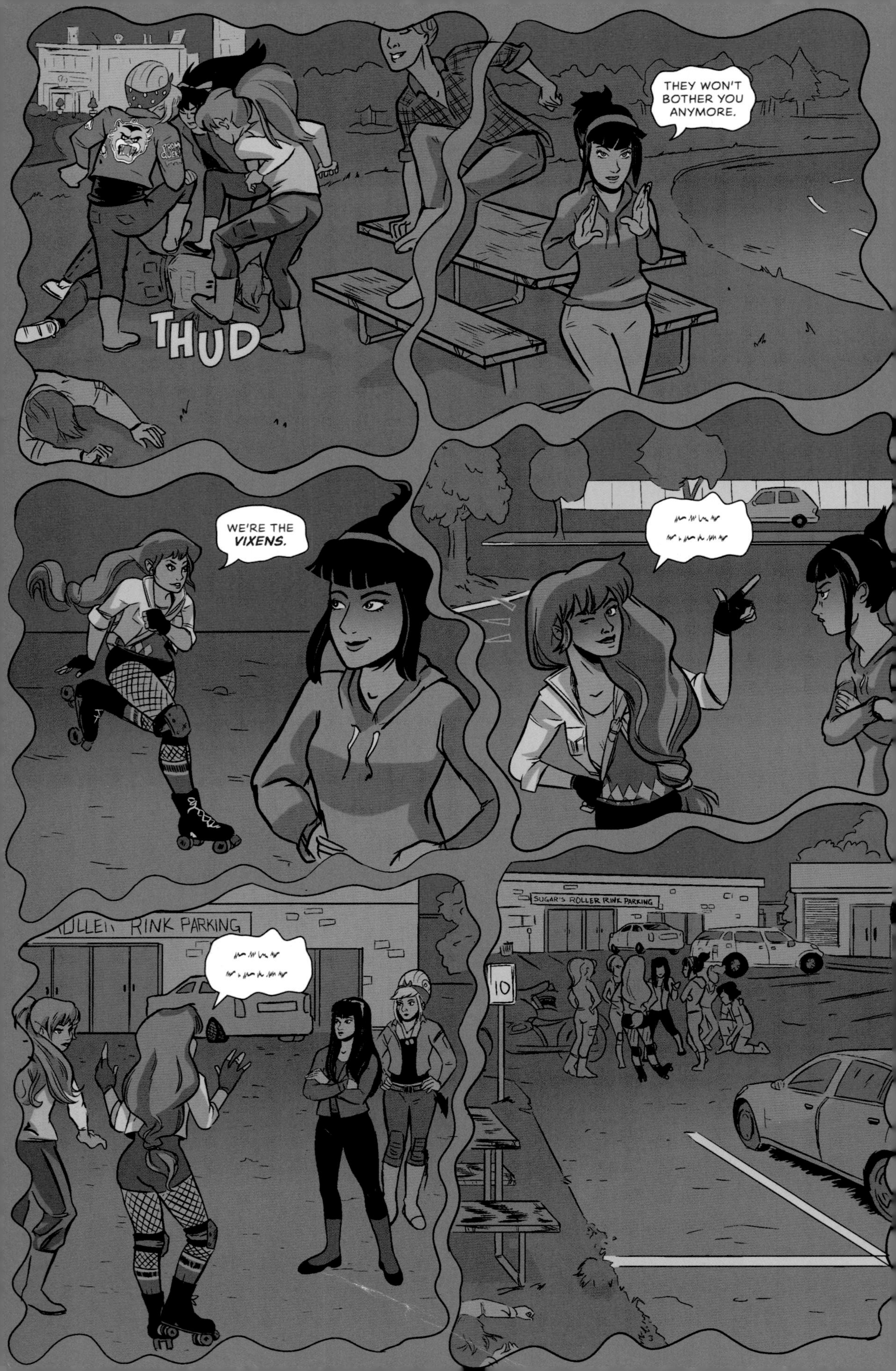
THUD
PROM QUEEN
THEY WON'T BOTHER YOU ANYMORE.
WE'RE THE *VIXENS.*
ROLLER RINK PARKING
SUGAR'S ROLLER RINK PARKING
10

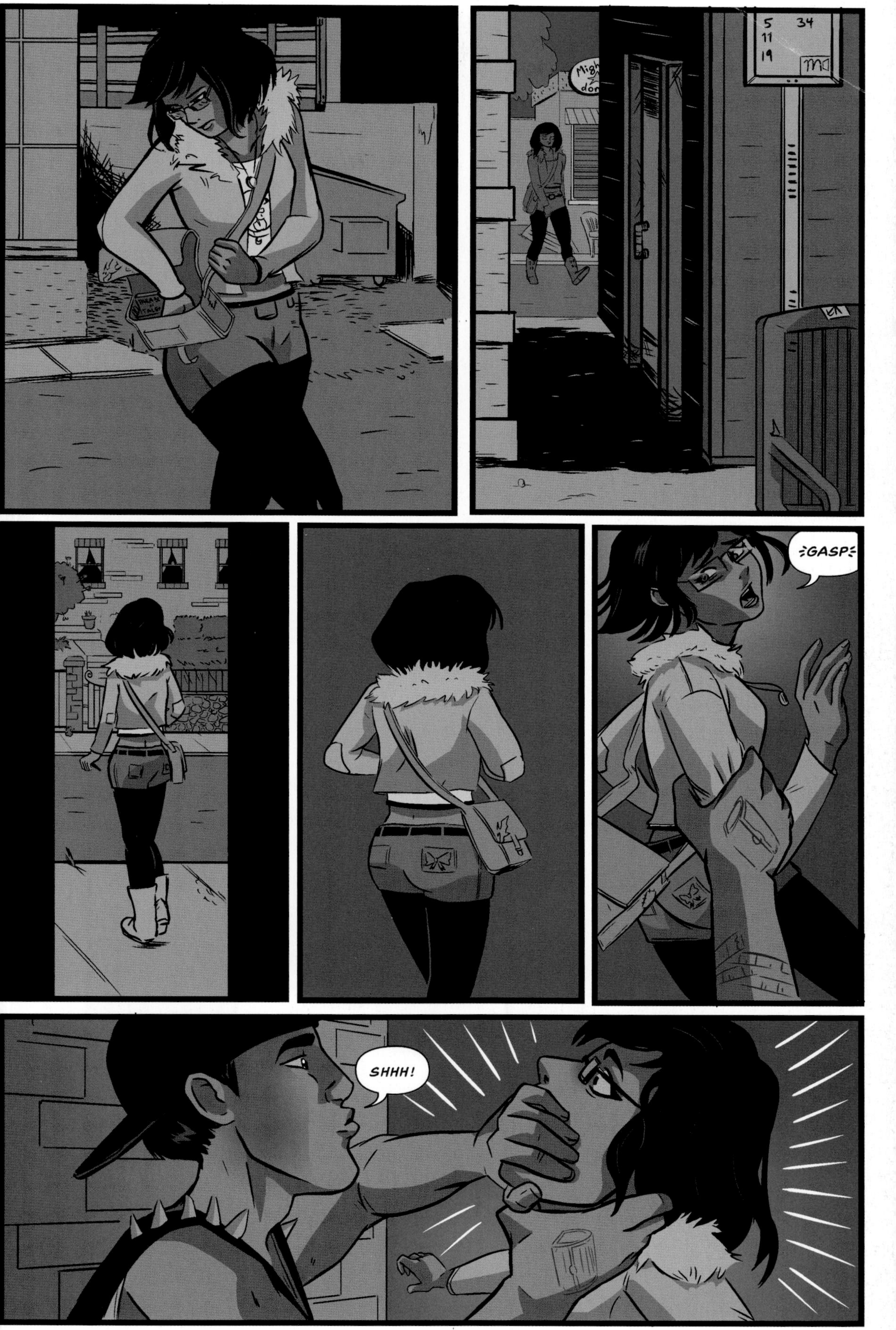
GASP
SHHH!

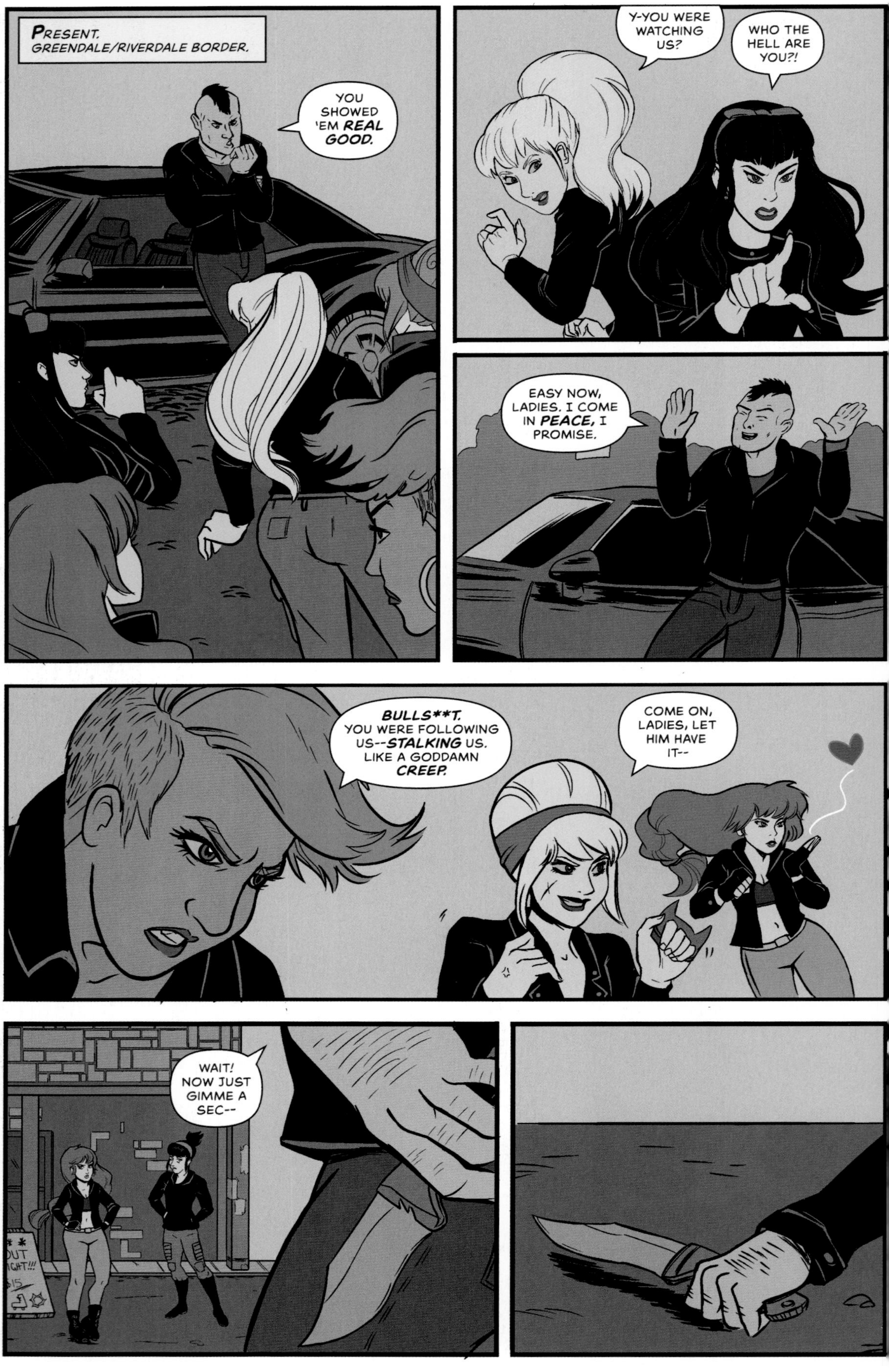
PRESENT.
GREENDALE/RIVERDALE BORDER.
YOU SHOWED 'EM REAL GOOD.
Y-YOU WERE WATCHING US?
WHO THE HELL ARE YOU?!
EASY NOW, LADIES. I COME IN PEACE, I PROMISE.
BULLS**T. YOU WERE FOLLOWING US--STALKING US. LIKE A GODDAMN CREEP.
COME ON, LADIES, LET HIM HAVE IT--
WAIT! NOW JUST GIMME A SEC--

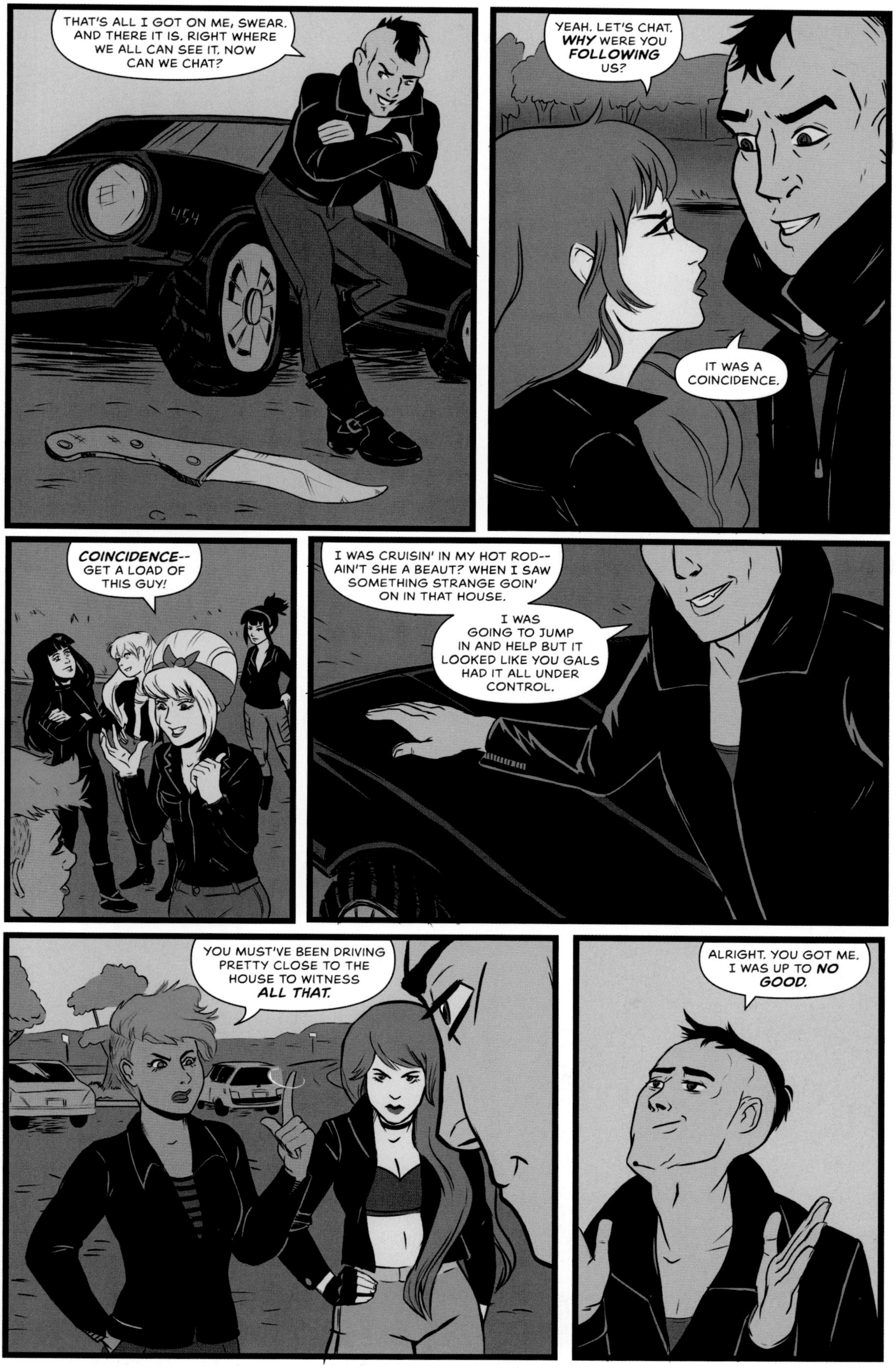
THAT'S ALL I GOT ON ME, SWEAR. AND THERE IT IS. RIGHT WHERE WE ALL CAN SEE IT. NOW CAN WE CHAT?
YEAH. LET'S CHAT. WHY WERE YOU FOLLOWING US?
IT WAS A COINCIDENCE.
COINCIDENCE-- GET A LOAD OF THIS GUY!
I WAS CRUISIN' IN MY HOT ROD-- AIN'T SHE A BEAUT? WHEN I SAW SOMETHING STRANGE GOIN' ON IN THAT HOUSE.
I WAS GOING TO JUMP IN AND HELP BUT IT LOOKED LIKE YOU GALS HAD IT ALL UNDER CONTROL.
YOU MUST'VE BEEN DRIVING PRETTY CLOSE TO THE HOUSE TO WITNESS ALL THAT.
ALRIGHT. YOU GOT ME. I WAS UP TO NO GOOD.

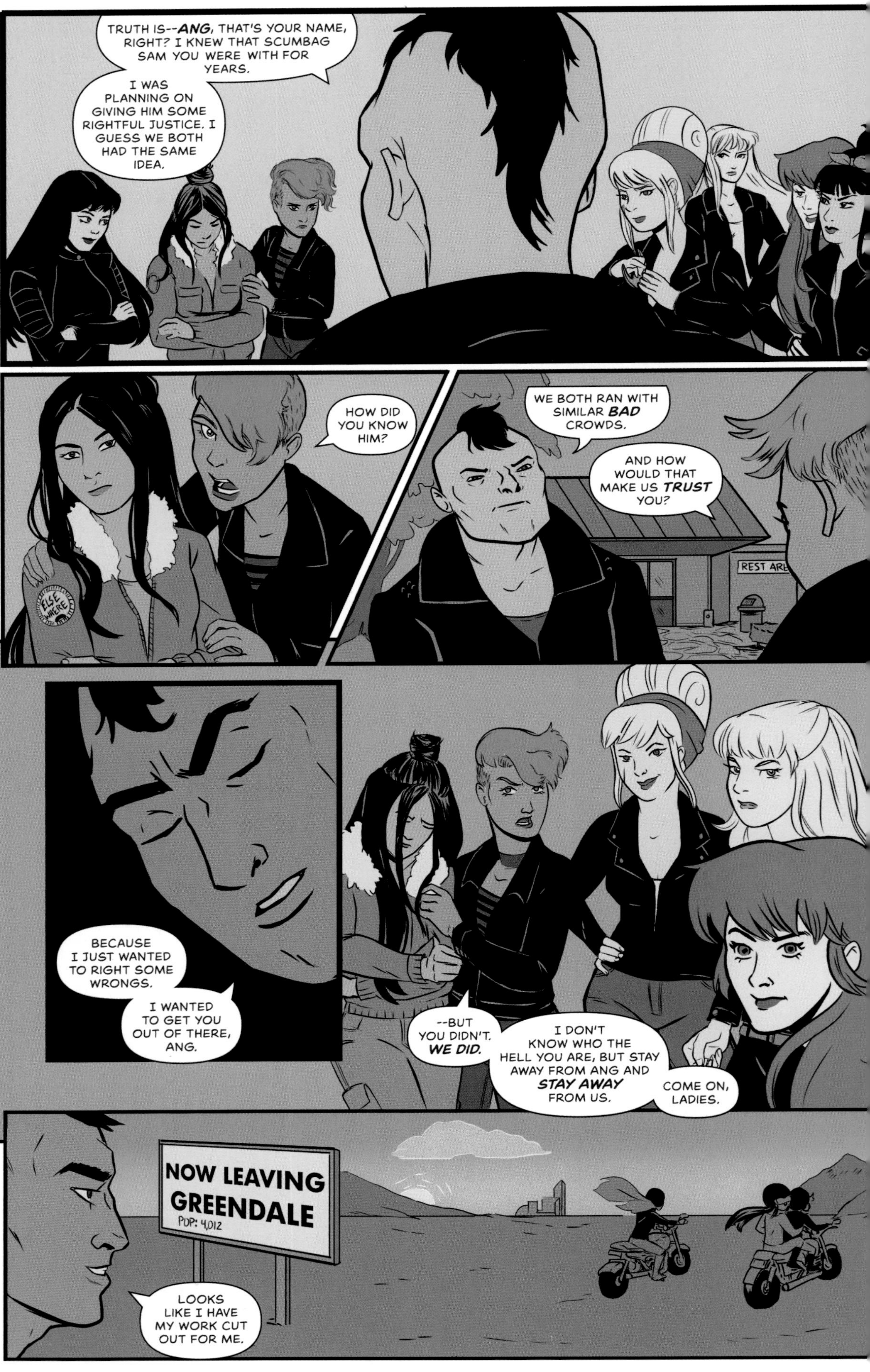
TRUTH IS--ANG, THAT'S YOUR NAME, RIGHT? I KNEW THAT SCUMBAG SAM YOU WERE WITH FOR YEARS.
I WAS PLANNING ON GIVING HIM SOME RIGHTFUL JUSTICE. I GUESS WE BOTH HAD THE SAME IDEA.
HOW DID YOU KNOW HIM?
WE BOTH RAN WITH SIMILAR BAD CROWDS.
AND HOW WOULD THAT MAKE US TRUST YOU?
REST ARE
BECAUSE I JUST WANTED TO RIGHT SOME WRONGS.
I WANTED TO GET YOU OUT OF THERE, ANG.
--BUT YOU DIDN'T. WE DID.
I DON'T KNOW WHO THE HELL YOU ARE, BUT STAY AWAY FROM ANG AND STAY AWAY FROM US.
COME ON, LADIES.
NOW LEAVING GREENDALE
POP: 4,012
LOOKS LIKE I HAVE MY WORK CUT OUT FOR ME.

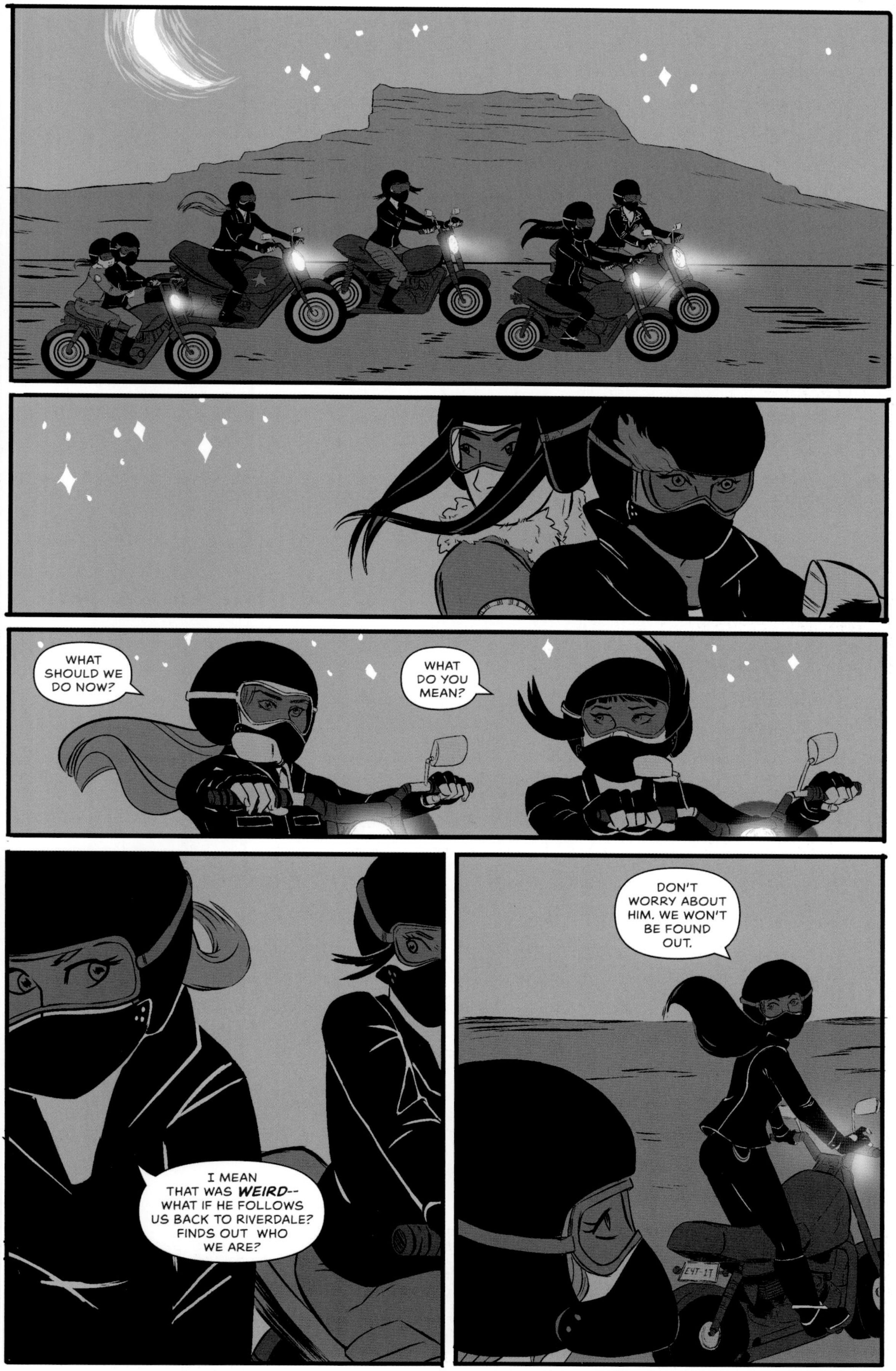
WHAT SHOULD WE DO NOW?
WHAT DO YOU MEAN?
I MEAN THAT WAS WEIRD-- WHAT IF HE FOLLOWS US BACK TO RIVERDALE? FINDS OUT WHO WE ARE?
DON'T WORRY ABOUT HIM. WE WON'T BE FOUND OUT.

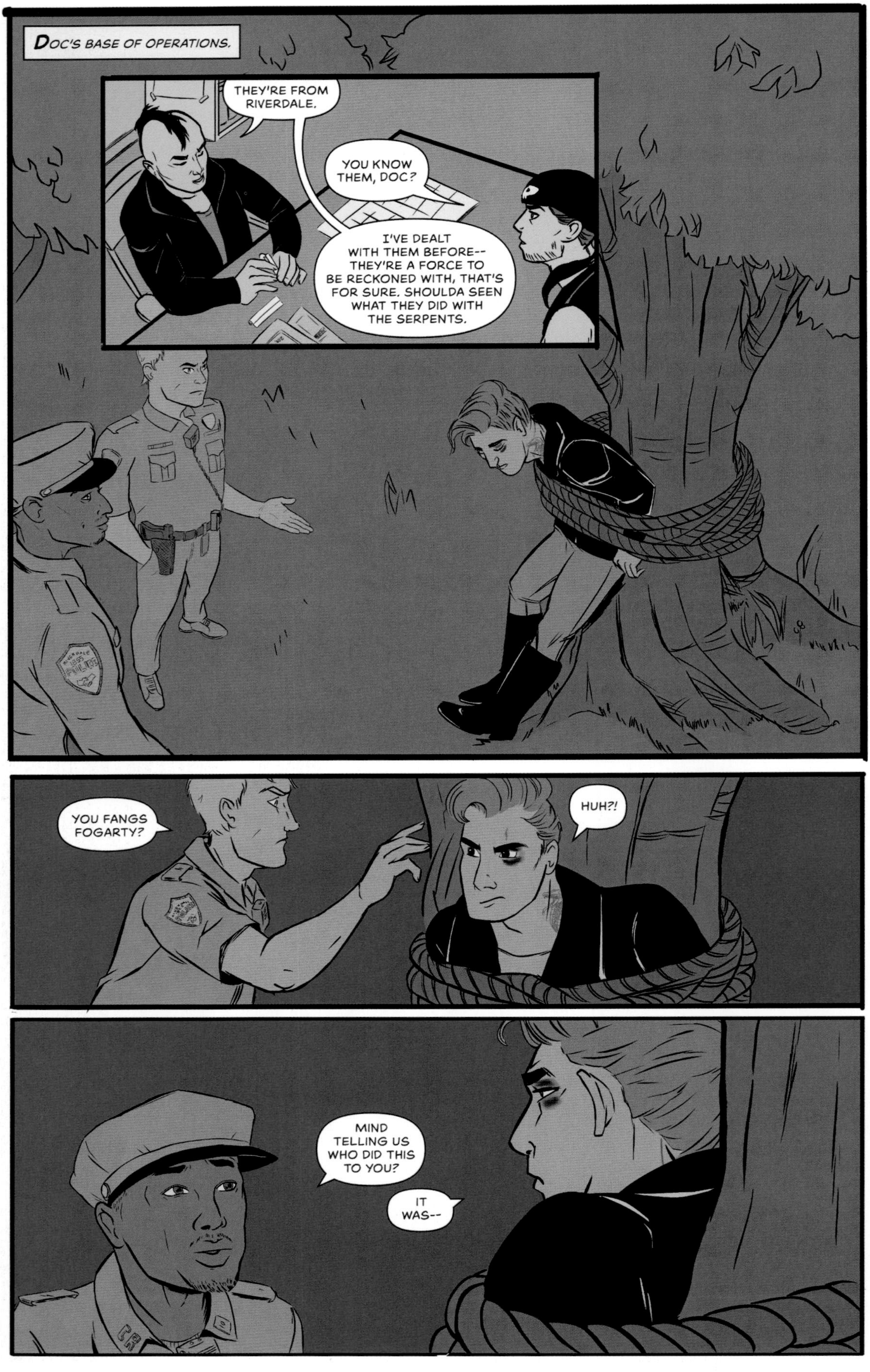
DOC'S BASE OF OPERATIONS.
THEY'RE FROM RIVERDALE.
YOU KNOW THEM, DOC?
I'VE DEALT WITH THEM BEFORE-- THEY'RE A FORCE TO BE RECKONED WITH, THAT'S FOR SURE. SHOULDA SEEN WHAT THEY DID WITH THE SERPENTS.
YOU FANGS FOGARTY?
HUH?!
MIND TELLING US WHO DID THIS TO YOU?
IT WAS--

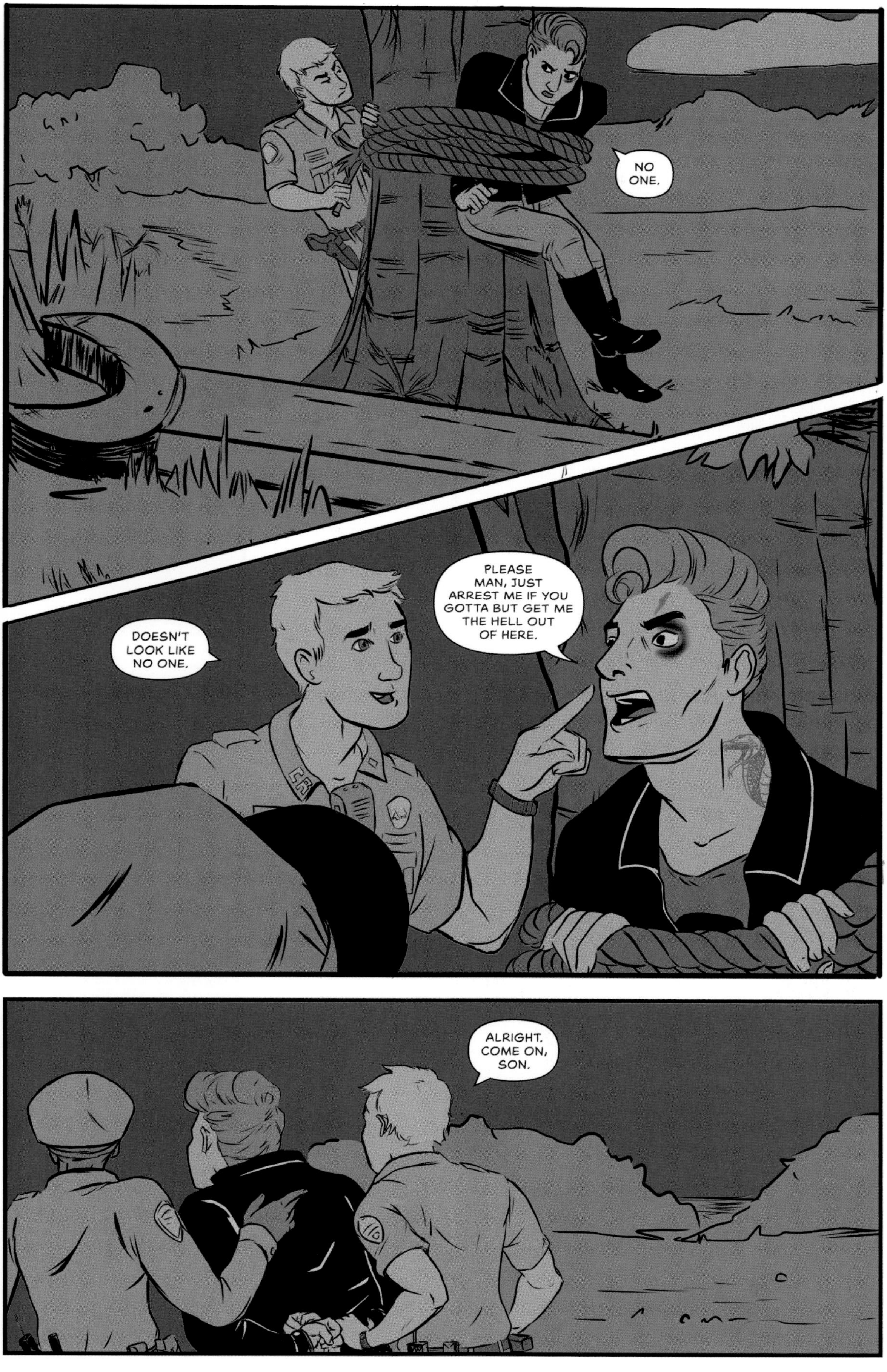
NO ONE.
DOESN'T LOOK LIKE NO ONE.
PLEASE MAN, JUST ARREST ME IF YOU GOTTA BUT GET ME THE HELL OUT OF HERE.
ALRIGHT. COME ON, SON.

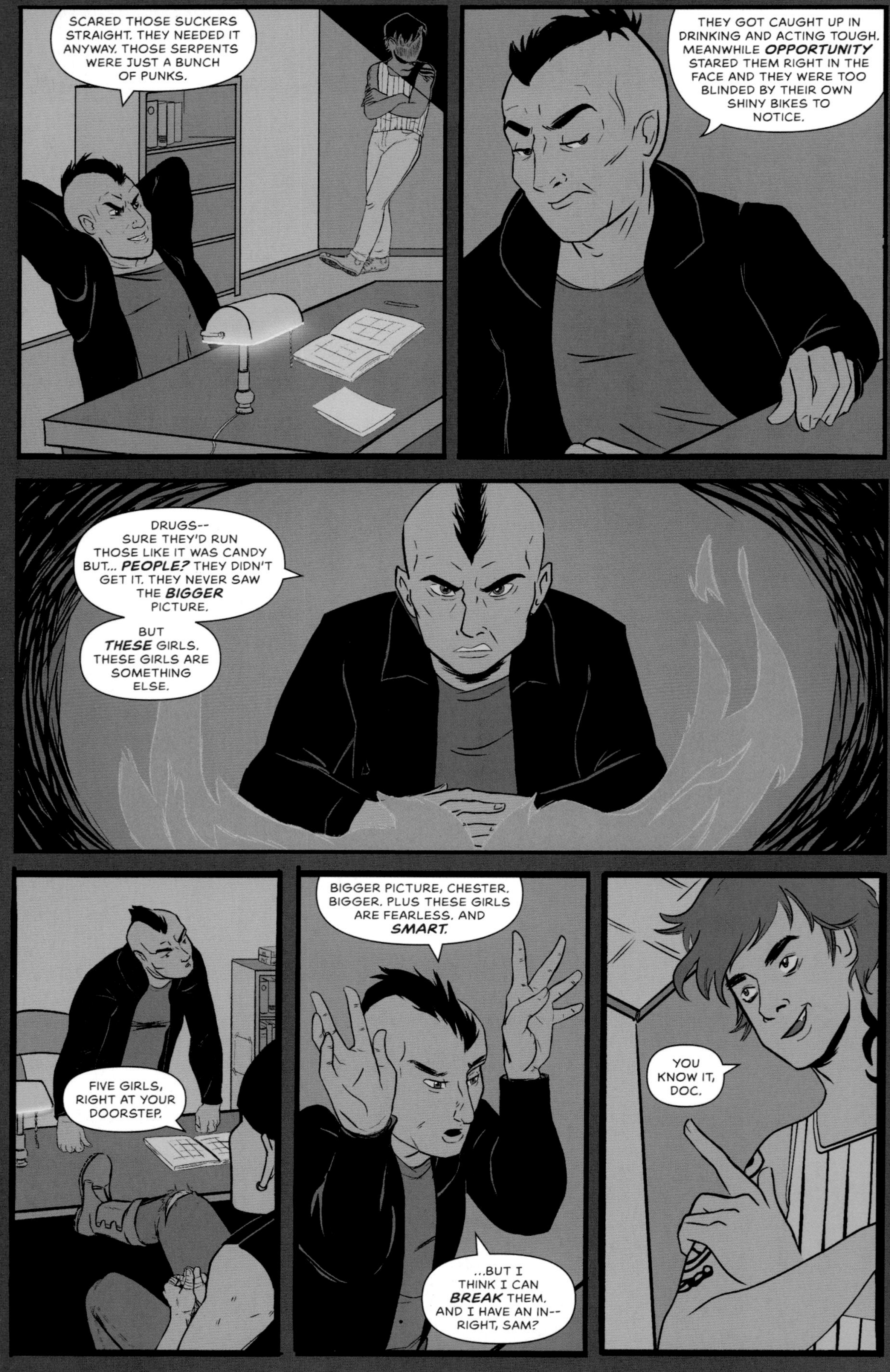
SCARED THOSE SUCKERS STRAIGHT. THEY NEEDED IT ANYWAY. THOSE SERPENTS WERE JUST A BUNCH OF PUNKS.
THEY GOT CAUGHT UP IN DRINKING AND ACTING TOUGH. MEANWHILE OPPORTUNITY STARED THEM RIGHT IN THE FACE AND THEY WERE TOO BLINDED BY THEIR OWN SHINY BIKES TO NOTICE.
DRUGS-- SURE THEY'D RUN THOSE LIKE IT WAS CANDY BUT... PEOPLE? THEY DIDN'T GET IT. THEY NEVER SAW THE BIGGER PICTURE.
BUT THESE GIRLS. THESE GIRLS ARE SOMETHING ELSE.
FIVE GIRLS, RIGHT AT YOUR DOORSTEP.
BIGGER PICTURE, CHESTER. BIGGER. PLUS THESE GIRLS ARE FEARLESS. AND SMART.
...BUT I THINK I CAN BREAK THEM. AND I HAVE AN IN-- RIGHT, SAM?
YOU KNOW IT, DOC.

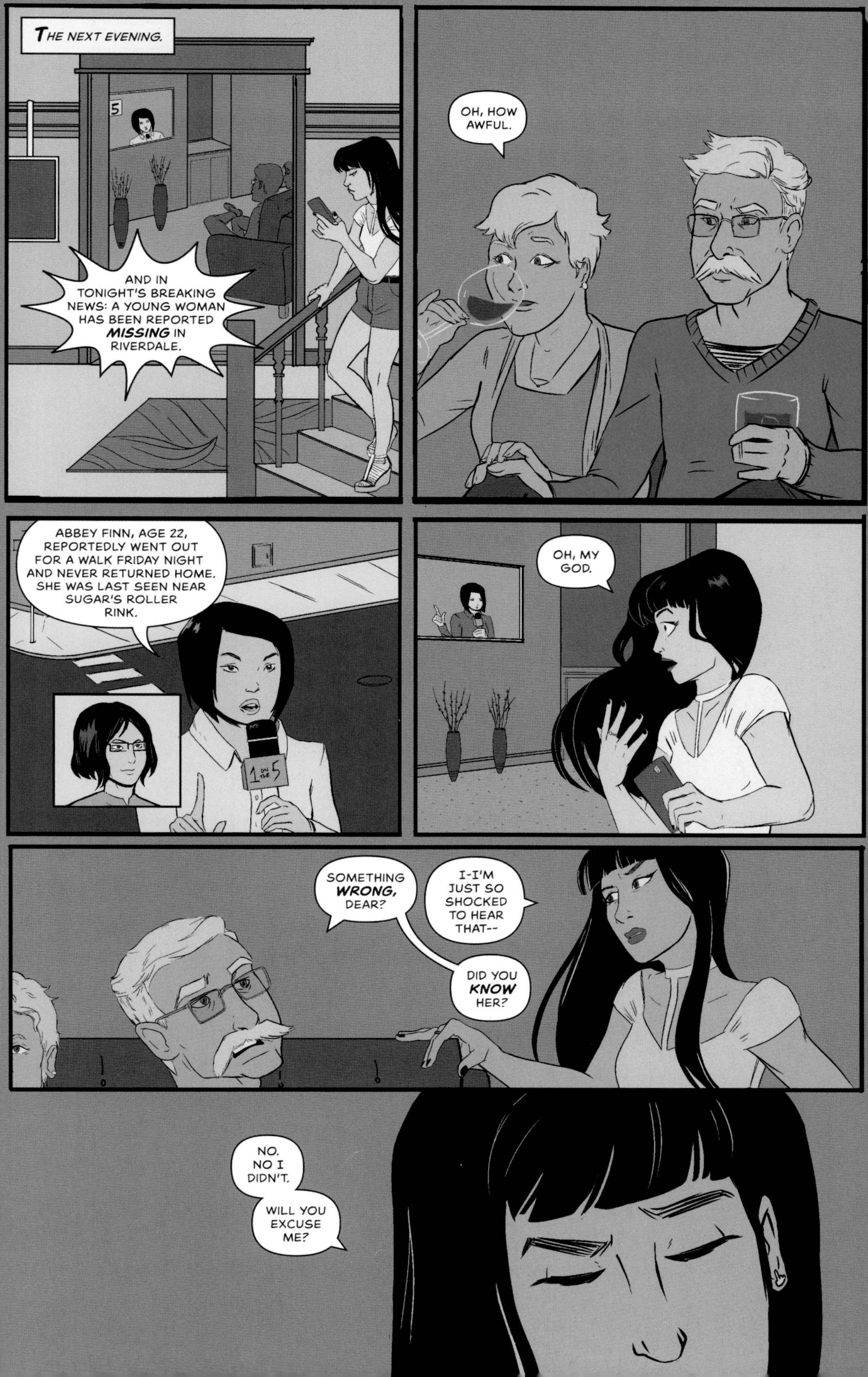
THE NEXT EVENING.
AND IN TONIGHT'S BREAKING NEWS: A YOUNG WOMAN HAS BEEN REPORTED MISSING IN RIVERDALE.
OH, HOW AWFUL.
ABBEY FINN, AGE 22, REPORTEDLY WENT OUT FOR A WALK FRIDAY NIGHT AND NEVER RETURNED HOME. SHE WAS LAST SEEN NEAR SUGAR'S ROLLER RINK.
1 ON THE 5
OH, MY GOD.
SOMETHING WRONG, DEAR?
I-I'M JUST SO SHOCKED TO HEAR THAT--
DID YOU KNOW HER?
NO. NO I DIDN'T.
WILL YOU EXCUSE ME?

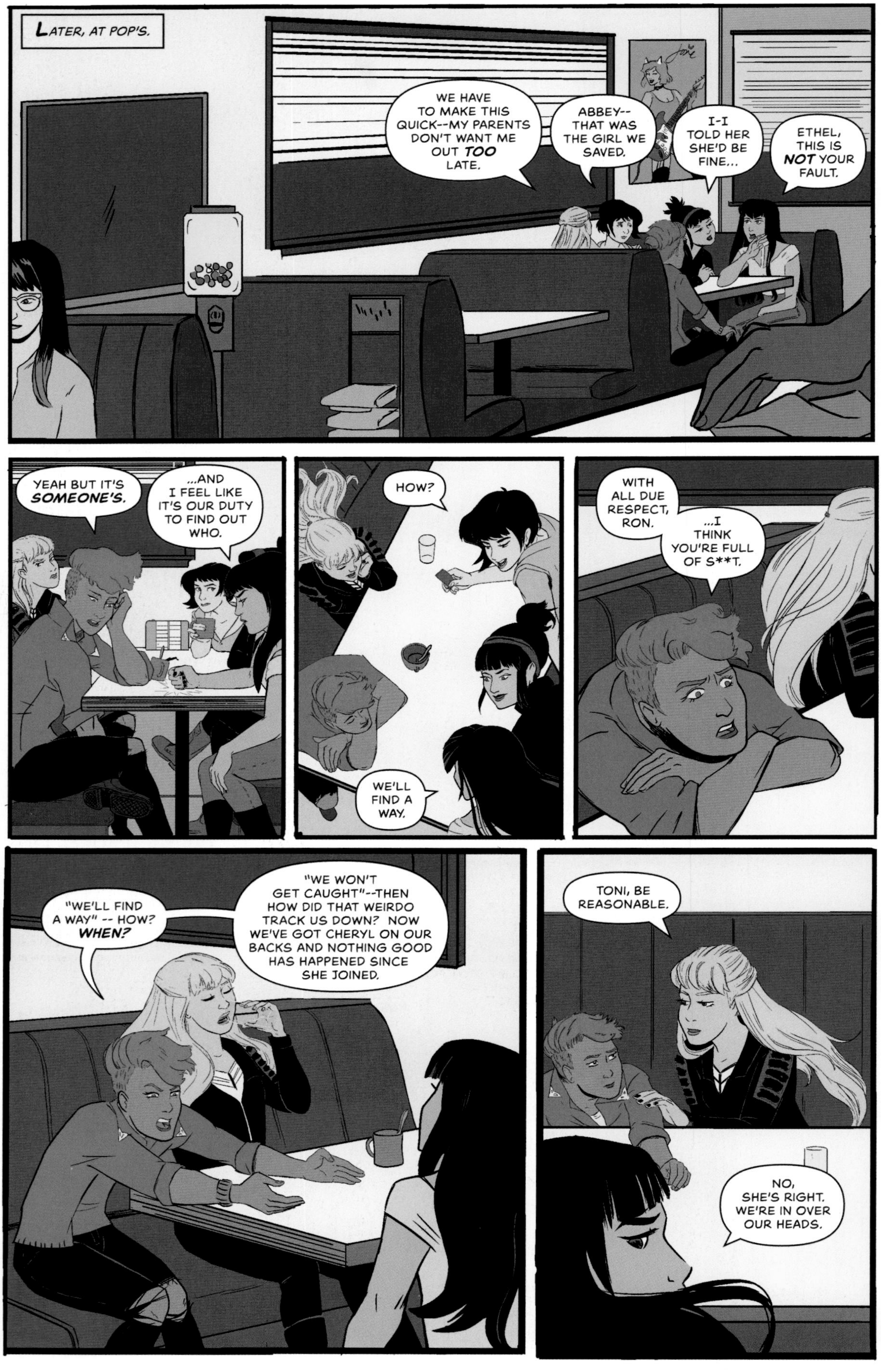
LATER, AT POP'S.
WE HAVE TO MAKE THIS QUICK--MY PARENTS DON'T WANT ME OUT TOO LATE.
ABBEY-- THAT WAS THE GIRL WE SAVED.
I-I TOLD HER SHE'D BE FINE...
ETHEL, THIS IS NOT YOUR FAULT.
YEAH BUT IT'S SOMEONE'S.
...AND I FEEL LIKE IT'S OUR DUTY TO FIND OUT WHO.
HOW?
WE'LL FIND A WAY.
WITH ALL DUE RESPECT, RON.
...I THINK YOU'RE FULL OF S**T.
"WE'LL FIND A WAY" -- HOW? WHEN?
"WE WON'T GET CAUGHT"--THEN HOW DID THAT WEIRDO TRACK US DOWN? NOW WE'VE GOT CHERYL ON OUR BACKS AND NOTHING GOOD HAS HAPPENED SINCE SHE JOINED.
TONI, BE REASONABLE.
NO, SHE'S RIGHT. WE'RE IN OVER OUR HEADS.

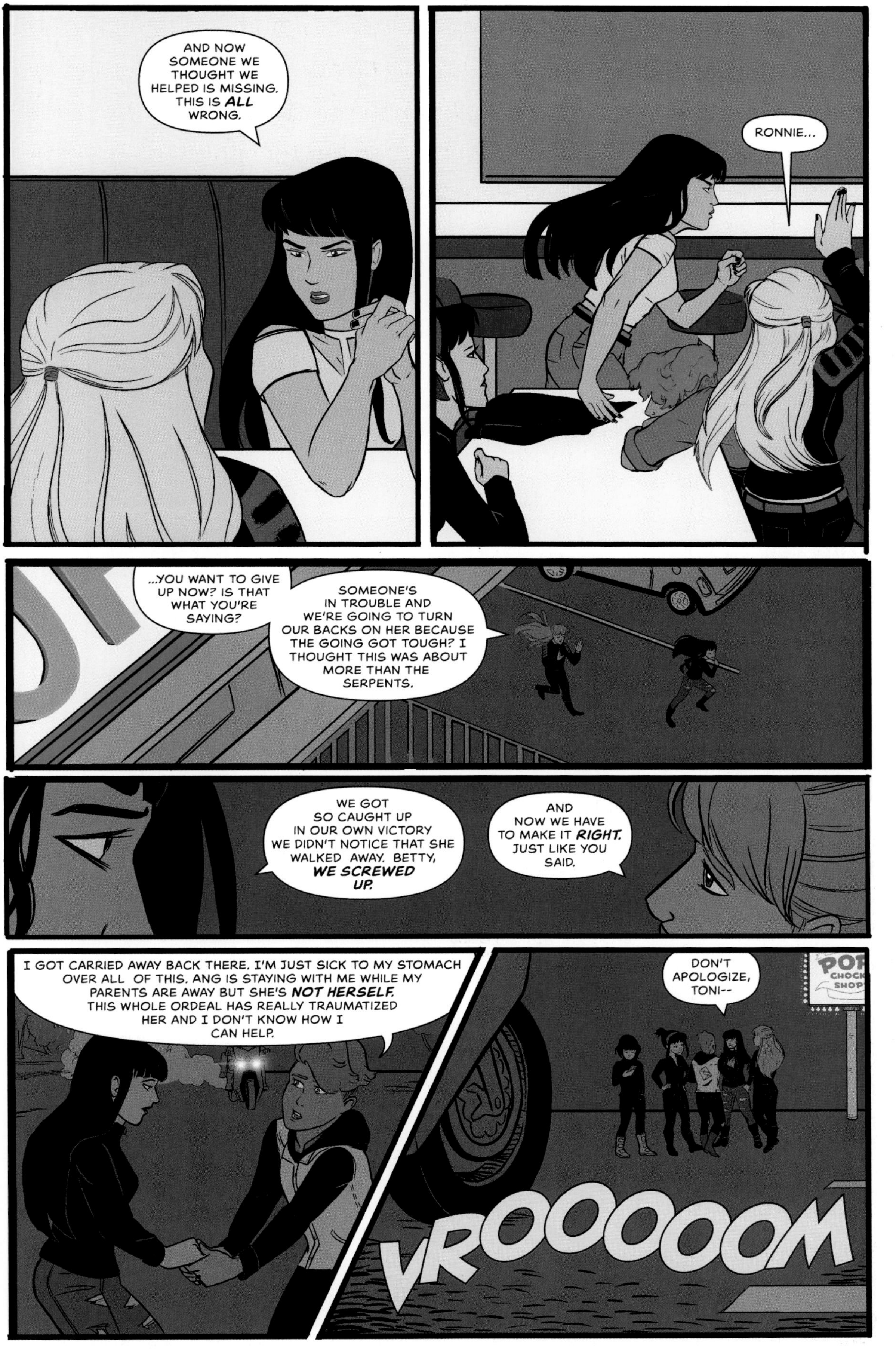
AND NOW SOMEONE WE THOUGHT WE HELPED IS MISSING. THIS IS ALL WRONG.
RONNIE...
...YOU WANT TO GIVE UP NOW? IS THAT WHAT YOU'RE SAYING?
SOMEONE'S IN TROUBLE AND WE'RE GOING TO TURN OUR BACKS ON HER BECAUSE THE GOING GOT TOUGH? I THOUGHT THIS WAS ABOUT MORE THAN THE SERPENTS.
WE GOT SO CAUGHT UP IN OUR OWN VICTORY WE DIDN'T NOTICE THAT SHE WALKED AWAY. BETTY, WE SCREWED UP.
AND NOW WE HAVE TO MAKE IT RIGHT. JUST LIKE YOU SAID.
I GOT CARRIED AWAY BACK THERE. I'M JUST SICK TO MY STOMACH OVER ALL OF THIS. ANG IS STAYING WITH ME WHILE MY PARENTS ARE AWAY BUT SHE'S NOT HERSELF. THIS WHOLE ORDEAL HAS REALLY TRAUMATIZED HER AND I DON'T KNOW HOW I CAN HELP.
DON'T APOLOGIZE, TONI--
VROOOOOOM

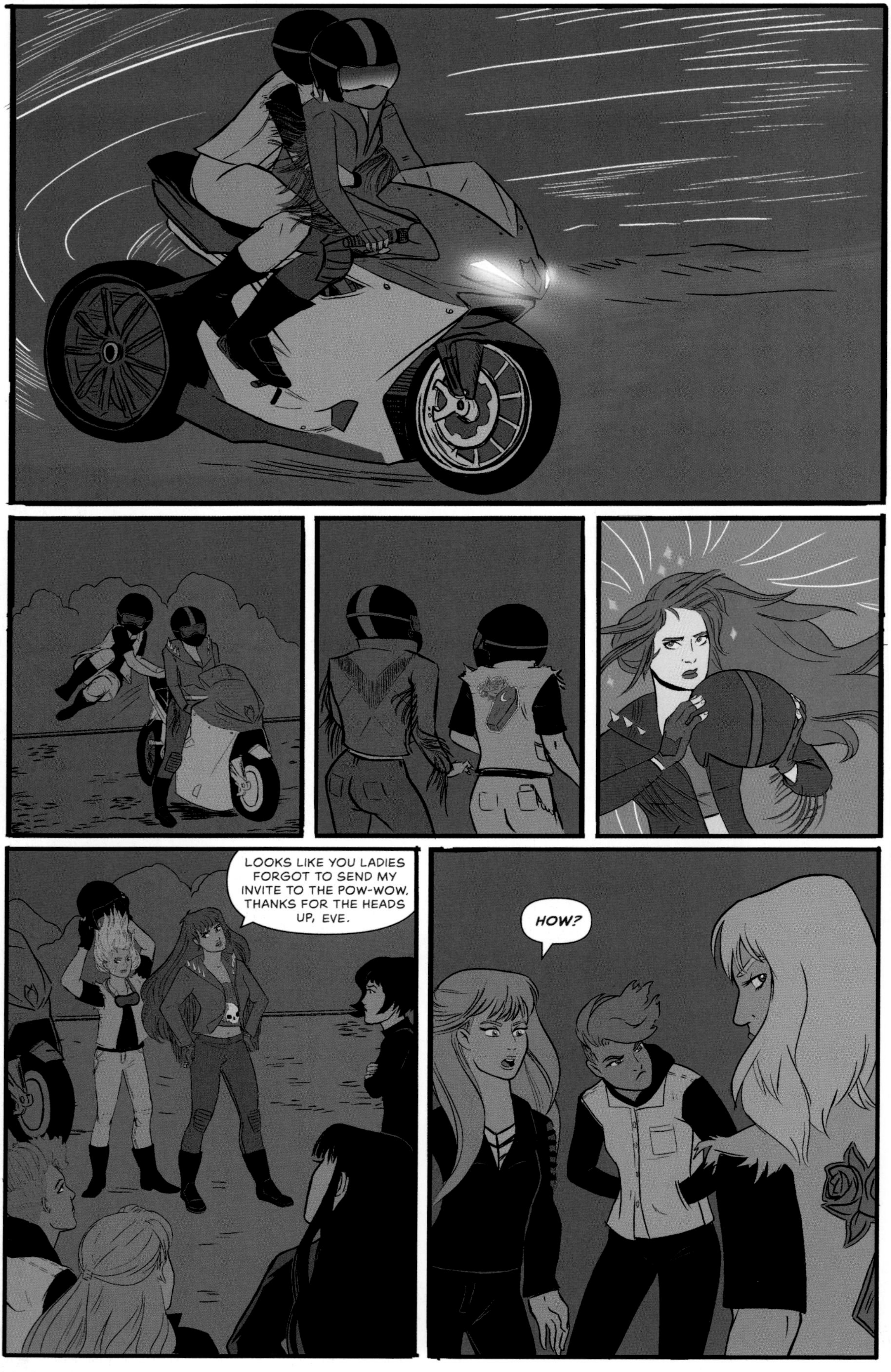
LOOKS LIKE YOU LADIES FORGOT TO SEND MY INVITE TO THE POW-WOW. THANKS FOR THE HEADS UP, EVE.
HOW?

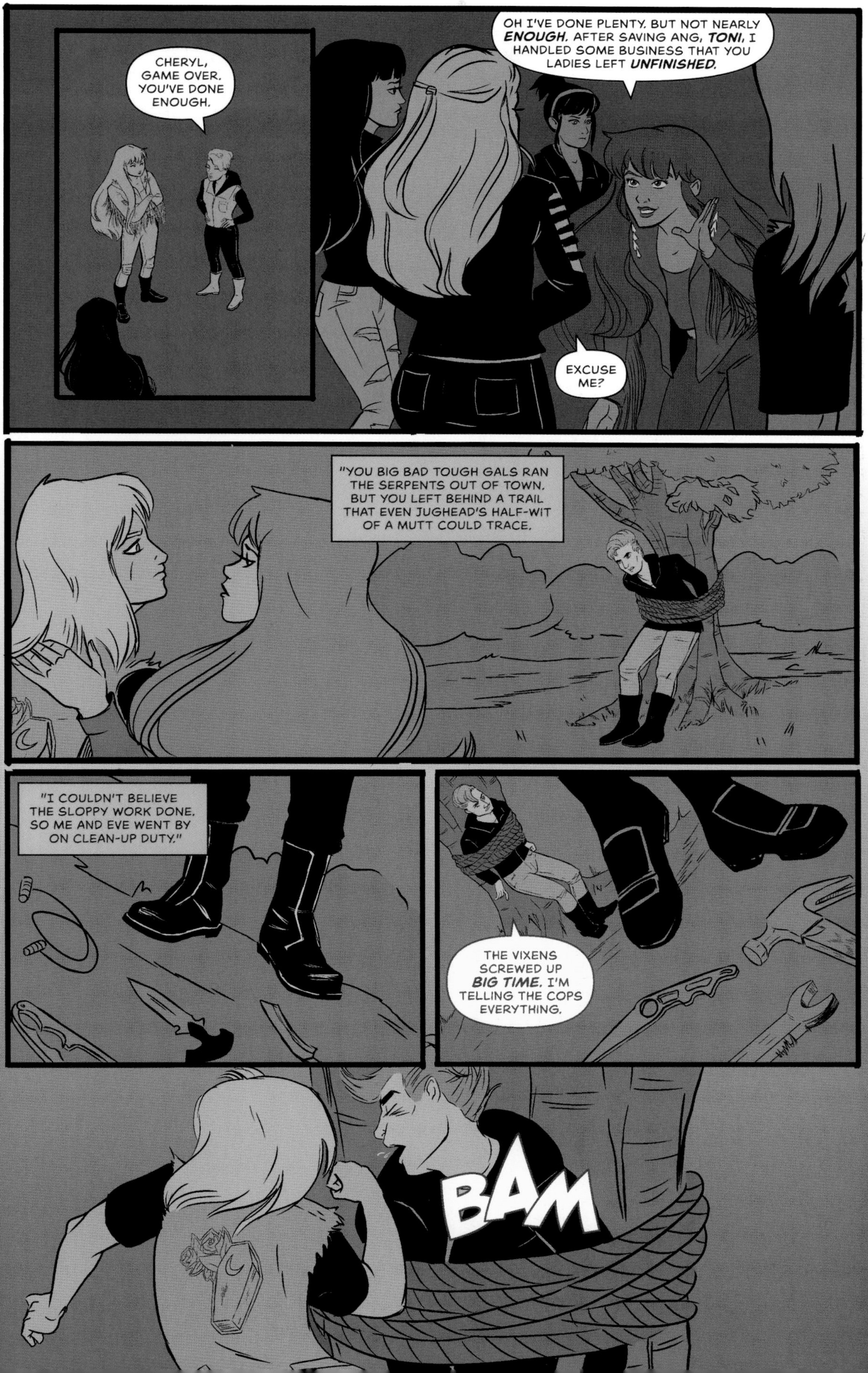
CHERYL, GAME OVER. YOU'VE DONE ENOUGH.
OH I'VE DONE PLENTY, BUT NOT NEARLY ENOUGH. AFTER SAVING ANG, TONI, I HANDLED SOME BUSINESS THAT YOU LADIES LEFT UNFINISHED.
EXCUSE ME?
"YOU BIG BAD TOUGH GALS RAN THE SERPENTS OUT OF TOWN, BUT YOU LEFT BEHIND A TRAIL THAT EVEN JUGHEAD'S HALF-WIT OF A MUTT COULD TRACE.
"I COULDN'T BELIEVE THE SLOPPY WORK DONE, SO ME AND EVE WENT BY ON CLEAN-UP DUTY."
THE VIXENS SCREWED UP BIG TIME. I'M TELLING THE COPS EVERYTHING.
BAM

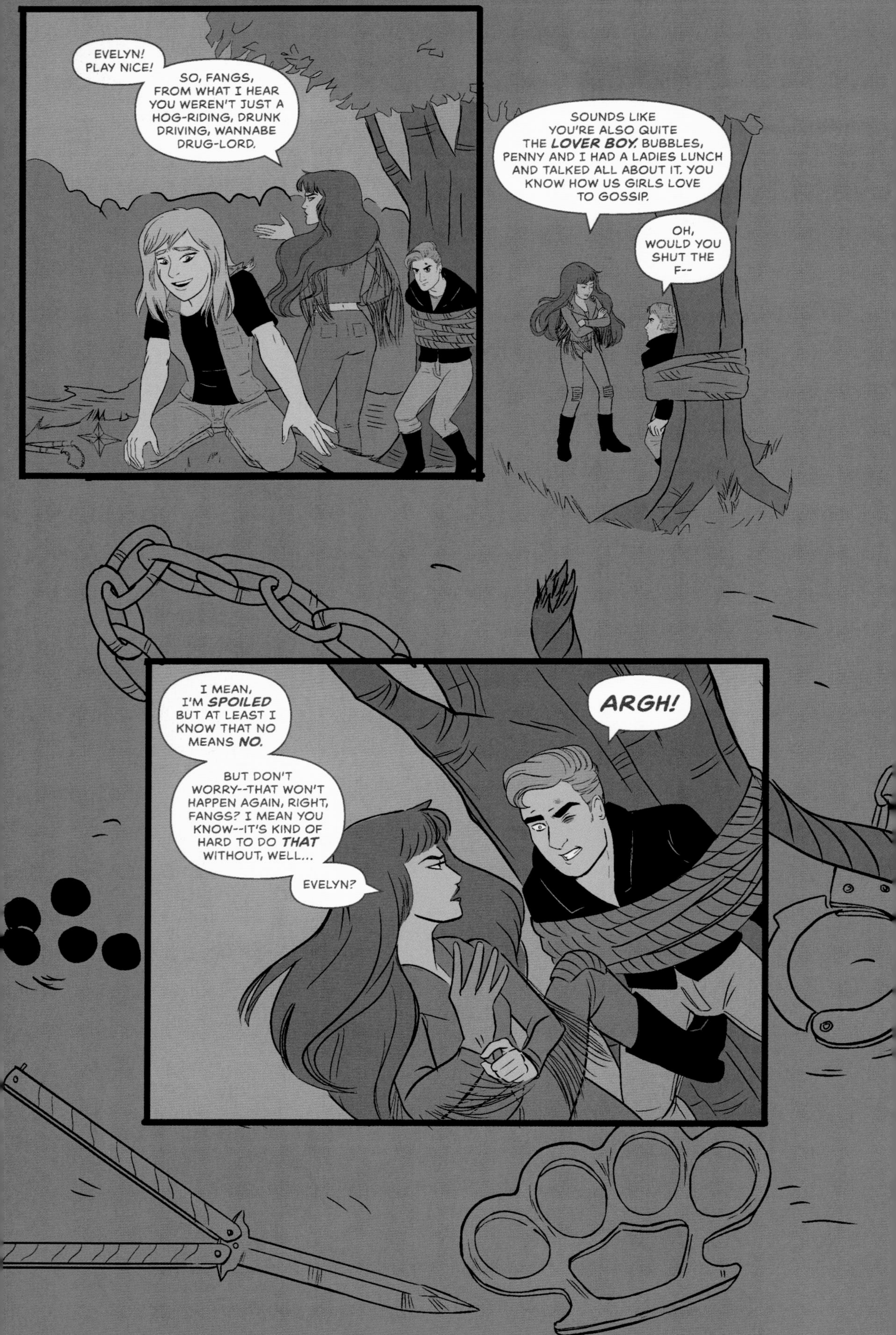
EVELYN! PLAY NICE!
SO, FANGS, FROM WHAT I HEAR YOU WEREN'T JUST A HOG-RIDING, DRUNK DRIVING, WANNABE DRUG-LORD.
SOUNDS LIKE YOU'RE ALSO QUITE THE LOVER BOY. BUBBLES, PENNY AND I HAD A LADIES LUNCH AND TALKED ALL ABOUT IT. YOU KNOW HOW US GIRLS LOVE TO GOSSIP.
OH, WOULD YOU SHUT THE F--
I MEAN, I'M SPOILED BUT AT LEAST I KNOW THAT NO MEANS NO.
BUT DON'T WORRY--THAT WON'T HAPPEN AGAIN, RIGHT, FANGS? I MEAN YOU KNOW--IT'S KIND OF HARD TO DO THAT WITHOUT, WELL...
EVELYN?
ARGH!

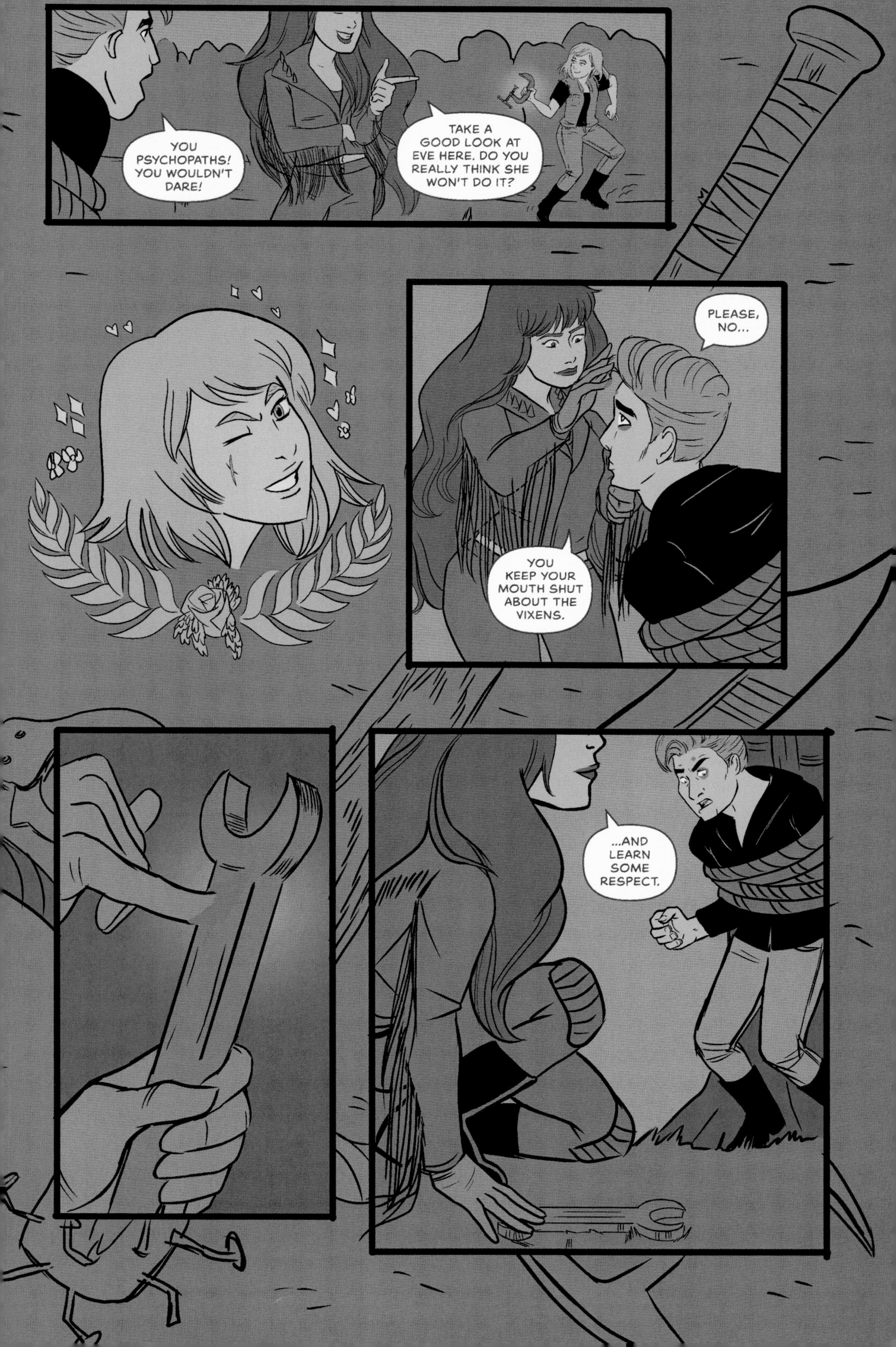
YOU PSYCHOPATHS! YOU WOULDN'T DARE!
TAKE A GOOD LOOK AT EVE HERE. DO YOU REALLY THINK SHE WON'T DO IT?
PLEASE, NO...
YOU KEEP YOUR MOUTH SHUT ABOUT THE VIXENS.
...AND LEARN SOME RESPECT.

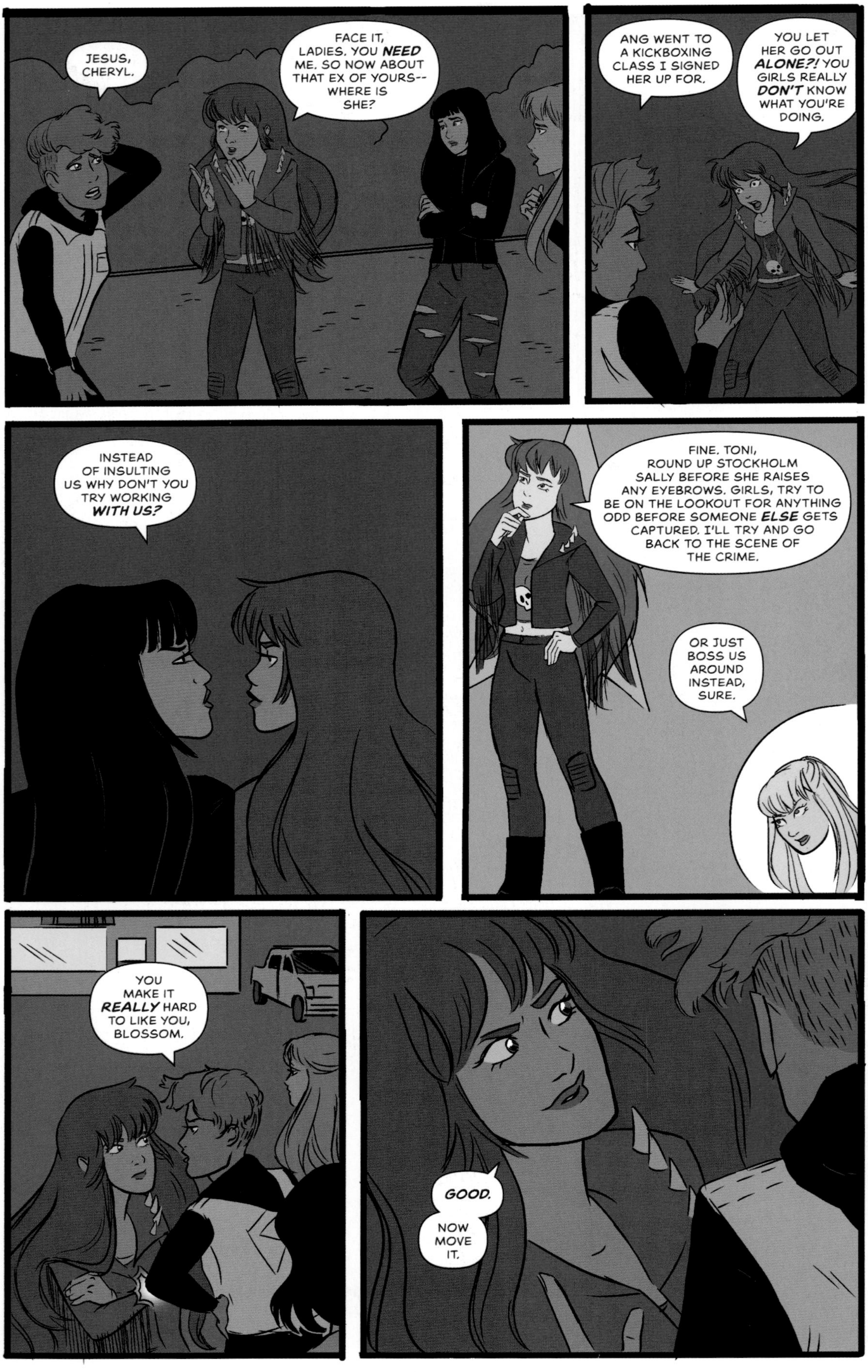

JESUS, CHERYL.
FACE IT, LADIES. YOU NEED ME. SO NOW ABOUT THAT EX OF YOURS-- WHERE IS SHE?
ANG WENT TO A KICKBOXING CLASS I SIGNED HER UP FOR.
YOU LET HER GO OUT ALONE?! YOU GIRLS REALLY DON'T KNOW WHAT YOU'RE DOING.
INSTEAD OF INSULTING US WHY DON'T YOU TRY WORKING WITH US?
FINE. TONI, ROUND UP STOCKHOLM SALLY BEFORE SHE RAISES ANY EYEBROWS. GIRLS, TRY TO BE ON THE LOOKOUT FOR ANYTHING ODD BEFORE SOMEONE ELSE GETS CAPTURED. I'LL TRY AND GO BACK TO THE SCENE OF THE CRIME.
OR JUST BOSS US AROUND INSTEAD, SURE.
YOU MAKE IT REALLY HARD TO LIKE YOU, BLOSSOM.
GOOD.
NOW MOVE IT.

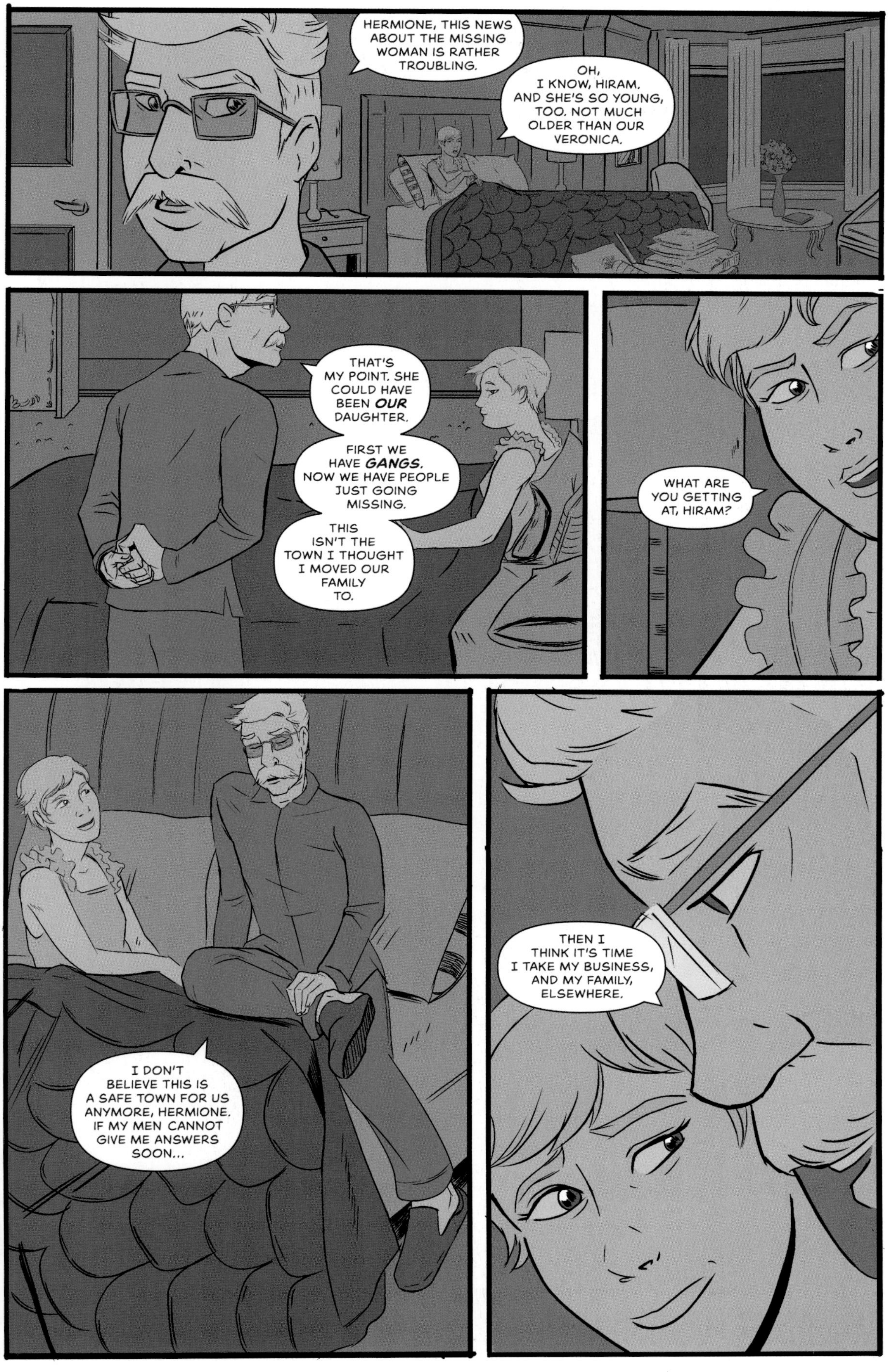
HERMIONE, THIS NEWS ABOUT THE MISSING WOMAN IS RATHER TROUBLING.
OH, I KNOW, HIRAM. AND SHE'S SO YOUNG, TOO. NOT MUCH OLDER THAN OUR VERONICA.
THAT'S MY POINT. SHE COULD HAVE BEEN *OUR* DAUGHTER.
FIRST WE HAVE *GANGS*. NOW WE HAVE PEOPLE JUST GOING MISSING.
THIS ISN'T THE TOWN I THOUGHT I MOVED OUR FAMILY TO.
WHAT ARE YOU GETTING AT, HIRAM?
I DON'T BELIEVE THIS IS A SAFE TOWN FOR US ANYMORE, HERMIONE. IF MY MEN CANNOT GIVE ME ANSWERS SOON...
THEN I THINK IT'S TIME I TAKE MY BUSINESS, AND MY FAMILY, ELSEWHERE.

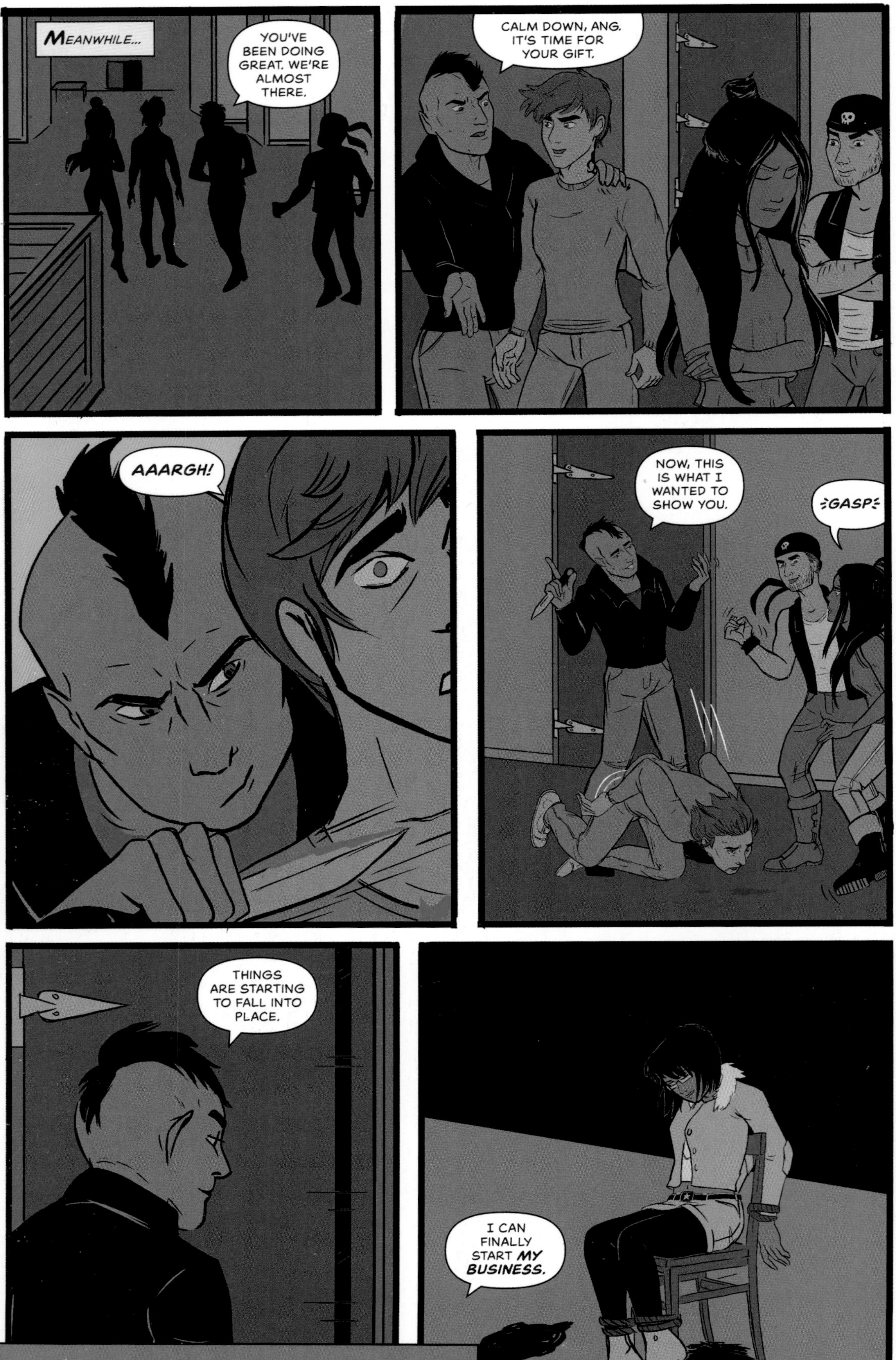
MEANWHILE...
YOU'VE BEEN DOING GREAT. WE'RE ALMOST THERE.
CALM DOWN, ANG. IT'S TIME FOR YOUR GIFT.
AAARGH!
NOW, THIS IS WHAT I WANTED TO SHOW YOU.
GASP
THINGS ARE STARTING TO FALL INTO PLACE.
I CAN FINALLY START MY BUSINESS.
BETTY & VERONICA: VIXENS
VOLUME 2 - ON SALE NOVEMBER 2018